WIMBLEDON

- 2019 -

CELEBRATING
No.1 COURT

THE CHAMPIONSHIPS
1 JULY - 14 JULY 2019

—

An illustration of No.1 Court, inspired by the flowers of The Championships

wimbledon.com/poster

IN PURSUIT *of* GREATNESS

#WIMBLEDON

The Championships' Official Poster 2019 celebrates the redevelopment of No.1 Court through its surrounding flora, inspired by the aspiration that visitors to the AELTC experience world-class tennis in an English garden environment

WIMBLEDON
- 2019 -

By Paul Newman

Published in 2019 by Vision Sports Publishing Ltd

Vision Sports Publishing Ltd
19-23 High Street
Kingston upon Thames
Surrey
KT1 1LL
www.visionsp.co.uk

ISBN: 978-1909534-91-9

Written by: Paul Newman
Additional writing by: Ian Chadband
Edited by: Jim Drewett and Alexandra Willis
Production editor: Ed Davis
Design consultation: Ikem Ononiwu
Proofreaders: Lee Goodall and Eloise Tyson

Photography: Bob Martin, Adam Warner, Andrew Baker, Anthony Upton, Ben Queenborough, Ben Solomon, Chloe Knott, David Gray, David Levenson, Dillon Bryden, Eddie Keogh, Florian Eisele, Ian Walton, Jed Leicester, Joe Toth, Joel Marklund, Jon Buckle, Karwai Tang, Paul Gregory, Simon Bruty, Thomas Lovelock, Tim Clayton

Picture editors: Neil Turner, Alice Trott, Lucy Ball, Richard Ward, Sammie Thompson
Picture research: Sarah Frandsen

All photographs © AELTC unless otherwise stated

Results and tables are reproduced courtesy of the AELTC

The All England Lawn Tennis Club (Championships) Limited
Church Road
Wimbledon
London
SW19 5AE
England

Tel: +44 (0)20 8944 1066
www.wimbledon.com

Printed in Slovakia by Neografia

This book is reproduced with the assistance of Rolex.

CONTENTS

—

FOREWORD

—

By Chairman Philip Brook CBE

I would like to welcome you all to the Official Annual of The Championships 2019, a celebration of the 133rd Championships.

It was a Championships of unbroken sunshine, fantastic matches, record attendances, new champions, and historic moments, a few of which I would like to highlight before you delve into the full tale of the Fortnight.

Firstly, the completion of the enhanced No.1 Court, with its retractable roof, additional seats, Living Walls, bigger screen, and new facilities for public, officials and hospitality guests. And while the new retractable roof wasn't needed to keep the rain away, it did make a valuable contribution helping us to complete matches after darkness on four evenings.

We are very proud to have welcomed Ann Jones and Rod Laver as our special guests, to mark 50 years since they won the singles titles at The Championships in 1969, which was also of course the year that Rod completed his second calendar Grand Slam.

Congratulations to all our champions, to Novak Djokovic on the occasion of a truly memorable fifth Wimbledon singles title, and to Simona Halep on her first Wimbledon title, the first Romanian to become a Wimbledon singles champion.

We witnessed two extraordinary five-set finals, both taking a record four hours and 57 minutes: the absorbing singles contest between Djokovic and Roger Federer, the first final to be decided by a tie-break at 12-12, and the phenomenal doubles match which saw Robert Farah and Juan Sebastian Cabal triumph over Nicolas Mahut and Edouard Roger-Vasselin.

Fifteen-year-old Cori Gauff was the story of the first week alongside Andy Murray's return to Wimbledon in the gentlemen's doubles as well as the mixed doubles with Serena Williams; we had British interest as Johanna Konta battled her way to a second Wimbledon quarter-final; and of course the 40th meeting of Federer and Rafael Nadal, their first at Wimbledon since the 2008 final.

Following last year's successful exhibition, we were delighted with the introduction of Quad Singles and Quad Doubles Championship events, and of course the excellent performance of our grass courts amid the beautiful sunshine and the many enhancements to our Grounds which successfully welcomed over half a million spectators.

Lastly, our commemorative coins returned from space to Centre Court, safely carried by astronaut Commander Drew Feustel to be used for the two singles finals coin tosses, expertly executed by our two young people from charities selected by the Wimbledon Foundation.

In conclusion, in my final year as Chairman, I would like to thank all of those who have competed in, attended, watched or worked at The Championships during my tenure, and I hope that once again this annual will prove to be a memorable and enjoyable read.

CENTRE COU

BJÖRN BORG 1980

ROLEX

THE CHAMPIONSHIPS, WIMBLEDON

The world of Rolex is filled with stories of perpetual excellence. At Wimbledon, the game's most honoured achievements continue to advance the sport. Defined by its greatest legends. And driven higher by the next generation of champions determined to take their place at the pinnacle of the game. Here, 140 years of memorable performances ensure Centre Court will remain tennis's ultimate stage. This is a story of perpetual excellence, the story of Rolex.

#Perpetual

THE CHAMPIONSHIPS, WIMBLEDON
THE ALL ENGLAND LAWN TENNIS CLUB, LONDON
1 TO 14 JULY 2019

ROGER FEDERER 2017

ANGÉLIQUE KERBER 2018

OYSTER PERPETUAL DATEJUST 41

ROLEX

INTRODUCTION

—

By Paul Newman

O n the eve of the 133rd edition of The Championships you might have been forgiven for thinking that time had stood still since Angelique Kerber and Novak Djokovic had lifted aloft their trophies 12 months earlier.

Serena Williams was still looking for the Grand Slam singles title she needed to equal Margaret Court's all-time record; Djokovic, Rafael Nadal and Roger Federer, statistically the three greatest male players of all time, filled the top three places in the world rankings, as they had for much of the previous decade; and Andy Murray's fitness, which had dominated the domestic media agenda in the build-up to The Championships 2018, was still a major subject of debate.

Away from tennis, much of the domestic sporting focus was again centred on a football World Cup, though this time it was the England women's team rather than the men who were seeking global glory. The men's Cricket World Cup, hosted by England, was also coming to a climax, with the home team keeping their hopes alive by beating India on the eve of The Championships.

The political landscape in Britain had not changed much either as Brexit still dominated the agenda. Theresa May, her hopes of leading an orderly exit from the European Union having been dashed, was in her last weeks as Prime Minister, with Boris Johnson and Jeremy Hunt locked in a leadership contest to succeed her.

It might have seemed as though the only difference compared with 12 months previously was the weather, the heatwave of 2018 having been replaced this year – in Britain if not in some other European countries – by a more typical June mixture of rain, overcast skies and occasional sunshine. Forecasters, nevertheless, were predicting a fine fortnight of weather for The Championships, which was surely all but guaranteed given that the All England Club had just unveiled its splendid new retractable roof over No.1 Court, the most visible aspect of a major three-year rebuilding and refurbishment project. Exactly the same scenario had played out 10 years earlier when the first Championships to be staged with a sliding roof over Centre Court had been blessed with glorious weather.

RAISING THE NEW ROOF

—

The anticipation surrounding the competitive baptism of the freshly refurbished No.1 Court, complete with splendid retractable roof, was palpable, especially as the Draw on the Friday before The Championships offered the prospect of some delicious matches to give this special arena a proper lift-off.

The expectation had only been heightened by the hugely successful 'No.1 Court Celebration' staged six weeks earlier, a wonderful May launch for the court featuring entertaining tennis and music, not to mention a drop or two of rain that offered the perfect backdrop for the official opening – and closing – of the roof.

What a sight it proved – 10 years since the unveiling of Centre Court's roof, here were the spectacular fruits of a three-year planning and design process and a three-year build.

"It was our largest ever project," Chairman Philip Brook explained. "A challenging and complex piece of engineering that was completed on time and on budget."

No wonder Martina Navratilova, one of the former champions invited to play in the celebration along with John McEnroe, Lleyton Hewitt, Venus Williams, Pat Cash, Goran Ivanisevic, Kim Clijsters and Jamie Murray, hailed it "an engineering marvel".

Singers Paloma Faith and Joseph Calleja (*right*), along with the Grange Park Opera chorus and the BBC Concert Orchestra, also 'raised the roof' on an enjoyable afternoon of entertainment that raised money for 'A Roof For All', the Wimbledon Foundation's new fund for the homeless.

Wimbledon raised the No.1 Court roof in style to a soundtrack provided by pop star Paloma Faith (far right), tenor Joseph Calleja, Grange Park Opera's chorus and the BBC Concert Orchestra (above)

There was entertaining tennis on show from a star-studded cast including John McEnroe, talking here to the BBC's Sue Barker (centre), and (clockwise from above left) Venus Williams, Goran Ivanisevic, Martina Navratilova, McEnroe, Kim Clijsters and Lleyton Hewitt among those competing

*Fifteen-year-old Cori Gauff (**above**) was the star of Qualifying at Roehampton, just as she was to become in The Championships itself*

First appearances, nevertheless, can be deceptive. The reality was that plenty had changed in tennis in the previous 12 months, nowhere more so than in the women's game. While Serena Williams had completed only six matches since the Australian Open because of a knee injury and Angelique Kerber had not won a title since The Championships 2018, a new wave of younger players had been prospering.

Naomi Osaka had won the US Open and Australian Open back-to-back and Ashleigh Barty had just conquered Roland-Garros and become world No.1 by winning the title in Birmingham. Three teenagers – Bianca Andreescu, Amanda Anisimova and Marketa Vondrousova – had been showing great promise, while eagle-eyed tennis fans might also have noticed that a 15-year-old had just become the youngest player ever to come through the Qualifying Competition for The Championships at Roehampton. We would be hearing more – much, much more – about Cori Gauff in the days to come.

In the men's game, too, younger players had been flexing their muscles. Alexander Zverev, for a while now the standard-bearer of the 'Next Gen' group, had enjoyed his biggest triumph at the year-end ATP Finals in London the previous November, and in an era dominated by 30-somethings there were four players (Stefanos Tsitsipas, Felix Auger-Aliassime, Denis Shapovalov and Alex de Minaur) aged 20 or under in the world's top 30 at the start of The Championships.

Above: Roehampton featured some familiar faces, with perennial crowd favourite Dustin Brown (***far left***) and 2013 finalist Sabine Lisicki (***left***) in action

GREENER THAN GREEN

It's one of the annual wonders of world sport how Neil Stubley, Wimbledon's Head of Courts and Horticulture, and his team manage, through meticulous preparation, to deliver such perfect grass courts for The Championships.

   Once again in 2019, the 18 courts, sown with 100 per cent perennial ryegrass and cut to a height of 8mm – optimal for play, durability and survival – looked a picture and ready for anything.

In Grand Slam competition, nevertheless, the old guard had refused to step aside. In the wake of his remarkable comeback triumph at The Championships 2018, Djokovic had won the US Open and Australian Open, only to fall at the semi-final stage at Roland-Garros in his quest to hold all four Grand Slam titles for the second time in his career. The champion in Paris, for a jaw-dropping 12th time, had been Nadal. Federer, meanwhile, arrived at Wimbledon having won more tour-level matches in the year than any other player after winning the titles in Dubai, Miami and Halle.

Murray, in contrast, had been happy just to be back on court given his travails of the previous two years. The Gentlemen's Singles Champion of 2013 and 2016 had been suffering with a hip injury for more than two years that had also forced his late withdrawal from The Championships 2018. At a tearful press conference at the Australian Open in January he had expressed fears that his career might be over, but hip resurfacing surgery later that month proved successful and in June, contrary to the expectations of many, the former world No.1 made his return in doubles at the Queen's Club alongside the veteran Spaniard, Feliciano Lopez. What a comeback it was too. Murray and Lopez beat the top seeds, Juan Sebastian Cabal and Robert Farah, in the first round and went on to win the title.

For the moment singles was off Murray's agenda as he rebuilt his fitness, but the 32-year-old Scot was throwing himself wholeheartedly into doubles. While playing with Marcelo Melo in the doubles at Eastbourne in the week before The Championships Murray revealed that he would be joining forces with Pierre-Hugues Herbert at Wimbledon and was also looking for a mixed doubles partner. Days of feverish speculation followed and by the eve of The Championships there was increasing talk of a dream partnership with Serena Williams. In the absence of Murray, the main home hope in singles play would be Johanna Konta, who had just reached the semi-finals at Roland-Garros at the end of her most successful clay court season.

Below: No, Andy Murray hadn't forgotten what tennis balls looked like (left). It was good to see the 2013 and 2016 champion back, and old friends like Novak Djokovic (right) couldn't have agreed more

ALL (ENGLAND) INCLUSIVE

—

The remarkable 75-year-old Billie Jean King, for so long a pioneer for both tennis and social justice, was thrilled to lead the way yet again by proving an inspiring figurehead at a special 'Inclusive Leadership' event staged at the All England Club on the Friday before The Championships, discussing sport, sexuality, empowerment and individuality.

The groundbreaking event was a collaboration between the AELTC, the Billie Jean King Leadership Initiative (BJKLI) and Pride Sports, an organisation working to challenge homophobia, biphobia and transphobia in sport and improve access to sport for all LGBT+ people across the world.

"It's incredible to be with these young leaders as we celebrate the power of being your authentic self," Billie Jean, six-times Ladies' Singles Champion, declared.

"Sports is a microcosm of society, and as athletes we need to ensure everyone feels they can bring all of themselves in any arena – sports, business or life. I'm inspired by this celebration of inclusive leadership and look forward to this becoming an annual event."

Young leaders from various local organisations and schools visited the Club to meet Billie Jean at this inspiring initiative, which was organised and hosted by Wimbledon Channel presenter Nick McCarvel, to celebrate June being 'Pride Month' around the globe and highlight sport's important role in encouraging

"Truth sets you free, it gives you power. Keep learning and keep learning how to learn," Billie Jean told her rapt audience of about 30 youngsters.

"Be a problem solver. That's what leadership is. Figure it out. Every one of you has something special. What is it? You have something extra. Every one of you." The applause told of just how inspirational her

For all those taking part, the next fortnight offered a chance to make history. In the build-up to The Championships, Wimbledon's promotional campaign, 'Join The Story', had focused on the many remarkable moments at the All England Club that had helped to frame history. In 1969, for example, man had walked on the Moon for the first time in the same year that Rod Laver had won his fourth gentlemen's singles title en route to completing his second calendar-year Grand Slam, a feat which no male player has matched since. It was fitting that Laver would be one of the Chairman's special guests at The Championships 2019 alongside Ann Jones, who in 1969 had finally won the ladies' singles title at her 14th and last attempt.

For those who had wanted to relive more recent history, in a new brand-building exercise there had been five showings on the weekend before The Championships of 'Wimbledon Rematch 1980'. Staged at the Troubadour Wembley Park Theatre, this immersive cinema experience, featuring live actors and period props, had recreated one of Wimbledon's most memorable Championships, which culminated in Bjorn Borg's extraordinary victory over John McEnroe.

Now it was time for the real thing. Would this be the first year since 2002 that someone other than Federer, Nadal, Djokovic or Murray would win the gentlemen's singles title? Would Barty and Osaka live up to their billing as the world's two best female players or could Serena Williams triumph for an eighth time and join Margaret Court at the head of the all-time list of Grand Slam singles champions? Let play begin.

You could not be serious! 'Wimbledon Rematch 1980' proved a unique immersive cinema treat, recreating those memorable Championships and Bjorn Borg's epic victory over John McEnroe

GENTLEMEN'S SINGLES SEEDS

—

1

Novak DJOKOVIC
(Serbia)
Age: 32
Wimbledon titles: 4
Grand Slam titles: 15

2

Roger FEDERER
(Switzerland)
Age: 37
Wimbledon titles: 8
Grand Slam titles: 20

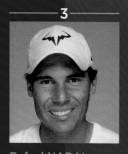

3

Rafael NADAL
(Spain)
Age: 33
Wimbledon titles: 2
Grand Slam titles: 18

4

Kevin ANDERSON
(South Africa)
Age: 33
Wimbledon titles: 0
Grand Slam titles: 0

5

Dominic THIEM
(Austria)
Age: 25
Wimbledon titles: 0
Grand Slam titles: 0

6

Alexander ZVEREV
(Germany)
Age: 22
Wimbledon titles: 0
Grand Slam titles: 0

7

Stefanos TSITSIPAS
(Greece)
Age: 20
Wimbledon titles: 0
Grand Slam titles: 0

8

Kei NISHIKORI
(Japan)
Age: 29
Wimbledon titles: 0
Grand Slam titles: 0

9

John ISNER
(USA)
Age: 34
Wimbledon titles: 0
Grand Slam titles: 0

10

Karen KHACHANOV
(Russia)
Age: 23
Wimbledon titles: 0
Grand Slam titles: 0

11
Daniil MEDVEDEV
(Russia)

12
Fabio FOGNINI
(Italy)

13
Marin CILIC
(Croatia)

14
Borna CORIC*
(Croatia)

15
Milos RAONIC
(Canada)

16
Gael MONFILS
(France)

17
Matteo
BERRETTINI
(Italy)

18
Nikoloz
BASILASHVILI
(Georgia)

19
Felix
AUGER-ALIASSIME
(Canada)

20
Gilles SIMON
(France)

21
David GOFFIN
(Belgium)

22
Stan WAWRINKA
(Switzerland)

23
Roberto BAUTISTA
AGUT
(Spain)

24
Diego
SCHWARTZMAN
(Argentina)

25
Alex DE MINAUR
(Australia)

26
Guido PELLA
(Argentina)

27
Lucas POUILLE
(France)

28
Benoit PAIRE
(France)

29
Denis
SHAPOVALOV
(Canada)

30
Kyle EDMUND
(United Kingdom)

31
Laslo DJERE
(Serbia)

32
Dusan LAJOVIC
(Serbia)

33
Jan-Lennard
STRUFF**
(Germany)

Withdrew due to injury
**Added to list of Seeds
due to Coric withdrawal*

LADIES' SINGLES SEEDS
—

1

Ashleigh BARTY
(Australia)
Age: 23
Wimbledon titles: 0
Grand Slam titles: 1

2

Naomi OSAKA
(Japan)
Age: 21
Wimbledon titles: 0
Grand Slam titles: 2

3

Karolina PLISKOVA
(Czech Republic)
Age: 27
Wimbledon titles: 0
Grand Slam titles: 0

4

Kiki BERTENS
(Netherlands)
Age: 27
Wimbledon titles: 0
Grand Slam titles: 0

5

Angelique KERBER
(Germany)
Age: 31
Wimbledon titles: 1
Grand Slam titles: 3

6

Petra KVITOVA
(Czech Republic)
Age: 29
Wimbledon titles: 2
Grand Slam titles: 2

7

Simona HALEP
(Romania)
Age: 27
Wimbledon titles: 0
Grand Slam titles: 1

8

Elina SVITOLINA
(Ukraine)
Age: 24
Wimbledon titles: 0
Grand Slam titles: 0

9

Sloane STEPHENS
(USA)
Age: 26
Wimbledon titles: 0
Grand Slam titles: 1

10

Aryna SABALENKA
(Belarus)
Age: 21
Wimbledon titles: 0
Grand Slam titles: 0

11
Serena WILLIAMS
(USA)

12
Anastasija
SEVASTOVA
(Latvia)

13
Belinda BENCIC
(Switzerland)

14
Caroline
WOZNIACKI
(Denmark)

15
Qiang WANG
(China)

16
Marketa
VONDROUSOVA
(Czech Republic)

17
Madison KEYS
(USA)

18
Julia GOERGES
(Germany)

19
Johanna KONTA
(United Kingdom)

20
Anett KONTAVEIT
(Estonia)

21
Elise MERTENS
(Belgium)

22
Donna VEKIC
(Croatia)

23
Caroline GARCIA
(France)

24
Petra MARTIC
(Croatia)

25
Amanda
ANISIMOVA (USA)

26
Garbiñe
MUGURUZA
(Spain)

27
Sofia KENIN
(USA)

28
Su-Wei HSIEH
(Chinese Taipei)

29
Daria KASATKINA
(Russia)

30
Carla SUAREZ
NAVARRO
(Spain)

31
Maria SAKKARI
(Greece)

32
Lesia TSURENKO
(Ukraine)

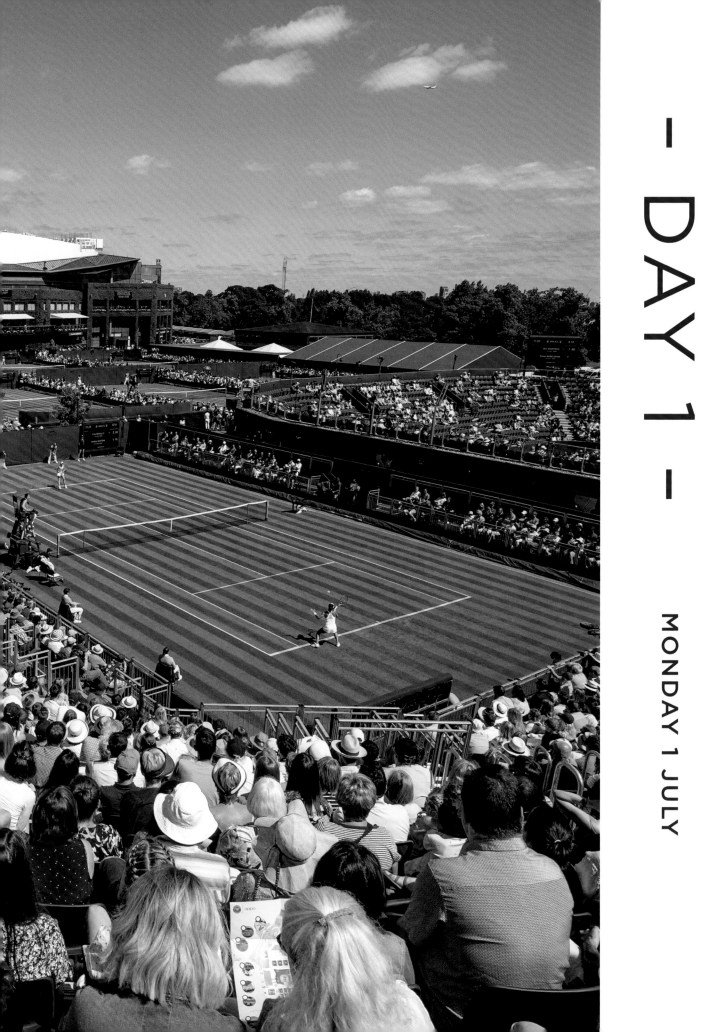

W

ith 32 seeds in Grand Slam singles competitions, headline-grabbing first round draws are a relative rarity these days. The Championships 2019, however, had produced a gem for the opening day.

The meeting of Cori Gauff and Venus Williams was an intriguing prospect: a 15-year-old making her debut in a Grand Slam tournament against a 39-year-old fellow American who had long been one of her idols; the youngest player in the ladies' singles field against the oldest; the teenager who had just become the youngest player ever to come through Qualifying against the five-times Ladies' Singles Champion making her 22nd appearance at Wimbledon. Williams had won two of her All England Club singles titles and appeared in four ladies' singles finals on Centre Court even before Gauff had been born.

The concluding match on No.1 Court more than lived up to its billing. Gauff, an outstanding junior who had won the girls' title at Roland-Garros at the age of 14, played with a maturity that belied her years to win 6-4, 6-4. From the start the teenager hit the ball confidently from the baseline, combining impressive power with consistent accuracy and intelligent point construction. Given Gauff's long limbs, thumping groundstrokes and serves struck at speeds of up to 116mph, Williams might have felt like she was facing her teenage self.

Has there ever been a more impressive Wimbledon debut? In the opening set Gauff made just two unforced errors and did not have to defend a single break point. When Williams rallied in the second set, recovering from a break down to level at 4-4, Gauff kept her nerve, although she needed four match points before closing out her victory. She made just eight unforced errors in the whole match, compared with Williams' 26.

While her parents, watching in the players' box, jumped for joy in celebration at the end, Gauff knelt to the ground as tears filled her eyes. At the net Gauff thanked Williams "for everything she's done for the sport" before joining the crowd in applauding her off the court. "I wouldn't be here if it wasn't for her," Gauff said later. "I told her she was so inspiring. I've always wanted to tell her that, but I've never had the guts to before."

Gauff said she had not gone into the match with a specific game plan. "My goal was just to stay calm and composed," she said. "I really believe that when I do that, I can do anything. I like to figure things out on the court. My parents always tell me: 'If you play your game, you can beat anyone.' I wouldn't say I didn't expect to win the match. I knew that I was going to go out there and play the way I play. I wasn't surprised that I won."

Asked how far she thought she could go in the competition, Gauff said: "My goal is to win it." She added: "I want to be the greatest. My dad told me that I could do this when I was eight... I think people limit themselves too much. Once you actually get your goal, then it's like: 'What do you do now?' I like to shoot really high." Williams, who had lost in the first round at The Championships on only one previous occasion, said of her conqueror's potential: "The sky's the limit. It really is."

In her post-match interviews Gauff demonstrated a bewitching mix of youthful confidence, common sense and good humour, without ever giving the impression that her maturity had come at the expense of how you might expect any 15-year-old girl to be. Before this match, when was the last time that she had cried? "The movie *Endgame*, when Iron Man died, I was crying," Gauff said. "Every time I think of it I get teary-eyed because I really liked Iron Man."

Before her last match in qualifying Gauff had had to sit a science test at 11pm UK time as part of her schoolwork. How had she fared then and how would she mark her performance against Williams? "On my science test I got a B," Gauff said with a smile. "Today I'd give myself an A."

On a day when five seeds in the ladies' singles and four in the gentlemen's singles were knocked out, the most significant scalp was Naomi Osaka, the

Following pages: The All England Club Grounds captured in all their glory against the spectacular backdrop of central London and looking ready for a wonderful Championships

Below: Venus Williams praised her 15-year-old conqueror Cori Gauff, saying "the sky's the limit" for the youngster

No.2 seed, who made 34 unforced errors in going down 6-7(4), 2-6 on Centre Court to Yulia Putintseva. Osaka went a break up in the opening set before her game fell apart as the world No.39 from Kazakhstan repeated her victory over the 21-year-old Japanese at Edgbaston the previous month. "To play on this amazing court, it's a great experience," Putintseva said afterwards. "I really loved it out there."

It was the latest setback in what had been a roller-coaster 11 months for Osaka. Having made her big breakthrough by winning the 2018 US Open, where she beat Serena Williams in the final, she won the Australian Open title in January, which took her to No.1 in the world rankings, a rise of 67 places in just over a year. Within days, however, Osaka parted company with Sascha Bajin, the coach who had guided her to the top, and her form suddenly dipped. She reached just one semi-final in her six tournaments between Melbourne and Roland-Garros, where she fell in the third round, and showed no signs of improvement on grass.

The pressures on Osaka were evident as she spoke in barely a whisper at her post-match press conference. Having admitted that she had not played well, she was asked how she had bounced back from defeats in the past. "The key for me was just learning how to have fun, kind of taking pressure off myself," she said. "I hope I can somehow find a way to do that." The press conference ended when she was asked how difficult it had been coping with her new level of fame. "Can I leave?" Osaka asked the moderator. "I feel like I'm about to cry."

Opposite: Novak Djokovic was in typically dynamic form as he opened the defence of his title with a win over Germany's Philipp Kohlschreiber

Below: Naomi Osaka, winner of two of the previous three Grand Slams, was left crestfallen after being knocked out on Centre Court by Kazakhstan's Yulia Putintseva

GETTING TO KNOW COCO
—

After her extraordinary breakthrough victory over her idol Venus Williams, everybody wanted to know all about this amazing 15-year-old schoolgirl Cori Gauff – and she obliged us all in the funniest, most charming fashion.

First things first, the girl from Delray Beach, Florida, likes to be known as Coco rather than Cori, which is pronounced the same way as her dad's name, Corey. "He likes to say every time they call me Cori, they're cheering for him," she smiled.

Coco has the right athletic genes, with Corey being a college basketball player at Georgia State University while mum Candi was a fine gymnast and track and field athlete at Florida State. Growing up idolising the Williams sisters, Cori was given the chance to train at the French tennis academy run by Serena's coach, Patrick Mouratoglou, who helped mould the girl who would become the youngest US Open girls' singles finalist at 13 and a Roland-Garros junior champion at 14. Her rare talent has seen her signed up by Roger Federer's management agency, Team8, with the great man himself taking a keen interest in her career.

"She's not a regular 15-year-old, she's completely driven, believes in herself incredibly and thinks she's going to be the greatest," said Mouratoglou. Yet away from tennis, said Coco, she is just a "goofy" teenager who loves cracking jokes and adores

her musical heroes Beyonce, Rihanna, Jaden and Kendrick Lamar.

And she was quite happy, she said, to not make a fuss about her skyrocketing career. "I'm not really the sort of person to talk about myself," she told The Wimbledon Channel. "I have three teachers who still don't even know I play tennis." That was a secret she wasn't going to be able to keep for long.

Magdalena Rybarikova, a semi-finalist two years earlier, crushed Aryna Sabalenka, the No.10 seed, 6-2, 6-4, while Marketa Vondrousova, the runner-up at Roland-Garros the previous month, was brought down to earth by Madison Brengle, who beat the No.16 seed 6-4, 6-4. Caroline Garcia, the No.23 seed, and Daria Kasatkina, the No.29 seed, were beaten by Shuai Zhang and Alja Tomljanovic respectively. Simona Halep twice needed on-court treatment after an awkward fall in her 6-4, 7-5 victory over Aliaksandra Sasnovich and admitted afterwards that she had been lucky to escape serious injury.

Novak Djokovic, playing the traditional opening match on Centre Court as the defending Gentlemen's Singles Champion, started with a double fault and a drop of serve before easing to a 6-3, 7-5, 6-3 victory over Philipp Kohlschreiber on a day when two of the game's best young men suffered surprising defeats to opponents ranked outside the world's top 100. Alexander Zverev, the No.6 seed, was beaten 6-4, 3-6, 2-6, 5-7 by Jiri Vesely, while Stefanos Tsitsipas, the No.7 seed, went down 4-6, 6-3, 4-6, 7-6(8), 3-6 to Thomas Fabbiano.

Zverev, whose performances at Grand Slam level have regularly failed to match his excellence elsewhere, admitted he was low on confidence. "It was kind of a typical Grand Slam match for me," the 22-year-old German said. "I started off well, then one or two things don't go my way and everything kind of a little bit falls apart."

Tsitsipas had been regarded by many as a dark horse for the title. In the previous 12 months the 20-year-old Greek had won three tournaments, played in two Masters 1000 finals, beaten Djokovic on

*Below: Two of the young stars of the game made a shock early exit but it was a good day for their conquerors, Italian Thomas Fabbiano (**left**), who beat No.7 seed Stefanos Tsitsipas, and Czech qualifier Jiri Vesely (**right**), victor over No.6 seed Alexander Zverev*

TO THE TENNIS

THE BEAUTIFUL SOUTH

A new attraction at Wimbledon was launched in the shape of the Southern Village, a spectacular public area featuring The Tennis Shop, food and drink outlets and a 'Wimbledon 2030' demonstration area offering a vision of a more sustainable future for the All England Club. Venus Williams was one of many who visited the innovative American Express Tennis Fan Experience located there (*right*), which gave spectators a chance to test their skills in a virtual reality test – the 'Champion's Rally' – against those of a certain Andy Murray.

a hard court and Rafael Nadal on clay, and reached the semi-finals of the Australian Open, knocking out Roger Federer along the way. However, he struggled throughout against Fabbiano, a 30-year-old Italian who had won only seven games in losing to Tsitsipas in the third round the previous year.

"People expected things from me and I didn't deliver," a disconsolate Tsitsipas said afterwards. "When you get so much support, so much energy, so much positivity from everyone and you just ruin everything by yourself, it's devastating." He added: "The way I played, it should have been in three sets, not five."

Gael Monfils, the No.16 seed, retired in the fifth set against Ugo Humbert because of an ankle injury, while Dusan Lajovic, the No.32 seed, was beaten by Hubert Hurkacz. The 2018 Gentlemen's Singles Runner-up, Kevin Anderson, playing in only his third tournament since January after suffering an elbow injury, beat Pierre-Hugues Herbert 6-3, 6-4, 6-2. Two Canadians celebrated Canada Day by meeting on Court 12 as 18-year-old Felix Auger-Aliassime beat Vasek Pospisil 5-7, 6-2, 6-4, 6-3 to become the first man born in the year 2000 or later to win a match at Grand Slam level. Another Canadian, Milos Raonic, progressed at the expense of India's Prajnesh Gunneswaran.

Heather Watson and Kyle Edmund, the only Britons in action on the first day, both won. Watson beat a 17-year-old qualifier, the American Caty McNally, 7-6(3), 6-2, but only after serving three double faults in the first game and saving two set points when McNally served at 6-5. Edmund, who had experienced a mixed first six months of the year, hit 46 winners in beating Spain's Jaume Munar 6-4, 6-4, 6-4. "It's pretty cool playing on Centre Court," he said afterwards. "You always remember every match you play there."

*Below: It was a bright start for the home challenge as the first two Britons in action, Heather Watson (**left**) and Kyle Edmund (**right**), both progressed to the second round with no alarms*

DAILY DIARY **DAY 1**

Feliciano Lopez enhanced his record for competing in the most consecutive Grand Slams as he made it 70 not out at Wimbledon with his opening day win over American qualifier Marcos Giron.

Yet the Spanish favourite (*above*), the 2019 singles winner at Queen's Club who also partnered comeback man Andy Murray to victory in the doubles, revealed that before Wimbledon he had feared his 17-year sequence could be at an end.

Step forward the All England Club. "I was out, I didn't make the cut," explained Lopez. "But the Club offered me the wild card to compete, so I'm very thankful."

It was great to see the elegant left-hander – "Deliciano" as Andy's mum, Judy, likes to call him – in such vintage form that the veteran himself could hardly believe it.

"It was obviously quite unexpected at 38 years old to be winning those titles at Queen's. I'm so proud," he added. The listening media agreed but nobody had the heart to tell him the really good news – he was actually only 37.

• It proved a landmark afternoon for one of Wimbledon's loftiest friends as Ivo Karlovic started his 15th Wimbledon with a victory over Italian qualifier Andrea Arnaboldi. Sixteen years since the giant Croat caused an opening day sensation by knocking out champion Lleyton Hewitt, Karlovic was back in the old boom-serving groove as he became – at 40 years and 123 days – the oldest men's singles competitor at Wimbledon since Ken Rosewall in 1975. Some things never change; the server of the most aces in history delivered 21 more to make it 13,399 and counting.

• Wimbledon cherishes its traditions but always recognises when it needs to move with the times. So it was on the opening day of the 133rd Championships that spectators and players no longer heard the time-honoured refrain of chair umpires referring to the marital status of female players when announcing scores during matches.

The All England Club announced that the honorifics 'Miss' and 'Mrs' would no longer be used in a bid to "achieve consistency" between the sexes. However, those titles were still used for code violation, medical time-out and Hawk-Eye challenge announcements.

• Pierre-Hugues Herbert revealed after his singles defeat by Kevin Anderson that he'd had a quad injury scare. So would he be fit to be Andy Murray's doubles partner? "I hope so," said the French four-times Grand Slam doubles champion, learning nervously about the expectations of teaming up with a national treasure. "I don't want to imagine having to say anything to Andy about an injury. I actually feel more pressure than ever!"

The victories of Kyle Edmund and Heather Watson on the first day had given British tennis the perfect start to The Championships and even better news was to follow. By the end of Day Two there were seven home singles players through to the second round, the most for 13 years.

Given the absence from singles competition of both Andy Murray, the country's standard-bearer for more than a decade, and Katie Boulter, who had been British No.2 earlier in the year until suffering a back injury which kept her out of both Roland-Garros and Wimbledon, it was a fine achievement. HRH The Duchess of Cambridge, Patron of the All England Club, could not have chosen a better day to visit SW19.

Dan Evans provided Britain's first victory of the second day when he beat Federico Delbonis 6-3, 7-6(5), 6-3 in his first appearance at Wimbledon for three years. Delbonis, a 28-year-old Argentinian ranked No.76 in the world, had failed to win a match in his four previous visits to The Championships and was in trouble from the moment he lost the first three games.

Evans had proved his grass court credentials the previous month by winning successive Challenger tournaments at Surbiton and Nottingham as he continued his impressive comeback following a one-year ban for a drugs offence. When Evans returned to competition in April 2018 he did not have a world ranking, but worked tirelessly to regain his place in the top 100 just 11 months later. By the start of The Championships he was world No.61, only 20 places below his career-high position.

After beating Delbonis, Evans recalled his situation 12 months earlier when he had practised at Roehampton during The Championships having lost in Qualifying. "Anyone who has played Wimbledon and is not involved, or when a Grand Slam is on, it's a difficult week to practise," the British No.3 said. "Your head's not there. You want to be at the tournament." Evans' coach, David Felgate, had stressed the importance of training that fortnight. "I have to give him credit for quite a lot of the last year," Evans said. "It's not easy when you're starting back from nothing."

Cameron Norrie, the British No.2 behind Edmund, had lost in the first round on both his previous appearances at The Championships but claimed a convincing 6-2, 6-4, 6-4 victory over Denis Istomin. Norrie had arrived at Wimbledon having lost five of his six previous matches, including a dispiriting defeat to the world No.273, Elliot Benchetrit, at Roland-Garros, but said the home crowd's support had lifted him.

Jay Clarke had also been looking for a first singles victory at The Championships. Having been given a wild card, the British No.4 took his chance with both hands, beating Noah Rubin, who was ranked 17 places lower than him at No.183 in the world, 4-6, 7-5, 6-4, 6-4. Clarke, aged 20, kept his composure despite losing the first set and seeing Rubin recover from 5-1 down to 5-5 in the second.

The win earned Clarke a second round meeting with Roger Federer, who had recovered from a slow start against South Africa's Lloyd Harris to win 3-6, 6-1, 6-2, 6-2. Clarke pointed out that Federer had won both the Wimbledon boys' singles and doubles titles the year that he had been born – 1998 – and said he had always looked up to him. "I tried to copy a lot of the stuff he does," Clarke said. "I actually gave up in the end because it was too tough to do."

On the day when England's footballers lost to the United States in the FIFA Women's World Cup semi-finals, Harriet Dart and Johanna Konta provided some home cheer. Dart, the world No.182, bridged a gap of 74 places in the rankings to beat Christina McHale, of the United States, 4-6, 6-4, 6-4. Dart said she had benefited from the experience of reaching the mixed doubles semi-finals 12 months earlier alongside Clarke, when they played on both Centre and No.1 Court. "I think all these

British youngster Jay Clarke booked a dream date against Roger Federer by winning his first round contest with American Noah Rubin

experiences are just helping me develop as a player and a person, just realising that I belong here," the 22-year-old Londoner said.

Konta, the British No.1, got off to an encouraging start in her eighth successive appearance at The Championships, beating Romania's Ana Bogdan 7-5, 6-2 on No.1 Court. Despite making 29 unforced errors, Konta broke serve three times and successfully defended the only two break points against her. "First rounds are always tricky in any tournament, but especially Slams," she said afterwards. "I was really pleased with how I served, how I just competed in general."

James Ward nearly provided a sixth British victory of the day but let slip a two-set lead over Nikoloz Basilashvili, the world No.16 winning 2-6, 4-6, 6-4, 6-4, 8-6.

HOLDING COURT

HRH The Duchess of Cambridge, Patron of the All England Club, enjoyed a full day at Wimbledon, not just meeting players, officials and support staff and visiting the Aorangi practice courts but also helping inspire a British tennis success story in an unlikely setting.

The Duchess did watch some of the action from her familiar Royal Box vantage point but also found time to pay a surprise visit to Court 14 to watch 22-year-old wild card Harriet Dart win her morning match with America's Christina McHale.

The Duchess, who was joined by British Fed Cup captain Anne Keothavong and another rising British player, Katie Boulter, sat among Ball Girls and Boys and Court Coverers and watched an hour of the match that Dart won in three sets.

The surprised and delighted Londoner Dart was left to later enthuse about the unexpected royal visit. "I was aware. The chair umpire mentioned it before the coin toss," said the Hampstead player.

"It's pretty cool to have royalty watching you. Such a privilege for me that she got to see me play... Hopefully, she'll come to many more of my matches."

Asked by reporters if it had been a career highlight, Dart could only smile: "I mean, it's pretty surreal. Any of you guys had the Duchess watch you play?"

HRH The Duchess of Cambridge chatted to players like Johanna Konta (top, left); support staff including Service Stewards (above); as well as current AELTC Chairman Philip Brook (left) and the incoming Chairman Ian Hewitt (top, right)

Paul Jubb, aged 19, making his Championships debut just six weeks after claiming the biggest prize in American college tennis, was beaten 0-6, 3-6, 7-6(8), 1-6 by the experienced Joao Sousa, while Katie Swan lost 2-6, 4-6 to Germany's Laura Siegemund, ranked 123 places higher than her at No.82 in the world.

Ashleigh Barty, the No.1 seed, beat Saisai Zheng 6-4, 6-2, but Donna Vekic, the No.22 seed, and Lesia Tsurenko, the No.32 seed, both went out, beaten by Alison Riske and Barbora Strycova respectively.

It was a day of mixed fortunes for past winners of the ladies' singles. Maria Sharapova, the champion in 2004, suffered another injury setback when she retired in the third set against Pauline Parmentier because of an arm problem, and Garbiñe Muguruza, the 2017 champion, was beaten 4-6, 4-6 by Brazil's Beatriz Haddad Maia, the world No.121. Angelique Kerber began the defence of her title by beating Tatjana Maria 6-4, 6-3 on Centre Court, while Petra Kvitova beat Ons Jabeur 6-4, 6-2 in her first match for six weeks. The champion of 2011 and 2014 had been a doubtful starter because of an arm injury that was still healing. "I will definitely be sore tomorrow," she said.

Serena Williams, aiming to win her eighth Wimbledon singles title, opened her campaign with a slightly stuttering 6-2, 7-5 victory over the world No.161, Giulia Gatto-Monticone, an Italian qualifier making her Wimbledon debut. At Roland-Garros 31-year-old Gatto-Monticone had become the oldest woman to play her first match at a Grand Slam tournament for 42 years.

During Williams' post-match press conference a reporter asked her about the continuing speculation as to whether she would play mixed doubles with Murray. "If you guys really want it, then maybe I'll do it," she said playfully. "We do really want it," the reporter responded. "All right, done, just for you guys," Williams said with a laugh. So was that a yes? "If you guys want it," she confirmed. "I really do," the reporter replied. "Just for you then," Williams smiled.

The American went on to describe Murray's work ethic as "off the charts" and said there were many reasons to admire him. "Above all, he really stands out, he really speaks up about women's issues, no matter what," she said. "You can tell he has a really strong woman in his life." Within an hour it was confirmed that Williams and Murray would indeed be in the following day's mixed doubles draw.

ANDY-ONE FOR TENNIS?

—

Andy Murray found his ideal mixed doubles match in Serena Williams but how spoilt for choice he had been with offers – some delightful and some deadly serious – from a host of suitors.

After world No.1 Ashleigh Barty turned Murray down because of her busy schedule, the Australian noted: "I'm sure he's got a million girls lined up and can take his pick."

Well, sort of. First came an offer from close to home as Murray's 85-year-old grandma Shirley Erskine (*right*) outlined her credentials on Twitter, saying: "Andy, you've got absolutely the right one here, no problem." Andy's mum, Judy, added invitingly: "She won't be able to hear a word u say + speed off the mark will be non existent but she will bring shortbread for changeovers + promises to watch her trams."

The great Billie Jean King, 75, was another such applicant, tweeting that she was "available and lacing up", while comedian Miranda Hart wooed Andy thus: "I'm VERY tall and the extra weight means I'm very grounded emotionally and physically."

Maria Sharapova retweeted a video of herself in doubles action, noting: "I heard Andy Murray was looking for a mixed dubs partner. Thanks US Open for sending in my resume today." CoCo Vandeweghe swore she'd brave injury to partner him, while Kirsten Flipkens, Murray's old SW19 partner, enquired: "Wimbledon 2006, Wimbledon 2019, Andy Murray?"

@judymurray

Fellow Brit Naomi Broady seemed keenest for the gig, telling Andy she would "totally ditch my own flesh and blood [brother and doubles partner Liam] to play with you". Alas, all their pleas were in vain.

Previous pages:
Roger Federer lost
a rare first round
set before kicking
his 21st consecutive
Wimbledon into gear
with victory over
young South African
Lloyd Harris on
Centre Court

Below: Maria
Sharapova, the
2004 Ladies' Singles
Champion, was
forced to retire with
an arm injury in the
third set of her match
against Pauline
Parmentier

There is widespread agreement within tennis that today's playing surfaces – whether grass, clay or hard courts – are more similar than they have ever been, but the meeting of Dominic Thiem and Sam Querrey demonstrated how some players still have distinct preferences. Thiem had been runner-up at Roland-Garros for the last two years but had gone past the second round at The Championships on only one previous occasion. The big-serving Querrey, meanwhile, had enjoyed some of his best results on grass and the 2017 semi-finalist duly won 6-7(4), 7-6(1), 6-3, 6-0. Querrey, who held his serve throughout, said afterwards: "I know grass is not his favourite surface, but he is still a great player who reached the French Open final a few weeks ago, so I felt like the pressure was on him." Denis Shapovalov was the only other men's seed to go out, losing 6-7(0), 4-6, 3-6 to Ricardas Berankis.

Bernard Tomic was crushed 2-6, 1-6, 4-6 by Jo-Wilfried Tsonga in 58 minutes, which made it the shortest completed men's match at The Championships for 15 years. Tomic was widely criticised for an apparent lack of effort and was subsequently fined £45,000 – his prize money as a first round loser – for not meeting the "required professional standard".

Rafael Nadal beat Yuichi Sugita 6-3, 6-1, 6-3 to earn what would be a much-anticipated second round meeting with Nick Kyrgios, who beat Jordan Thompson 7-6(4), 3-6, 7-6(10), 0-6, 6-1. There had been little love lost between Kyrgios and Nadal in the past. After Nadal lost to Kyrgios in Acapulco earlier in the year the Spaniard had accused him of lacking respect, while the Australian said the former world No.1 was "super salty" in defeat. Asked here about their relationship, Kyrgios insisted they had mutual respect but stressed: "Not sure that me and Rafa could go down to the Dog & Fox and have a beer together." Nadal refused to rise to the bait. "I'm too old for all that stuff," he said.

DAILY DIARY DAY 2

The historic moment caught everyone a little by surprise as there was not a drop of rain in the air, but at 9.10pm on Tuesday No.1 Court's splendid new retractable roof (*above*) was put into action for the very first time during The Championships.

As bad light descended near the end of the first round match between Donna Vekic and Alison Riske, it was decided the roof should be closed to enable the exciting contest – locked at 5-5 in the final set – to be completed under lights.

When play resumed at 9.25pm, it didn't take long for Riske to seal the 3-6, 6-3, 7-5 victory, leaving the American delighted to have earned an unexpected place in Wimbledon annals.

"I've been waiting to have my place in history, so I'm glad I finally made it!" the American laughed, little knowing that this would not be her only surprise contribution of the Fortnight.

• Paul Jubb's story captured everyone's imagination. The 19-year-old British wild card and world No.431 was naturally disappointed to lose his debut match on Court 17 in four sets to the experienced Portuguese Joao Sousa but could look back with pride on his special journey to get there.

The teenager had taken the most unlikely route from a Hull council estate to becoming America's college champion and one of the bright new prospects of British tennis.

Jubb's parents both died when he was young, leaving his grandmother Valerie to use her pension and family

allowance to look after the youngster, who got his feel for tennis by playing Swingball in his aunt's garden.

Imagine then 77-year-old Valerie's pride as she sat at courtside alongside other family members. "She's played a huge role in my life, being a rock ever since I was four," Jubb said of his gran. "She's led me in the right direction from day one. She means the world. I love her very much."

• The dramatic progress of England's football 'Lionesses' at the World Cup was followed avidly by many at Wimbledon who tuned in to watch their semi-final clash with holders USA.

Johanna Konta was one, sending them a filmed message from SW19 – "I'm really rooting for you guys. Let's go Lionesses!" – while even Serena Williams was left admiring the "amazing" English team, having met them at their World Cup training base in Paris.

"Obviously I'm rooting for USA, though. I love the team," said Williams. Alas for the Lionesses' fans, Serena proved – as she so often does – the winner, with her compatriots winning the big match in Lyon 2-1.

— DAY 3 —

WEDNESDAY 3 JULY

Cori Gauff had indicated on Day One that she preferred her nickname of 'Coco' to Cori, which was clearly a godsend for headline writers the world over. For three days now the media had been going 'loco for Coco' following her remarkable victory over Venus Williams.

Given all the attention on the 15-year-old, the question now was whether she would be able to maintain her focus in the second round against Magdalena Rybarikova, a 30-year-old Slovakian who was a proven performer on grass. There was already huge interest in the match, but it was given an extra dimension when Andrew Jarrett, the Referee, moved it to be played under the No.1 Court roof because of the late-running programme on No.2 Court. The roof had been used briefly the previous evening at the end of Alison Riske's victory over Donna Vekic, but this would be the first match to be played from start to finish under cover on No.1 Court.

From the outset it was evident that Gauff would once again take everything in her stride. Rybarikova, a semi-finalist at The Championships in 2017, tried to play her normal attacking game, but was repeatedly forced back by the quality of Gauff's groundstrokes. The teenager made only 10 unforced errors and did not have to defend a single break point, while Rybarikova was regularly under pressure on her serve. Moving smoothly around the court, Gauff broke to love to go 4-2 up, dropped only one point in her next two service games to take the opening set and was soon 3-1 up in the second. After just an hour and 10 minutes a third break of serve secured her 6-3, 6-3 victory.

Gauff said afterwards that she had been surprised by the interest in her following her victory over Williams. "It was honestly so hard just with social media and everything trying to focus on my next match because people are still posting about Venus," she said. "I wasn't expecting any of this." Gauff said she had been "kind of star-struck" by the number of direct messages she had received from celebrities, but found social media helped to relax her before she went on court. "I just watch YouTube videos," she said. "It gets me in a laughing spirit."

What advice had her parents and coaches been giving her? "They just told me: 'You have another match. The tournament's not over. Don't focus too much on what happened.' My goal is to win it. They just told me: 'Keep yourself grounded.' I think I've always just done a good job of that." Corey Gauff, her father, told the Reuters news agency: "This is not the first time she has had to deal with pressure, but she surprises me with some of the fight she comes up with. My words to her today were: 'Just keep it simple and make sure you hit the ball hard, and hit it in the corners.'"

Gauff said that she had been working particularly hard in her practice sessions in recent weeks, doing extra sprinting sessions and telling her sparring partner to hit the ball harder at her. "It just shows if you really work hard, you can get where you want to go," she said. "Last week around this time, I didn't know I was coming here. It just shows you have to be ready for everything." Gauff said she had also worked on her "off-court thinking" and on "how I can improve myself and improve the way I act on court". She added: "You can kind of fake it till you make it. But I'm not faking it, at least right now."

The teenager was one of only two American women left in the bottom half of the draw after two seeds went out. Madison Keys, the No.17 seed, was beaten 2-6, 4-6 by Slovenia's Polona Hercog, who would be Gauff's next opponent, while Sofia Kenin, the No.27 seed, who had knocked Serena Williams out of Roland-Garros a month earlier, went down 5-7, 6-4, 3-6 to Ukraine's Dayana Yastremska. However, Danielle Collins, a semi-finalist at the Australian Open in January, secured her place in the third round for the first time by beating Latvia's Anastasija Sevastova, the No.12 seed, 4-6, 6-4, 6-3.

Below: No.1 Court's roof was closed for an entire match for the first time at The Championships, leaving Cori Gauff and Magdalena Rybarikova to play the court's maiden 'indoor' blockbuster (following pages)

51

Caroline Wozniacki and Karolina Pliskova progressed with straight-sets victories over Veronika Kudermetova and Monica Puig respectively, while two other former world No.1s, Simona Halep and Victoria Azarenka, set up a heavyweight showdown in the third round. Halep was made to work for a 6-3, 4-6, 6-2 victory by her fellow Romanian, Mihaela Buzarnescu, but Azarenka, back at her highest place in the world rankings for more than two years at No.40, brushed aside Australia's Ajla Tomljanovic, winning 6-2, 6-0.

Heather Watson and Kyle Edmund were unable to build on the previous day's British triumphs as both lost after promising starts. Watson broke Anett Kontaveit in the opening game and was still in contention at 5-5 in the first set, but the No.20 seed won eight of the last nine games to take the match 7-5, 6-1. "I thought in general I was too defensive," Watson said afterwards. "I didn't use my variety enough, coming to the net."

Edmund, the No.30 seed, appeared to be on his way to the third round for the second year in a row when he won the first two sets against Fernando Verdasco and led 3-0 in the third, only for the 35-year-old Spaniard to fight back and win 4-6, 4-6, 7-6(3), 6-3, 6-4. In what had been an injury-troubled year for Edmund, the 24-year-old Briton appeared to struggle with his right knee after slipping on the baseline. Edmund, who had underlined his position as British No.1 by beating Cameron Norrie and Dan Evans en route to the semi-finals in Eastbourne the previous week, refused to blame the defeat on his injury and said that he need to be physically stronger. "Obviously I've been dealing with a problem, but it's not really an excuse," he said. "When you are in sport, you play at a level. I've got to be able to play for longer

with the intensity I started the match with. I definitely didn't play with the same intensity at the end. These are not excuses. These are just things I've got to get a bit better at. I was in a position to win and didn't."

Verdasco's sixth victory in his career from two sets down set up a third round meeting with the 5ft 8in Italian Thomas Fabbiano, who beat the 6ft 11in Croatian Ivo Karlovic 6-3, 6-7(6), 6-3, 6-7(4), 6-4. Reilly Opelka, another 6ft 11in man mountain, had better luck over five sets, beating Stan Wawrinka, the No.22 seed, 7-5, 3-6, 4-6, 6-4, 8-6. Opelka, who was Wimbledon Boys' Singles Champion in 2015, hit serves at speeds of up to 142mph, but showed he had plenty more to his game. "I've always been a pretty good mover – under-rated, actually," the 21-year-old American said. "I think sometimes when I play guys for the first time, they don't expect it. It helps me win so many points." Wawrinka, who had been steadily improving since undergoing knee surgery in 2017, described it as "a tough loss" but added: "I'm really happy [with] the way I'm playing."

*Defending Gentlemen's Singles Champion Novak Djokovic (**top**) made short work of American Denis Kudla, winning in straight sets, but Britain's No.1 Kyle Edmund (**above**) suffered a five-set Centre Court defeat to the ever-dangerous Fernando Verdasco (**left**)*

STAIRWAY TO HEAVEN

—

Let's hear it for the lads and lasses on the ladders, the scoreboard operators who keep a Wimbledon tradition alive while keeping thousands of spectators informed about the results around the Grounds.

In this digital age, isn't there something timelessly reassuring about the sight of these manually operated Order of Play and results boards still being tended by a seven-strong team so dedicated that they never get a chance to actually watch any tennis?

Mind you, they know better than anyone who's won what – and where – as they monitor the scores on a computer screen from their headquarters near Court 17 before springing into action to make the 1,500 or so daily journeys up and down the wooden ladders to insert the right name plates and scores. The results are up there in a flash.

"People love the manual scoreboards and draw boards, because they're handmade and a tradition that has continued down the years," the team's manager, Sean Pontin, who's been in the role at 31 Championships, told wimbledon.com.

"In total, we put up 1,358 match results on the Order of Play boards, 1,230 results on the 13 main draw boards – more than 2,500 results in total."

It's hard work but fun and very worthwhile. "We are proud to be at the best tennis tournament in the world," says Pontin, "and we're committed to making sure every score we put up is correct and tells the story of the tournament to visitors."

Kevin Anderson, the 2018 Gentlemen's Singles Runner-up, beat Janko Tipsarevic 6-4, 6-7(5), 6-1, 6-4, while Novak Djokovic, the man he had lost to in the final, reached the third round for the 11th year in a row by beating Denis Kudla 6-3, 6-2, 6-2. The only man with more consecutive appearances in the last 32 in the Open era is Jimmy Connors, who made 14 between 1972 and 1985. "I guess consistency was one of the keys and focus points of my Grand Slam career going back 10 years," Djokovic said after his 93-minute victory. "I always aim to play my best in Grand Slams. I guess the quality of tennis that I produce in the Slams is pretty high. That's what allows me to have the results like this."

Many a year has passed since the draw for the mixed doubles was so eagerly awaited as Andy Murray and Serena Williams learned that Germany's Andreas Mies and Chile's Alex Guarachi would be their first opponents. Murray revealed that his partnership with Williams had come about after his coach, Jamie Delgado, had been approached by Patrick Mouratoglou, the American's coach. Murray said that because Williams had had a knee problem both sides had wanted to see how she came through her opening singles match the previous day before confirming their partnership.

"With everything that has gone on the last couple of years you don't know what's coming next or what's around the corner," Murray told a group of reporters. "The opportunity to play with Serena, one of the best tennis players of all time and one of the biggest female athletes ever, was something that I may never get another chance to do again. Potentially I might not play mixed doubles again, so if I'm going to do it once the chance to play with her is obviously brilliant."

A lovely panorama, taken from the roof of the AELTC Museum building with, in the foreground, Court 17 hosting a ladies' doubles match featuring Lidziya Marozava and Storm Sanders against Victoria Azarenka and Ashleigh Barty

DAILY DIARY DAY 3

A tall story unfolded on No.2 Court as the giant American Reilly Opelka caused a shock by knocking out Stan Wawrinka amid a barrage of 23 aces.

Opelka (*above*), Boys' Singles Champion in 2015, was asked afterwards exactly how tall he was and shrugged, explaining that he wasn't sure if it was 6ft 11in or whether he may even tip 7ft. Either way, he was certainly the most towering figure left in the tournament after Ivo Karlovic, also listed at 6ft 11in, was knocked out by Thomas Fabbiano.

Naturally, being that lofty has its big-serving advantages but away from the court, as Opelka explained, it can be trying. While at the pre-Wimbledon tournament in the "kinda like an older town" of Eastbourne, he revealed with a sigh that he couldn't really fit in his bed.

So why, he was asked, wasn't he playing top-flight US basketball instead? "Good question," he pondered, adding with a smile: "I wish I was. I regret it every day..."

• After the exit of so many of the sport's young guns over the first three days – Alexander Zverev, Stefanos Tsitsipas and Denis Shapovalov – there was much talk about exactly when the next generation of men's stars might make that long-awaited breakthrough.

Novak Djokovic, one of the seemingly eternal 'Big Three' along with Roger Federer and Rafael Nadal, was happy to offer a reassuring answer. "There is time. I understand that people want to see a new winner of a Grand Slam. They don't want to see three of us

dominating. Eventually it's going to come," said the 15-time Slam champion.

Yes, but when exactly, Novak? "In about 25 years," he grinned. "Then we'll all be happy."

• During his defeat to Opelka, Stan Wawrinka again demonstrated his charm. Having accidentally hit a female line judge with his racket as he was stretching to retrieve one of Reilly Opelka's monster serves, he felt terrible. "I was sure she had some pain and was not happy," noted Stan, "so I gave her a little hug." A gentleman to the last.

• Karolina Pliskova, the most prolific ace server in women's tennis, had an extra incentive to bang down a few more untouchable efforts as she had promised a £100 contribution to a charitable cause for every ace she sent down. Another nine whistled past Monica Puig in their second round match, taking her tournament total to 15 and ensuring her charity would collect at least a £1,500 pay-out. By the end of her tournament the Czech was able to write a cheque for £3,600.

— DAY 4 —

Controversy surrounds Nick Kyrgios wherever he goes, to the point where one essential fact is sometimes forgotten: when he puts his mind to it, the 24-year-old Australian can be a wonderful tennis player. The second round of the gentlemen's singles provided a vivid reminder of that as Kyrgios and Rafael Nadal fought out a memorable duel on Centre Court.

Above: Nick Kyrgios was in spectacular form as he attempted to beat the two-times champion Rafael Nadal

Previous pages: Kyrgios and Nadal prepare to do battle in the most eagerly awaited early showdown of The Championships 2019

It had everything, including glorious shot-making, breath-taking rallies, Kyrgios arguing with the umpire and evidence of the friction that exists between the two players. Five years after Kyrgios had announced his arrival on the world stage by beating Nadal on the same court, the Spaniard turned the tables with a 6-3, 3-6, 7-6(5), 7-6(3) victory.

When asked earlier in the week about his relationship with Nadal, Kyrgios had suggested they were unlikely to share a beer in the Dog & Fox in Wimbledon Village. The Spaniard was certainly nowhere to be seen when Kyrgios visited the pub the evening before this encounter. Whether or not it was down to their respective pre-match preparations, Nadal was soon in charge, breaking serve at the first attempt and then serving out for the opening set. By the second set Kyrgios was becoming frustrated at what he saw as the umpire's failure to control the time Nadal was taking between points. "Feels good up there with all the power, does it?" Kyrgios asked Damien Dumusois, who gave the Australian a code violation for unsportsmanlike conduct after he mimicked being hit by an electric shock. "You're no one," Kyrgios told him. "You think you're important. You have no idea what's going on. You're a disgrace."

Conflict, nevertheless, can bring the best out of Kyrgios, who took the second set after appearing to unsettle Nadal by aiming a ferocious forehand straight at him. In the third set emotions boiled over. When Kyrgios drove another thunderbolt forehand direct at his opponent Nadal gave him a long stare across the net and celebrated lustily when he went on to win the game. The set went to a tie-break in which Nadal played immaculately and Kyrgios made crucial errors. It was much the same story in the fourth set tie-break as Kyrgios missed what should have been a routine smash on the opening point while Nadal was a model of consistency.

"He played really well today," Kyrgios said afterwards. "He plays every point. He doesn't take one point off. I feel like we're the polar opposites. I struggle so hard to just play every point with a routine."

Nadal was asked what Kyrgios might achieve if he could play with the same intensity. "If, if, if," Nadal said. "Sometimes what is important is your love and passion for this game. Without really loving this game that much, it's difficult to achieve important things. With his talent and with his serve, he can win a Grand Slam, of course. He has the talent to do it. It's true that things can be completely different for him if he wants to play all the matches the same way that he tried today."

Kyrgios did not see himself as a current contender for Grand Slam honours. "I'm a great tennis player, but I don't do the other stuff," he said. "I'm not the most professional guy. I won't train day in, day out. I won't show up every day. There are a lot of things I need to improve on to get to that level."

Rafael Nadal demonstrated all his fighting qualities as he prevailed in four entertaining sets against his mercurial opponent

When asked about Kyrgios thumping the ball at him, Nadal said his only concern had been that it could have endangered officials or spectators. Kyrgios admitted that he had been trying to hit Nadal and could not understand why he might have been expected to apologise. "Why would I apologise?" he said. "I mean, the dude has got how many Slams, how much money in the bank account? I think he can take a ball to the chest."

Six more seeds went out of the gentlemen's singles. John Isner hit 34 aces but could not find a way past Mikhail Kukushkin, who won 6-4, 6-7(3), 4-6, 6-1, 6-4. Isner, a semi-finalist 12 months earlier, was playing his first tournament for three months following a foot injury. "It stinks going out early," he said afterwards. "My lack of preparation certainly showed."

However, two of Isner's fellow Americans celebrated Independence Day by knocking out seeds as Tennys Sandgren beat Gilles Simon 6-2, 6-3, 4-6, 3-6, 8-6 and Steve Johnson outlasted Alex de Minaur, winning 3-6, 7-6(4), 6-3, 3-6, 6-3. Marin Cilic's difficult year took another turn for the worse as the 2017 runner-up was beaten 4-6, 4-6, 4-6 by Portugal's Joao Sousa, while Laslo Djere sank to a 3-6, 2-6, 1-6 defeat by John Millman.

Dan Evans handed out a lesson in grass court tennis to Nikoloz Basilashvili, the No.18 seed, as the 29-year-old Briton enjoyed his best moment since returning from a one-year suspension for a drugs offence. Basilashvili can outpower opponents, but the 27-year-old Georgian could not handle the variety in Evans' game. Evans, who by the end of the day was the only Briton left in the gentlemen's singles, won 6-3, 6-2, 7-6(2) and had tears in his eyes as he raised his hands to the sky at the end.

"A lot of my friends were here, people who have helped me so much," Evans said afterwards. "It's a big deal to be winning matches in the best tournaments in the world, especially here at Wimbledon, at your home Slam, with so much tradition at the tournament. I want to go as far as I can here. For me it's the best Grand Slam."

Two-times Ladies' Singles Champion Petra Kvitova served her way to an impressive win against the dangerous Kristina Mladenovic on No.1 Court

TALES OF THE UNEXPECTED

—

It was in 2014 that a gangling youngster with a carefree air and preposterous talent blew onto Centre Court and dispatched world No.1 Rafael Nadal amid a blizzard of 37 aces, 70 winners and the odd wonder 'tweener'. In teenager Nick Kyrgios that day, we saw a starburst of rare brilliance.

So, now we were back five years on for a thrilling repeat and perhaps another crazy tale of the unexpected from the 24-year-old Australian who's never stopped being compulsive viewing.

As so it proved again. This time, amid the blitzed winners, a behind-the-back volley and one booming forehand that smacked straight into Nadal, who could forget the moment Kyrgios feathered, from nowhere, the underarm ace that left even the stranded Spaniard summoning a pained laugh?

Kyrgios had already produced his 'signature weapon' against Nadal in Acapulco earlier in 2019 but no one could recall such audacity on Centre Court. It prompted cheers; then, when he repeated the dose to win another point, jeers.

So, yes, Kyrgios can be polarising but, even in defeat here, what a gift! Not only did he deliver the slowest first serve in Championships annals - too gentle even for IBM to record a speed - he also struck Wimbledon's fastest-ever second serve, a 143mph ace that proved the quickest of the Fortnight and the second-swiftest second serve in ATP history. And all off the back of an evening in the Dog & Fox! Now that's entertainment.

WONDER WALLS

Beautiful and biodiverse, two five-metre-tall 'living walls' of 14,344 plants covering 245 square metres on the side of No.1 Court – horizontally flanking either side of the big screen – quickly proved a spectacular attraction. The walls, five years in the planning and thriving through a high-tech automatic irrigation system, quickly demonstrated how they could enhance biodiversity within the Grounds when goldfinches were seen nesting amid the purple, white and green plants there just a week after the installation earlier in 2019.

Cameron Norrie enjoyed the "unbelievable experience" of playing on Centre Court for the first time and remained upbeat despite his 4-6, 4-6, 0-6 defeat by Kei Nishikori. "I was just really happy with the way I handled myself," the 23-year-old Briton said.

Jay Clarke, the British No.4, faced a daunting task against Roger Federer, who eased to a 6-1, 7-6(3), 6-2 victory. In a match dominated by serves, Federer, crucially, converted four of his five break points. After a nervous start 20-year-old Clarke said that he had learned a lot from the experience, while Federer gave the impression that he had barely moved out of third gear. "The tank is full," the eight-times champion said afterwards. "I came here with a lot of confidence. The first few matches haven't been very taxing physically."

Two Britons reached the third round of the ladies' singles as Johanna Konta beat the Czech Republic's Katerina Siniakova 6-3, 6-4 and Harriet Dart beat Brazil's Beatriz Haddad Maia 7-6(4), 3-6, 6-1. Siniakova, the world No.38, had beaten Konta in their only previous meeting, but struggled to handle her serve. Konta dropped only 11 points on serve and did not have to defend any break points. "I definitely felt like I served well today," Konta said. "Overall I was just pleased again with how I handled my opponent."

Dart followed up her maiden Wimbledon singles victory with a spirited performance against Haddad Maia, who had knocked out Garbiñe Muguruza in the previous round. "I'm just learning from all the experiences I'm having this year," Dart said afterwards. "This is my second Wimbledon. I'm still finding my feet. I'm definitely proving that my tennis is definitely right up there with the level." Dart's victory secured a third round meeting with Ashleigh Barty, who beat Alison Van Uytvanck 6-1, 6-3, and made up for her disappointment at not playing in the mixed doubles after Clarke, with whom she reached the semi-finals in 2018, made a late decision to play instead with Cori Gauff.

Above: Poland's Magda Linette roared her delight following her victory over US teenager and Roland-Garros semi-finalist Amanda Anisimova on Court 12

Left: American Lauren Davis pulled off one of the Fortnight's big shocks by coming from a set down to knock out Angelique Kerber on No.2 Court

Previous pages:
A picturesque peep at
Court 17 as Tamara
Zidansek prepares to
receive serve during
her second round
defeat by Qiang Wang

Below: Andy
Murray was
given a champion's
welcome as he made
a winning comeback
to Wimbledon after
a two-year injury
absence in his first
round gentlemen's
doubles match on No.1
Court with French
partner Pierre-
Hugues Herbert

Amanda Anisimova, the No.25 seed, was beaten 4-6, 5-7 by Magda Linette, while the biggest upset of the day saw Angelique Kerber, the defending champion, go down 6-2, 2-6, 1-6 to Lauren Davis, the world No.95, who had lost in Qualifying but appeared in the main draw as a lucky loser. The 25-year-old American hit 45 winners to Kerber's 13 and broke the German's serve eight times. Kerber said afterwards that she had been short of energy. "I won the first set, but I was not really feeling like I was playing well," she said. "She was going for it. She took the match in her hands. I was too defensive in the important moments."

Serena Williams has never lost to a player ranked outside the world's top 100 at The Championships but that record seemed in danger when Kaja Juvan, an 18-year-old Slovenian making her Wimbledon debut, took the opening set. The world No.133 broke serve twice and converted her first set point when Williams made a mess of a smash. However, Williams, watched by her friend HRH The Duchess of Sussex, quickly restored order and went on to win 2-6, 6-2, 6-4. "I play best when I am down sometimes," Williams said afterwards. "I am a fighter."

Andy Murray, playing his first match at The Championships for two years, and Pierre-Hugues Herbert made a successful start in the gentlemen's doubles, beating Ugo Humbert and Marius Copil 4-6, 6-1, 6-4, 6-0. After a nervous start Murray and Herbert soon took charge, to the delight of the vast majority of the crowd on No.1 Court.

Murray was simply elated to be back on court given that he had feared his career might be over when he decided to have a hip resurfacing operation in January. "Every time I'm on the court now, it's great," he said. "I'm just playing tennis again. Pain-free, healthy. It's nice. It's what I have enjoyed doing since I was a kid. At times over the last few years, I was not getting any enjoyment out of it. The fun is back."

DAILY DIARY DAY 4

Wimbledon bid a fond farewell to a popular figure who was hanging up his racket after a distinguished 16-year career. And what a wonderfully flamboyant way Marcos Baghdatis (*above*) chose to bow out.

After losing his second round encounter with Matteo Berrettini, the 34-year-old Cypriot, given a wild card to compete in his 14th Wimbledon, celebrated his goodbye with a rare old party on No.2 Court where he was the one handing out the retirement presents.

After the inevitable tears came the laughter as he gave away all his rackets, towels and kit – yes, even the shoes he was wearing – to the cheering crowd while parading around the court in his socks.

To the end, the crowd adored him. "I think I will be remembered as a happy, enjoyable person, as a person of the people," he smiled later. "That's the biggest gift any athlete can have."

The former Australian Open finalist and Wimbledon semi-finalist always had that gift. As tributes to Baghdatis flooded in from peers like Roger Federer and Stefanos Tsitsipas, the man himself reflected: "On 4 July 2004, Greece won soccer's European Championship and that gave me the impact that if I can believe in myself, [that] I can achieve anything.

"I'm retiring on 4 July 2019. Me coming from a small country shows that anything is possible." Thanks, Marcos, we'll miss you.

• Hmmm, who was that familiar-looking face playing in the Junior Qualifying Competition at Roehampton? The

long blond locks, the Viking good looks, that classy double-fisted backhand – yes, didn't 16-year-old Leo Borg look eerily like his legendary dad Bjorn?

It was 47 years since Borg Senior won the boys' title at 16, and the great man wisely stayed away from Roehampton in 2019, not wishing to heap more pressure on the world's 356th-ranked junior as the cameras zoomed in on him.

Leo was beaten by Frenchman Loris Pourroy 6-1, 6-4, but the future looks bright for the young Swede. "Today was not my day," Borg stated calmly, but we're sure that, just like his dad, he'll be back, stronger and icier.

• Decisions, decisions. Judy Murray had a family dilemma with both her lads in action simultaneously in the gentlemen's doubles, with Andy on No.1 Court and Jamie on Court 18. Who to watch? Judy plumped for Jamie, prompting a droll response from Andy: "Jamie is the No.1 son, so he used to get all the good presents. I always kind of got the hand-me-downs since we were young, so I'm used to that…"

– DAY 5 –

FRIDAY 5 JULY

Another day, another landmark for Cori Gauff. Having won her first two matches on No.1 Court, the 15-year-old American would now have her first taste of the biggest stage of all. With the eyes of the sporting world on her, Gauff faced Polona Hercog, a 28-year-old Slovenian, on Centre Court, the winner to meet Simona Halep, a former world No.1 and Roland-Garros champion, in the fourth round on Manic Monday.

Above: Big-hitting Slovenian Polona Hercog proved Cori Gauff's toughest challenge yet, earning two match points against the teenager

Previous pages: Come on Coco! The Hill was in a state of high excitement as supporters roared on both players

Neither Gauff nor Hercog had ever reached the second week of a Grand Slam tournament, but that was about where the similarities between the two players ended. Hercog was making her 36th appearance at a Grand Slam event while Gauff was making her debut.

On the face of it the world No.60 posed less of a threat than either of Gauff's previous opponents, Venus Williams and Magdalena Rybarikova. However, it soon became clear that this would be a backs-to-the-wall scrap. Gauff struggled on her serve in the opening set and was broken twice. At 3-5 she dropped her serve to love after hitting three double faults.

Trailing 5-2 in the second set, it seemed that the Gauff fairytale was about to end, but a clever backhand saved a first match point and Hercog double-faulted on the second. The set went to a tie-break, in which Hercog led 5-3, only for Gauff to fight back once again and eventually convert her third set point. Hercog's nerves were fraying, while Gauff was reaping a regular dividend from her sliced backhands. In the deciding set Hercog recovered an early break to level at 4-4, but at 5-6 a forehand

error took Gauff to match point. Emboldened, Gauff attacked the net, forcing Hercog into a lob which landed beyond the baseline. As Centre Court erupted, Gauff dropped her racket to the floor and leapt into the air in celebration of her 3-6, 7-6(7), 7-5 victory.

Gauff said afterwards that she had not felt any nerves walking out on to Centre Court – which she described as "one of the most sacred courts in the world" – and had kept believing in herself. "When I was down 5-2, I was just like: 'I can fight back. Just need to hold serve, break, then we'll see what happens from there'," she said. "I was just thinking: 'I need to go for my shots. I can't play pushing'."

Why did Gauff think she had made 43 unforced errors against Hercog compared with a total of just 18 in her first two matches? "I think I made more errors today because she was playing really well," Gauff said. "I felt like I had to go bigger because she was hitting so many forehand winners. I knew that I had to hit bigger. I think I was trying to hit too big to a point where I was missing a lot."

Gauff appreciated the crowd's support. "It's just crazy," she said. "I remember before I played Venus, there are people waiting when you walk to leave the practice courts. One little kid asked me for a picture. Then the next day, after I played Venus, everybody was screaming my name. It was pretty surreal how life changes in a matter of seconds."

Once again Gauff's reaction in victory was a mixture of teenage excitement and cool-headed analysis as she switched from talking about social media in one breath to discussing in the next how she did not believe in fate and destiny. "I feel like you can change your own world," she said. "I'm always hearing:

*Top: Cori Gauff savours the moment of victory after putting mum Candi and dad Corey (**above**) through the emotional mill over two and three-quarter hours*

'You're going to do this one day, do that one day.' If I relax now, that won't happen. I try not to think of it like that. I take it just one tournament at a time."

When told she had won £176,000 in prize money so far, Gauff described it as "cool" and said she might buy some hoodies with her earnings. "I love wearing hoodies," she said. "My mum banned me from buying hoodies for two months. Every week I was getting new hoodies sent to the house."

At 15 years and four months Gauff became the youngest player to reach the fourth round of the singles competition since 14-year-old Jennifer Capriati in 1990. Capriati's subsequent struggles to cope with 'teenage burn-out' were one of the reasons why the Women's Tennis Association (WTA) introduced its 'Age Eligibility Rule' in 1995, restricting the number of professional tournaments girls can play before they reach 18. For example, 15-year-olds are allowed to play in only 10 tournaments a year, though in Gauff's case that number had been raised to 14 because of her success at junior level.

Gauff's achievements and the way she was handling the public and media attention inevitably prompted debate over whether the restrictions were justified. Her father, Corey, suggested to *The New York Times* that restricting the number of matches rather than tournaments might be better, while Roger Federer, whose management company represents Gauff, had told the WTA that they should "loosen up" the rules. "I think it would be nice if they could play more," he said. "I feel like in some ways it puts extra pressure on them every tournament they play."

The pressure would surely rise in the next round against Halep, who played what the 27-year-old Romanian described as her best match of the year to beat Victoria Azarenka 6-3, 6-1. Halep, who won 11 of the last 12 games, had often been at her best on clay in the past, but said she felt confident on all surfaces. "I have a chance everywhere I play," she said. "I just have to fight and have the desire to win every match I play."

Caroline Wozniacki, who has never gone beyond the fourth round at The Championships, again made an early departure despite winning the first four games on No.2 Court against China's Shuai Zhang. "No.2 Court over the years hasn't really been my friend," the 28-year-old Dane said after losing 4-6, 2-6. "I was hoping to strike up a friendship this year. It wasn't to happen." Wozniacki was unhappy with a number of Hawk-Eye verdicts, calling them "crazy", "ridiculous" and "absurd", but a subsequent examination of the technology showed that it was in full working order.

Karolina Pliskova has a similarly modest record at The Championships, despite having won three titles on grass away from Wimbledon, but the two-times Eastbourne champion beat Su-Wei Hsieh 6-3, 2-6, 6-4 to earn a fourth round meeting with her fellow Czech, Karolina Muchova, who beat the No.20 seed, Anett Kontaveit, 7-6(7), 6-3. "I'd love to call myself a specialist on grass," said Pliskova afterwards. "This year I'm doing better and I've made the second week."

Novak Djokovic had coasted through his first two matches in straight sets but needed three hours to dispose of Hubert Hurkacz, who appeared to surprise the world No.1 and defending champion with an

Caroline Wozniacki's disappointing sequence of early Wimbledon exits continued as the former world No.1 lost to Shuai Zhang on her bogey No.2 Court in the third round

LOCO FOR COCO

—

From the mass exhilaration on The Hill to the fevered excitement gripping Centre Court, the enthusiasm for the latest of young Cori Gauff's amazing adventures in Wimbledon wonderland recalled the headiest days of 'Murraymania'.

Yet while the standing ovation and delighted whoops from Spice Girl Geri Horner (*above*) and fellow Royal Box guests greeted the 15-year-old's amazing win from two match points down against Polona Hercog, the cheers were actually resonating far beyond SW19 as the Coco glory story went global.

Nothing reflected that better than the tweet from America's former First Lady Michelle Obama who said simply "Coco is terrific!" That response left Gauff reflecting later: "I was super excited. She's one of my role models. So it was just cool to see that she knows I exist."

And as Coco soaked up the praise from the likes of her musical hero Jaden – "Shout Out @CocoGauff You're The One" he tweeted - it was wonderful to see her transformed from the focused athlete on court to a star-struck schoolgirl off it.

"Miss Tina Knowles, Beyonce's mom, posted [about] me on Instagram. I was, like, screaming," she explained. "I hope Beyonce saw that. I hope she told her daughter about me because I would love to go to a concert!"

And the best thing of all for Coco? Her mum Candi

her cheering from the players' box. "She's going to go viral, I know!" beamed Coco. "She's going to be a

THE FUTURE IS GREEN

Wimbledon's continuing commitment to sustainability was made clear through a series of highly visible initiatives during an unusually warm and dry Fortnight.

Leading up to the tournament, Wimbledon had signed up to the UN Sports for Climate Action Framework, and the AELTC further championed the environment with the launch of the 'Sustainability at Wimbledon' area in the Southern Village.

The first 100 per cent recycled, 100 per cent recyclable water bottles from evian, Official Water of The Championships, were introduced while a transformation in the racket stringing operation meant 4,500 fewer plastic bags used over the Fortnight.

A team of 'Eco Champions' (*left*) around the Grounds helped champion sustainability and guide people to discard waste into the appropriate bins, while the percentage of recycled content in food and drink packaging was increased, with containers for strawberries and cream made from 70 per cent recycled plastic.

The Wimbledon Foundation's link-up with the charity WaterAid (*left*) was also highlighted by a stunning fountain made from 2,631 tennis balls, representing the number of lives that could be saved each day if everyone worldwide had access to clean water and good hygiene.

array of bold attacking shots. Throwing himself around the court Boris Becker-style, the 22-year-old Pole levelled the match by winning a thrilling tie-break at the end of the second set before Djokovic restored order to close out a 7-5, 6-7(5), 6-1, 6-4 victory and reach the fourth round for the 12th time, a record bettered in the Open era only by Federer and Jimmy Connors.

Guido Pella knocked out the previous year's runner-up for the second year in a row when he followed up his 2018 victory over Marin Cilic by beating Kevin Anderson 6-4, 6-3, 7-6(4) to reach the fourth round of a Grand Slam tournament for the first time. Anderson, who had only recently returned to competition following a three-month break because of an elbow problem, had not dropped his serve in his first two matches but was broken three times by the 29-year-old Argentinian.

Ugo Humbert came out on top in a meeting of the two youngest players left in the men's singles as the 21-year-old Frenchman beat the 18-year-old Canadian Felix Auger-Aliassime 6-4, 7-5, 6-3 in convincing fashion. Humbert said he had played "maybe the best match of my career", while Auger-Aliassime described his performance as "pretty embarrassing" and said the pressure of the occasion had got to him. Russia's challenge in the men's singles petered out as Karen Khachanov and Daniil Medvedev, seeded No.10 and No.11 respectively, lost to Roberto Bautista Agut and David Goffin, while Milos Raonic came out on top in a big-serving showdown with Reilly Opelka, winning 7-6(1), 6-2, 6-1.

The gentlemen's doubles draw had thrown up the possibility of Andy and Jamie Murray being on opposite sides of the net in the third round, but Jamie and Neal Skupski fell at the first hurdle, losing 6-2, 6-7(2), 6-3, 1-6, 4-6 to Ivan Dodig and Filip Polasek. The Britons were playing their first Grand Slam tournament together following Jamie's split with Bruno Soares, who had been his partner for the previous three and a half years. In the mixed doubles, meanwhile, Eden Silva and Evan Hoyt proved that experience need not count for everything. The Britons, playing in The Championships for the first time, had a combined age of 47, while their opponents, Samantha Stosur and Leander Paes, appearing in The Championships for the 16th and 24th times respectively, had a combined age of 81. The result? A 6-4, 2-6, 6-4 victory for the younger generation.

*Below: Canadian teenager Felix Auger-Aliassime (**left**) is touted as one of the sport's next superstars but another promising youngster, French 21-year-old Ugo Humbert (**right**), won their No.1 Court duel*

DAILY DIARY DAY 5

It never rains but it does occasionally pour. Well, at least it did on Court 15 when, amid an otherwise wonderfully dry and sun-blessed Championships, a rogue sprinkler ensured the mixed doubles partnership of German Laura Siegemund and New Zealander Artem Sitak (*above*) were left scrambling for cover, narrowly avoiding a drenching.

The pair were sat down during an otherwise uneventful changeover during their match with Ken Skupski and Darija Jurak when the offending sprinkler head malfunctioned and a jet of water erupted just behind them, knocking over Sitak's chair as the players scrambled to drag their kit bags out of the way.

Then, just when groundstaff thought they had halted the spray by stepping on the sprinkler head, a second stream of water prompted another swift evacuation.

Both players were quite unfazed by the brief downpour and when the match had to be moved to neighbouring Court 16 because 15 had simply become too wet, Sitak and Siegemund quickly regained their equilibrium to run out 3-6, 6-3, 6-4 winners.

• The eagerly awaited Centre Court debut of Andy Murray and Serena Williams had to be put on hold after the schedule overran but there was still time to enjoy another eye-catching mixed doubles act as Serena's big sister, Venus, joined forces with rising US star Frances Tiafoe – 18 years her junior – on Court 12.

The pair made a convincing debut as they beat the British pair of Scott Clayton and Sarah Beth Gray 6-2, 6-3 and sounded so enthused by the new partnership that afterwards they were already wondering if, in 2020, it might just be an Olympic-winning one. "There is definitely time [to qualify for the Tokyo Games], but I think this could work, right?" mused Venus. To which Tiafoe, who reckoned that it was just an honour to share a court with someone he's looked up to all his life, could only enthuse: "Yeah, I'd love that. I'd love that!"

• The 'Special One' met the special Championships as Jose Mourinho visited the All England Club, not just cheering on his Portuguese compatriot Joao Sousa but also taking some time out to talk to The Wimbledon Channel about another Iberian who would, in his opinion, have been a sensational footballer.

"I'm happy he didn't become one but I think Rafael Nadal could have been a fantastic player," Mourinho, a keen tennis fan, explained. "His uncle [Miguel Angel Nadal] was my player at Barcelona in 1996 and I know Rafa can play football well. With his physicality, mentality and skill, he could have been a player but thank so much that he wasn't. Because in tennis, he can do anything!"

– DAY 6 –

SATURDAY 6 JULY

Middle Saturday, when all third round singles matches are due to be completed, can be a lonely place if you are a British player. In the 19 editions of The Championships staged since the turn of the century there had been 11 years when only one Briton reached the third round in singles and just three occasions when three or more home players had made it to the last 32. At The Championships 2007 no British singles players at all survived beyond even the second round.

Previous pages:
England cricketers
past and present in the
Royal Box on Sporting
Saturday. Take a bow
Tom and Sam Curran,
Jimmy Anderson, Eoin
Morgan, Andrew
Strauss, Stuart Broad,
Jonny Bairstow and
Joe Root

This year, nevertheless, Middle Saturday crackled with anticipation for home fans. Three Britons – Johanna Konta, Harriet Dart and Dan Evans – were through to the third round and all would be playing on the same day. There was even the huge bonus of Andy Murray, so often the lone flag-bearer in singles, playing twice in the day, firstly with Pierre-Hugues Herbert in the gentlemen's doubles and then with Serena Williams in their long-awaited mixed doubles debut. With some of the country's finest sportsmen and women filling the Royal Box, as has become the tradition on Middle Saturday, the stage was set for a memorable day.

When Dart opened the programme on Centre Court, nevertheless, it was the 22-year-old Briton's misfortune to face the form player in the women's game. Ashleigh Barty was on a winning streak of 14 consecutive victories after a remarkable six weeks. The 23-year-old Australian had claimed her first Grand Slam title at Roland-Garros, risen to the top of the world rankings by winning at Birmingham

and dropped just 10 games in her first two matches at The Championships. It was no surprise when she overpowered Dart, winning 6-1, 6-1 in just 53 minutes to reach the fourth round at The Championships for the first time.

At least the world No.182 avoided a repeat of her 0-6, 0-6 mauling by Maria Sharapova when making her Australian Open debut, in the Rod Laver Arena, at the beginning of the year. The Briton insisted she was "super happy" with her performances over the week. "Not many people can say you played the third round of Wimbledon against the world No.1 on Centre Court," she said. "It was pretty special to be out there. I definitely enjoyed every minute."

Konta, playing on No.1 Court, faced a familiar foe in Sloane Stephens, having already beaten the world No.9 three times in 2019, most recently at Roland-Garros. The 26-year-old American nevertheless took the opening set after becoming the first player of the week to break Konta's serve and continued to make inroads into the Briton's

Opposite: Ashleigh Barty looked every inch the world No.1 as she raced past Harriet Dart and into the last 16 on Centre Court

Above: Dart found Barty too tough as she succumbed 6–1, 6–1 in 53 minutes but Johanna Konta (left) won to ensure a British presence in the ladies' singles fourth round

SPORTING SATURDAY SIRS

A veritable panoply of sporting stars were given a wonderful ovation in the traditional Saturday Royal Box parade of champions, including four knighted Olympian greats with 16 gold medals between them – Sir Chris Hoy (*above, left*); Sir Mo Farah and Lord Sebastian Coe (*above, right*); and Sir Ben Ainslie.

It was an enjoyable break for some of England's cricketers during their bid to win the World Cup, with captain Eoin Morgan joining Yorkshire batting duo Jonny Bairstow and Joe Root (*right*) in taking the acclaim of the Centre Court crowd. Bairstow arrived off the back of scoring two successive centuries to guide England into the following week's semi-final.

Another major event, the Netball World Cup, was about to start in Liverpool the following week, and one of the sport's biggest names, Ama Agbeze (*right*) – who led England to Commonwealth Games glory – took a deserving bow.

Manager Gareth Southgate and midfielder Eric Dier represented England's 2018 World Cup football semi-finalists, while coach Eddie Jones joined Dylan Hartley, Jonny May and Maro Itoje from England's 2019 Rugby World Cup hopefuls.

Among the many other guests were tennis Grand Slam legends Martina Navratilova, Billie Jean King, Ann Jones and Rod Laver and GB Davis and Fed Cup captains Leon Smith and Anne Keothavong.

service games at the start of the second set. Konta held firm, however, and the match turned when she broke for the first time as Stephens served at 4-5. The former US Open champion won only 13 points in the deciding set as Konta closed out a 3-6, 6-4, 6-1 victory in just over two hours.

Through to the second week of successive Grand Slam tournaments for the first time, Konta said she had been pleased with the way she had varied her game in an effort to knock Stephens out of her stride. "The more opportunities I get to be in the latter stages of Grand Slams, the more experience I gain," she added. "Experience can only bring good things."

Evans and Joao Sousa followed Konta and Stephens onto No.1 Court and served up one of the matches of the Fortnight. The two men were separated by just eight places in the world rankings, with 29-year-old Evans at No.61 and 30-year-old Sousa at No.69. A contest full of spectacular shot-making ended with the Briton winning 167 points to his Portuguese opponent's 166, but the only statistic that mattered was the scoreline as Sousa won 4-6, 6-4, 7-5, 4-6, 6-4.

Although Evans made the first break of serve in all five sets, he paid the price for converting only seven of his 24 break points and dropping his own serve eight times. With the light fading, the roof was closed for the final set and after nearly four hours Sousa converted his first match point when Evans, serving at 4-5 and 30-40, netted a backhand.

"Playing under the roof was an amazing experience," Evans said afterwards. "I loved every minute of it out there, apart from losing. Last year I wasn't here playing the tournament, so I have to put everything into perspective."

Asked how long it would take him to get over the defeat, Evans said: "In about 45 minutes I'll be over it. It has to be done, doesn't it? I can't go back and ruin everyone else's [day]. I'll be home in 45 minutes. I just have to park it, then get on. It's not the end of the world. I lost. Joao was too good. It just hurts to lose that match really, but what can I do? Feeling sorry for myself is not going to do anything for anyone, is it?"

Sousa's reward for reaching the fourth round for the first time would be a meeting with Rafael Nadal, who swept aside Jo-Wilfried Tsonga, winning 6-2, 6-3, 6-2. Tsonga was never in contention once the Spaniard had made his first break of serve in the fourth game. "I think I played a great match," Nadal said afterwards. "I was returning well, playing aggressively with the forehand and the backhand. I think I did a lot of things well."

Two men's seeds were beaten by unseeded opponents as Fabio Fognini and Jan-Lennard Struff lost to Tennys Sandgren and Mikhail Kukushkin respectively, while Roger Federer reached two significant landmarks with his 7-5, 6-2, 7-6(4) victory over Lucas Pouille. The Swiss became the first player of either sex to win 350 singles matches at Grand Slam tournaments and the first in the Open era to reach the fourth round at The Championships 17 times, eclipsing the record set by Jimmy Connors. His next opponent would be Matteo Berrettini, who beat Diego Schwartzman 6-7(5), 7-6(2), 4-6, 7-6(5), 6-3 after more than four and a quarter hours.

Joao Sousa raises his hands in triumph but Britain's Dan Evans cuts a dejected figure after losing their epic late-finishing five-setter under the No.1 Court roof

MIXED DOUBLES MANIA

—

It felt like the dream team pairing of Andy Murray and Serena Williams had brought a whole new level of allure to the mixed doubles at Wimbledon.

This rare teaming of two Grand Slam-winning greats, described as "great fun" by both Andy and Serena but layered with a deadly serious competitive edge, set the trend for a host of other fascinating double acts to take the stage.

Andy's brother, Jamie, who had partnered Victoria Azarenka to the previous year's final, this year joined forces with American Olympic mixed doubles champion Bethanie Mattek-Sands (*opposite, top left*), while Venus Williams, who's won three Olympic doubles gold medals alongside her sister, Serena, was left thinking of Tokyo 2020 as she partnered the young American hot-shot Frances Tiafoe (*below, right*).

Jay Clarke, fresh from his singles clash with Roger Federer, and teen sensation Cori Gauff (*opposite, middle left*) made a notable duo, as did the ever-entertaining Nick Kyrgios who asked American Desirae Krawczyk to partner him (*opposite, middle right*).

"I didn't want to come off like a creep when I asked her. I just genuinely wanted to play," explained Kyrgios. "I just love doubles a lot. I wanted to play."

Alas, they didn't last long, getting knocked out in the first round. "I take these losses harder than I do in singles matches," promised Kyrgios. "It hurts to not win. I really wanted to."

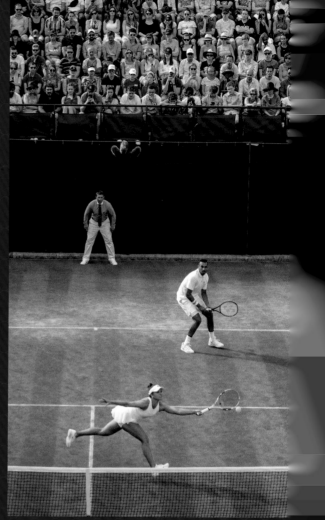

Starry mixed double acts are nothing new at Wimbledon, but don't guarantee success. Jean Borotra 'the Bounding Basque' and 'La Divine' Suzanne Lenglen were famed French champions in 1925, but the 1974 campaign of sweethearts Jimmy Connors and Chris Evert (left) lasted only one match before they withdrew to concentrate on their singles triumphs In 1999, Stefanie Graf pulled out before the semis, leaving her partner, one John McEnroe, not best pleased

Kiki Bertens, the No.4 seed, was the most notable loser in the ladies' singles. The 27-year-old Dutchwoman, a quarter-finalist in 2018, was beaten 5-7, 1-6 by Barbora Strycova and admitted afterwards that she needed to play more aggressively on grass. Belinda Bencic was another to come unstuck against an opponent with a game more suited to the surface as Alison Riske beat the No.13 seed 4-6, 6-4, 6-4.

Petra Kvitova, who beat Magda Linette 6-3, 6-2 to record her third successive straight-sets victory, reported continuing improvement with the arm injury which had marred her preparations for The Championships, while Serena Williams produced her best performance of the first week to beat Julia Goerges 6-3, 6-4 and reach the second week for the 16th time. Serving with consistent power, Williams won with single breaks of serve in both sets. "I just need to keep it up," Williams said. "Each match for me really counts."

A lack of matches in the first six months of the year had contributed to Williams' decision to play alongside Murray in one of the most exciting mixed doubles partnerships for many a decade. Both players had already played one match – Williams in singles, Murray in men's doubles – when they took on Germany's Andreas Mies and Chile's Alexa Guarachi for the day's finale on Centre Court. For Murray it was a welcome return to his greatest stage, the Scot having last played there when he limped to defeat against Sam Querrey in 2017.

The crowd gave the players a rapturous reception and the volume barely dipped as Murray and Williams won 6-4, 6-1. The fact that they had had minimal time together on the practice court hardly seemed to matter as Williams struck big blows from the baseline and Murray demonstrated his all-court craft. You would never have guessed that they had been recovering from a knee injury and hip surgery respectively.

"For me it was a great experience being back on Centre Court with Serena after the last year or so being tough," Murray said. Williams agreed, saying she wanted to do well but "have fun at the same time", though she added: "At some point I started feeling a lot of pressure: 'Oh, my God, I have to do well because this match is so hyped that I want to see it.' I didn't even want to be in it, I kind of just wanted to watch it. Maybe I'll try to get a video of it or watch it somewhere." Murray said he had been impressed with Williams' enduring will to win at this stage of her career. Asked who had been in charge on court, Murray replied: "We're both younger siblings and we're used to being bossed by the older one."

Earlier in the day Murray and Herbert were beaten 6-7(4), 6-4, 6-2, 6-3 by Nikola Mektic and Franko Skugor, the No.6 seeds, in the second round of the men's doubles. The turning point came when Herbert was broken serving at 4-5 in the second set. "It's not a blow really in the grand scheme of things," Murray insisted. "The first two sets I felt like we were the better team. If we had got the second set I think we would have run away with it."

There's often a sting for those dreaming of making the second week at Wimbledon – but this fellow will definitely 'be' there

DAILY DIARY **DAY 6**

How marvellous it was to see the great Rod Laver (*above*), special guest of Chairman of the All England Club Philip Brook alongside Ann Jones, back on Centre Court 50 years since winning the last of his four singles titles here in 1969 en route to a second calendar-year Grand Slam.

The 'Rocket' is always a popular visitor to the Club, as evidenced on the eve of The Championships when – on a tour of the Grounds – he was greeted warmly by greats like Roger Federer and Novak Djokovic, who even had a little swish with Rod's old wooden racket before noting admiringly: "That's a beauty!"

On the afternoon when great sports figures take a bow in the Royal Box, it felt especially poignant that this 80-year-old legend should be presented with a special replica of the Gentlemen's Singles Trophy by Brook.

"The celebrations this year have reignited so many wonderful memories, shared with friends and fans worldwide," said the great Australian.

• Fabio Fognini, known for his volcanic temperament on court, let his irritation get the better of him during his defeat by Tennys Sandgren on Court 14.

The Italian ended up saying sorry for his muttered suggestions in his native tongue on court about how he wished "a bomb would explode on this club", comments that he later said had stemmed from his frustration.

However, the No.12 seed's apology for his explosive outburst didn't stop him later receiving a $3,000 (£2,400) fine for unsportsmanlike conduct.

• When the Red Arrows are performing their wondrous aerobatics, it's hard not to be awe-struck. That presumably wasn't Harriet Dart's reaction, however, when the iconic display team chose an awkward moment to jet over the All England Club to mark the 2019 Pride in London parade.

The fly-past occurred over Centre Court at deuce in Dart's first service game against world No.1 Ashleigh Barty, with Dart having just served a fault. After a delay following the crowd's prolonged applause, the Londoner resumed only to complete a double fault. Barty quickly snaffled the break point to lead 2-0, the beginning of a quick end.

• Harriet could be forgiven a wry smile after a tough day when fellow Briton Jay Clarke, her former mixed doubles partner who elected at late notice to compete instead with new sensation Cori Gauff, was defeated alongside his new 15-year-old partner in the first round by Robert Lindstedt and Jelena Ostapenko. With Dart, Clarke had done rather better the previous year, reaching the semi-finals.

MIDDLE SUNDAY.
OPENED UP.

MEGA MIDDLE SUNDAY

As the Championship courts enjoyed their vital day of rest and watering, neighbouring Wimbledon Park buzzed with activity thanks to the first 'Middle Sunday Opened Up' free tennis festival. A series of activities entertained and educated hundreds through the day with special guests leading the sessions, including Judy Murray (*right*), who ran a course aimed at young girls and teenagers. Stars like Harriet Dart (*below*), double Gentlemen's Wheelchair Singles Champion Stefan Olsson (*above*) and former ladies' singles finalist Andrea Jaeger (*above, right*) also helped make it a spectacular success.

For most 15-year-olds Monday meant a return to school, but Cori Gauff would be putting away her textbooks for at least another day. The American's name might have meant little to most tennis fans just seven days earlier, but after her remarkable performances in the first week Gauff was one of the key characters in the cast of 'Manic Monday' as all 32 players left in the two singles competitions vied for places in the quarter-finals.

Having already beaten a legend of the game in Venus Williams and two seasoned professionals in Magdalena Rybarikova and Polona Hercog, Gauff now faced Simona Halep, the previous year's champion of Roland-Garros, a recent world No.1 and the current No.7. The 27-year-old Romanian was the first top 10 opponent to cross Gauff's path.

If Gauff looked nervous in dropping serve in the opening game on No.1 Court, she was not the only one feeling the tension. Halep made four unforced errors to drop her own serve in the next game and then held for 2-2 despite three successive double faults. However, it was Gauff who continued to make the most mistakes as Halep took the opening set following another break of serve. After a further exchange of breaks at the start of the second set Gauff called for the doctor because she felt unwell and at 2-3 four successive unforced errors handed Halep her fifth and final break. Serving at 2-5, Gauff – to huge cheers from the crowd – saved two match points, but Halep held her nerve and her serve in the following game to win 6-3, 6-3.

Halep praised Gauff's "great performance" and added: "I think if she keeps going, she will be top 10 soon. She will be a very tough opponent for everybody. If she keeps doing what she did here, she's going to get a lot of confidence and she can win big tournaments soon."

Gauff said the best memory of her Championships debut would be the support of the crowd. "You don't really expect this kind of support when you're in another country, not your home country," she said. "I really did feel like I was probably playing in New York somewhere." She added: "I learned how to play in front of a big crowd. I learned what it was like to be under pressure. I learned a lot and I'm really thankful for this experience."

What did Gauff hope the crowd had learned about her? "That I'm a fighter. I'll never give up. I hope they learned from me that anything is possible if you work hard and just continue to dream big." Gauff was pleased with the way she had fought for every point and stressed: "I'm only 15. I've not nearly gotten or developed my game. I started tennis at six. I'm so excited to see, if I continue to work hard, what other success I can have."

As for the immediate future, Gauff said that schoolwork and a short holiday beckoned. She also confirmed that she would not be giving up her studies. "I'm going to do it online," she said. "I still want to go to college. Kind of like a requirement, I guess, from my parents." And her next goal in tennis? "To win the next tournament I play." As for The Championships, Gauff was already thinking about her next appearance. "These past two weeks have been amazing," she said. "I'm excited to be back next year."

By the end of the day Halep was the highest-ranked player left in the ladies' singles after Ashleigh Barty, Karolina Pliskova and Petra Kvitova all lost. Barty, the world No.1, went down 6-3, 2-6, 3-6 to Alison Riske, the world No.55. Barty hit aces on the first four points of the match, but Riske worked her way back in the second set, profiting from frequent forays into the net. It was the 29-year-old American's fourth successive three-set match. At nine hours and five minutes, her time on court so far was the longest by any ladies' singles quarter-finalist at The Championships for 17 years.

Simona Halep commiserates with Cori Gauff at the net after ending the 15-year-old's Wimbledon adventure

*This page: Three shock winners enjoyed a massive Monday, with Karolina Muchova (**above**) knocking out compatriot Karolina Pliskova; fellow Czech Barbora Strycova (**right**) defeating Elise Mertens; and Alison Riske (**far right**) knocking out world No.1 Ashleigh Barty*

Opposite: Johanna Konta celebrates after her Centre Court triumph from a set down against two-times Ladies' Singles Champion Petra Kvitova

Riske, who had won the grass court titles at 's-Hertogenbosch and Surbiton in the build-up to The Championships, was to marry her fiancé, Stephen Amritraj, less than two weeks later. "I wish I could get married more often," she said with a smile. "Maybe we'll have to renew our vows because it's worked out well having that on the horizon."

She added: "We both love Wimbledon equally as much. We love London. We would love to live here, love to be a member of the All England Club. Just throwing it out there!"

Barty, who had won 21 sets in a row until she lost the second set to Riske, was philosophical in defeat. "Today wasn't my day," she said. "I didn't win a tennis match. It's not the end of the world." She added: "It's disappointing right now, but give me an hour or so and we'll be all good. The sun's still going to come up tomorrow."

Pliskova had a chance of replacing Barty at the top of the world rankings at the end of the Fortnight, but the No.3 seed was beaten 6-4, 5-7, 11-13 by her fellow Czech, Karolina Muchova, in the longest ladies' singles match of The Championships 2019 at three hours and 17 minutes. Muchova, aged 22, became the first player for 13 years to reach the quarter-finals on her debut in the main draw. The world No.68 had hit 147 winners so far, more than any of the other quarter-finalists in the ladies' singles.

Kvitova lost 6-4, 2-6, 4-6 to Johanna Konta in a meeting of two of the game's best ball strikers. The world No.6, who had been a doubtful starter before The Championships because of an arm problem, started confidently and took the first set by breaking when Konta served at 4-5. The world No.18's response, however, could not be faulted. Konta took early charge of both the second and third sets with double breaks of serve and faltered only when she led 5-1 in the decider. Kvitova, going for her shots, brought the score back to 5-4 before Konta secured her place in the quarter-finals of a Grand Slam tournament for the fifth time.

It was Konta's 13th win in the 15 matches she had played in 2019 which had gone to deciding sets. "That's something I can be really proud of," she said. "It's a good feeling to have as a player. It definitely comes with match fitness, as well as playing a lot of them."

Serena Williams overpowered Carla Suarez Navarro, winning 6-2, 6-2 in just 64 minutes to reach the quarter-finals for the 14th time. The former world No.1 also learned something new when she lost a point for leaning over the net to hit a volley. "I didn't realise it was a rule,"

CLOSE ENCOUNTERS

The chance of a close encounter with a sporting great is one of Wimbledon's enduring pleasures. Like these Chelsea Pensioners (*above*), taking a post-match picture with Simona Halep after her Centre Court victory over Victoria Azarenka, or the privilege of watching Roger Federer and Rafael Nadal work their magic in practice (*opposite*). If you wear the right hat you might get an autograph from Federer (*left*) or a snap with Karolina Pliskova (*below, left*). And if you're really lucky, Novak Djokovic (*below*) might even take the selfie for you!

Guido Pella made it to his first Grand Slam quarter-final at the 20th attempt, coming from two sets down to oust 2016 finalist Milos Raonic on No.3 Court

she said afterwards. "I don't want to make that mistake in our 'Murena' doubles match," Williams added, confirming her preferred name for her mixed doubles partnership with Andy Murray, who had previously suggested 'SerAndy'. Williams insisted: "I like Murena. My vote is still for Murena."

With Barbora Strycova and Shuai Zhang also through, three of the eight quarter-finalists would be 30-somethings. In the men's draw, meanwhile, only three of the quarter-finalists would be under the age of 30, with the youngest 28-year-old David Goffin. It would be the third year in a row that 30-somethings outnumbered their younger counterparts in the quarter-final line-up.

Novak Djokovic, Roger Federer and Rafael Nadal in particular were showing no signs of a weakening of their domination. In the fourth round the so-called 'Big Three' dropped a total of 19 games and defended just one break point between them. Djokovic beat 21-year-old Frenchman Ugo Humbert 6-3, 6-2, 6-3, Federer crushed Italy's Matteo Berrettini 6-1, 6-2, 6-2 in just 74 minutes and Nadal beat Portugal's Joao Sousa 6-2, 6-2, 6-2.

Djokovic, who had demonstrated his continuing desire to improve by adding Goran Ivanisevic to his coaching team at The Championships, said it was hard work that kept the 'Big Three' on top. "It takes hours of training, preparation, recovery. It's a lifestyle really. Dedication truly pays off. I guess each one of us top three guys is different, but I think what we share in common is that we just love the game and we are very dedicated to it. We have high aims all the time. I don't think any one of us plays for fun or to just be part of the tour. We play there to be the best in the world."

He added: "Young guys will eventually replace us at the top spots of the world. This is going to happen. When? Hopefully not too soon, but it's going to happen."

Berrettini had been enjoying his best season, climbing from No.54 in the world rankings at the end of 2018 to No.20 by the start of The Championships, and had just claimed his first grass court title, at Stuttgart, but won only 11 points on Federer's serve and was broken six times. "I was expecting a tough match and a close one with not many chances," a matter-of-fact Federer said afterwards. "It was actually quite the opposite."

Nadal, who made just 10 unforced errors against Sousa, was asked afterwards by a journalist if he thought it was right that he had been playing on Centre Court while Barty, the world No.1, played on No.2 Court. "I am the world No.2 and I won 18 Grand Slams," a forthright Nadal replied. "In the world of tennis today, honestly, my feeling is I am little bit more than Ashleigh Barty, even if Ashleigh Barty is the first player of the world and she already won in the French Open and is playing unbelievably well."

As for the 'youngsters' who reached the last eight, Guido Pella made the comeback of the day, beating Milos Raonic 3-6, 4-6, 6-3, 7-6(3), 8-6 to reach his first quarter-final at a Grand Slam tournament, Kei Nishikori reached his 12th by beating Mikhail Kukushkin 6-3, 3-6, 6-3, 6-4, and Goffin beat 35-year-old Fernando Verdasco 7-6(9), 2-6, 6-3, 6-4. Goffin said it was "an amazing feeling" to enjoy his best run at his favourite tournament. He would do well to savour the moment while he could, bearing in mind his next opponent: a certain Novak Djokovic.

DAILY DIARY DAY 7

As Johanna Konta reached the quarter-finals amid hope she could end the long wait for a British Ladies' Singles Champion, there was an inspiration for her over the Fortnight in the shape of a smiling tennis legend in the Royal Box.

It hardly felt 50 years ago since the nation cheered Ann Jones (*above*) to victory, beating the legendary Billie Jean King in the 1969 final that gripped a nation.

Special guest of the AELTC Chairman alongside Rod Laver, Ann, now 80, enjoyed meeting up again with the great Billie Jean, who had won their 1967 final before the Midlander gained revenge two years later and became the first left-handed female player ever to win the title.

Ann was, of course, hoping Konta could join that most elite of clubs, the three post-war British Ladies' Singles Champions: Angela Mortimer (1961), Jones herself and Virginia Wade (1977).

• Ashleigh Barty's defeat by Alison Riske was the sensation of 'Manic Monday' but it was nice to see the Australian world No.1 maintaining her sense of humour on a tough day as she owned up to some first-week mischief with the media.

For a bit of fun, Barty had been including a quote from a Disney film into each post-match press conference. So, after her first round, she shrugged: "Came into it thinking kind of like 'hakuna matata', just relax…"

Next round, she borrowed from *Toy Story's* Buzz Lightyear to say: "I chat to my niece. Over and over she

tells me you can go to infinity and beyond."

Then, quizzed on her shot-making choices in the third round, she referenced *The Little Mermaid*, nodding sagely: "Sometimes, I play a shot, I think the seaweed is always greener in someone else's lake."

Ash couldn't help teasing reporters: "You guys caught on the third time around!" By which time, of course, we felt she should '*Let It Go*'.

• Karolina Muchova was perhaps not the most familiar name to fans before her shock victory over No.3 seed Karolina Pliskova, but one movie star already knew all about the rising 22-year-old.

Rebel Wilson, the Australian comedienne and star of *Pitch Perfect*, was cheering on Muchova from her No.2 Court players' box, leaving the young Czech laughing about the "crazy" way they had become such unlikely friends.

"She texted me on Twitter last year when I beat Garbiñe Muguruza in the US Open. I was, like, 'Wow!' I was surprised," reflected Muchova. "She's just super chill and a super nice person. And, whatever she says, super funny!"

DAY 8 –

TUESDAY 9 JULY

Two years after her memorable run to the semi-finals, Johanna Konta was within one victory of a repeat performance. There had been times, nevertheless, in the intervening 24 months when the British No.1's fortunes had dipped sharply.

Above: Johanna Konta's Wimbledon dream ended at the hands of an in-form Barbora Strycova

Previous pages: Elina Svitolina leapt with delight after her No.1 Court triumph over Karolina Muchova that sent her to her first Grand Slam semi-final

Having risen to No.4 in the world rankings on the back of her Wimbledon success in 2017, she won only two more matches that year before parting company with her coach, Wim Fissette, and appointing Michael Joyce in his place. After The Championships 2018, where she lost in the second round, Konta fell to No.50 in the world.

Joyce lasted less than a year in his post and by the time Konta played her final tournament of 2018 she was working with the Frenchman Dimitri Zavialoff. Confirmation that she was back on track came when her six successive victories in singles rubbers helped to take Britain back into the Fed Cup's World Group for the first time in 26 years. She then enjoyed her best clay court season, reaching the finals in Rabat and Rome and the semi-finals at Roland-Garros, where she led 5-3 in both sets against Marketa Vondrousova before losing 5-7, 6-7(2).

After reaching the quarter-finals of The Championships by beating two top 10 players in Sloane Stephens and Petra Kvitova, Konta now had a chance to make further progress against Barbora Strycova. A 33-year-old Czech whose only previous Grand Slam singles quarter-final had been at The Championships 2014, the world No.54 had nevertheless beaten three higher-ranked players to reach the last eight.

Konta, the quarter-finalist with the best serving record over the Fortnight having being broken only three times, flew into a 4-1 lead but was soon struggling in the face of Strycova's clever variations of pace and spin and her smart volleys. As Konta's mistakes multiplied, particularly on her forehand, Strycova broke back in the seventh game and went on to take the opening set, though she had to come back from 5-4 down in the tie-break.

In the preceding months Konta had repeatedly turned matches around after losing the first set, but there was to be no such fightback here. Strycova raced into a 3-0 lead in the second set and broke again to lead 5-1 as Konta hit a wild drive volley beyond the baseline. The match ended in appropriate fashion when Konta made her 34th unforced error on match point, hitting a backhand long to give Strycova her 7-6(5), 6-1 victory.

Konta said afterwards that Strycova had been "a very difficult player to play on this surface". She added: "My best today just wasn't good enough. But every decision that I made, every thought process, every opportunity that I gave myself, everything, I have no regrets in doing."

When a reporter pointed out her high number of unforced errors and asked her whether she needed to "look at yourself a little bit", a tense exchange followed. "I don't think you need to pick on me in a harsh way," Konta said. "I say how I feel out there. If you don't want to accept that answer or you

Czech veteran Barbora Strycova screamed for joy at finally reaching a Grand Slam singles semi-final at the 53rd attempt

don't agree with it, that's fine." The reporter said he was posing the question as she was a player "who presumably wants to go on from here, learn from this, win a Grand Slam one day". Konta asked her questioner not to patronise her. "In the way you're asking your question, you're being quite disrespectful and you're patronising me," she said. "I'm a professional competitor who did her best today – and that's all there is to that."

Strycova, who had previously indicated that this might be her last year on tour, had become the oldest first-time Grand Slam semi-finalist in the Open era. "It was always my dream to play well at this tournament," she said. "I set this goal at the beginning of this year, that Wimbledon would be where I wanted to really play well."

The Czech, who completed a memorable day by reaching the quarter-finals of the ladies' doubles alongside Su-Wei Hsieh, said that Wimbledon was her favourite tournament and London her favourite city. "I was two years old when my grandpa took me to the museum here," she said. "I saw the trophy. I was like: 'I'm going to play here.' Right now here I am at 33, which is incredible."

Next up for Strycova would be Serena Williams, who was pushed all the way by Alison Riske, her fellow American. Riske, who broke the former champion's formidable serve five times, was playing in her first quarter-final at any Grand Slam tournament but had won 14 of the 15 matches she had played on grass in 2019. The world No.55 was immediately into her stride, breaking serve at the second attempt. Williams, nevertheless, broke twice to take the opening set and was two games from victory at 4-4 in the second, only for Riske to raise her game. A winning volley gave the 29-year-old a break, after which she served out to love to level the match.

Midway through the deciding set Williams did her hair up because the wind was blowing it across her face. "I just needed to get it out of the way, put the business bun up and get to business," she said later. It was an ominous sign for Riske, who double-faulted on break point at 3-4 before Williams hit

UMPIRE STRIKES BACK!

Wimbledon unearthed a new star after umpire Jamie Crowson was persuaded by the incorrigible Henri Leconte during a Gentlemen's Senior Invitation Doubles match to let him take over the umpiring while the official replaced him as Patrick McEnroe's playing partner. Not content with just one winning volley, our blazered Boris then struck another while simultaneously tumbling over theatrically, prompting Leconte to tell him over the chair mic: "You're definitely my hero!"

her 18th and 19th aces of the match in the final game to secure her 6-4, 4-6, 6-3 victory and a place in the semi-finals for the 12th time. "I just needed to fight," Williams said afterwards. "She was not giving it to me. I needed to step up and take it."

At her post-match press conference Williams was asked about a $10,000 fine imposed on her for damaging one of the practice courts with her racket before The Championships began. "I just threw my racket," she said. "I have always been an Avenger in my heart. Maybe I'm super strong."

China's Shuai Zhang, who had reached her second Grand Slam quarter-final at the age of 30, threatened to pull off a major surprise when she led Simona Halep 4-1. The world No.50 struck the ball beautifully at the start, but Halep soon found her rhythm and started forcing her opponent into mistakes. In securing a 7-6(4), 6-1 victory, the Romanian booked her place in the semi-finals for the first time since 2014. Halep said she was a different person compared with five years previously. "I'm more confident," she said. "I love grass. It's the first time that I can say that." Halep said she had developed a better feel for grass "in my hands, in my legs, and also in my mind".

Elina Svitolina became the first Ukrainian woman to reach the semi-finals of a Grand Slam tournament when she beat the Czech Republic's Karolina Muchova 7-5, 6-4. The world No.8 is generally at her best on slower surfaces, but recovered from a gradual start to take charge with some consistent ball-striking as her opponent started to feel the effects of her three-hour marathon the previous day. Much had been expected of Svitolina at Grand Slam level when she won more titles

Below left: Czech Karolina Muchova, the world No.68, was a surprise quarter-finalist, the lowest-ranked of all eight players, as she tackled Elina Svitolina

Below right: Ukrainian Svitolina was clearly delighted to have got past the last-eight in a Grand Slam at the fifth attempt

Having a ball. Andy Murray and Serena Williams enjoyed plenty of laughs amid some excellent tennis as they beat Fabrice

Martin and Raquel Atawo in the mixed doubles second round during Serena's second visit of the day to Centre Court

– nine – than any other woman in 2017 and 2018, but a knee injury hampered her progress in 2019 and she had arrived at The Championships having lost seven of her last eight matches. However, the 24-year-old felt she had benefited from flying under the radar. "Going into Roland-Garros a couple of times, I had lots of expectations, lots of pressure," she said. "Here I probably just had the pressure from myself and I've handled it pretty well."

History was made on Court 12 as Henri Kontinen and John Peers became the first winners of a final set tie-break at The Championships. Tie-breaks at 12-12 in the final sets had been introduced for the first time this year. Kontinen and Peers beat Rajeev Ram and Joe Salisbury 7-6(2), 6-4, 3-6, 4-6, 13-12(2) in the third round of the gentlemen's doubles after nearly four and a half hours. Lukasz Kubot and Marcelo Melo, the top seeds, lost 6-7(3), 7-6(5), 3-6, 3-6 to Nicolas Mahut and Edouard Roger-Vasselin.

Williams, who had kicked off the Centre Court programme, returned later in the day to partner Andy Murray in the second round of the mixed doubles. Once again the former world No.1s provided great entertainment, beating Raquel Atawo and Fabrice Martin 7-5, 6-3. "I am having a blast," Williams said afterwards, having celebrated winning points with roars and fist pumps and hit some stunning return winners off huge serves by Martin. "Do not expect that to ever happen again," she said afterwards with a smile. "I'm convinced that was once in a lifetime. I just never hit returns like that in my life."

Murray's brother, Jamie, who won the mixed doubles title in 2007 with Jelena Jankovic and in 2017 with Martina Hingis, and was runner-up in 2018 with Victoria Azarenka, went out in the second round. Mate Pavic and Gabriela Dabrowski beat Murray and Bethanie Mattek-Sands 6-4, 3-6, 6-3. However, the British wild cards Evan Hoyt and Eden Silva continued their good run by reaching the quarter-finals with a 5-7, 7-6(5), 6-4 victory over Joran Vliegen and Saisai Zheng.

There was a moment of history on Court 12 as John Peers and Henri Kontinen won Wimbledon's first-ever final set tie-break in their gentlemen's doubles match against Rajeev Ram and Joe Salisbury

DAILY DIARY **DAY 8**

The 'Lionesses' (*above*) returned home after their World Cup heroics in France to be treated to an invitation to the Royal Box along with their manager, Phil Neville, his wife, Julie, and Baroness Sue Campbell.

Everybody from Judy Murray to double Olympic champion Dame Kelly Holmes enjoyed the chance to be pictured with the country's new footballing stars.

Serena Williams also took the opportunity for a brief reunion with her Parisian hotel mates following her mixed doubles match with Andy Murray.

• Elina Svitolina, one of the tour's true fighters, reached her first Grand Slam semi-final by defeating Karolina Muchova and then revealed how boxing was playing a big part in honing her tough, battling spirit.

The Ukrainian, a huge fan of the country's boxing heroes, the Klitschko brothers, while growing up and now a devoted follower of British heavyweight star Anthony Joshua, explained how, when training in the gym at one of her regular London bases, she loves taking her on-court frustrations out on punch bags.

"From a long time ago, I start doing boxing with my brother and then just continued. It's a great workout because sometimes you just need to let go the negative things in your head," she said.

• Another name familiar to football fans could be spotted out on Court 11. Jorge Burruchaga, whose 84th-minute goal won the 1986 World Cup final for Argentina in the 3-2 win over Germany, was watching his son Roman Andres getting beaten in the boys' singles second round 5-7, 6-7(3) by Japan's Shintaro Mochizuki. Jorge's goal, set up brilliantly in Mexico City's Aztec Stadium by Diego Maradona, was followed by his ecstatic celebrations. Emotions were very different here for a 56-year-old dad as he admitted to "suffering" as Roman Andres slipped to defeat.

• It's rare a player will offer such a genuine, effusive tribute to someone who has just defeated them, but fresh from her quarter-final loss to Simona Halep, China's Shuai Zhang revealed exactly why she hoped her conqueror would go on to win Wimbledon – and it said a lot about the popular Romanian.

"I wish she can win the tournament because she's the best player I like," said Zhang. "I like Simona not only because she play good tennis, [but also] because she's great person. You can see in her eyes how nice. And also, when I beat her twice, she [was] still very nice to me!"

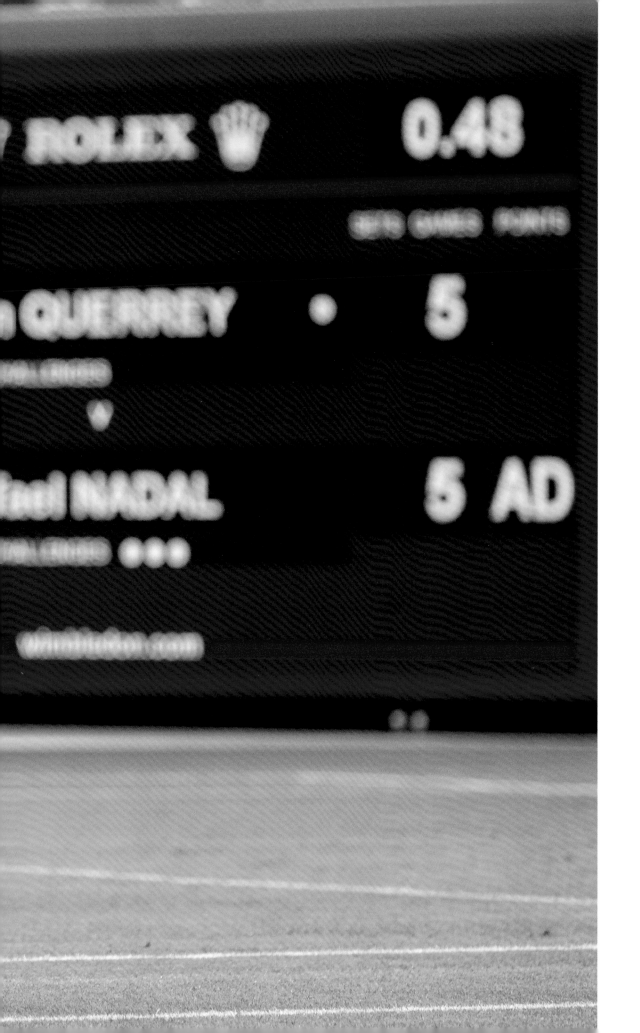

E ver since the draw for the gentlemen's singles had been made 12 days earlier, tennis fans the world over had been speculating about the possibility of Rafael Nadal and Roger Federer meeting at The Championships for the first time since their unforgettable final in 2008.

Above: Two-times Gentlemen's Singles Champion Rafael Nadal made it to the semi-finals for a second straight year on No.1 Court

Previous pages: An intense Nadal celebrates a crucial point in the first set of his quarter-final win over Sam Querrey

Going into the quarter-finals, we were now just one round away from seeing arguably the two greatest male players in history lock horns once again. Indeed, given their current form (with 36 victories each, no other man could equal their total of match wins in 2019) and their past results against their opponents in the last eight, it would be a surprise if we were not looking forward to a 40th showdown between the Spaniard and the Swiss by the end of the day. Nadal was facing Sam Querrey, who had lost four of their five previous meetings, while Federer was up against Kei Nishikori, who had lost six of his last seven encounters with the eight-times Gentlemen's Singles Champion.

When Nadal lost in the fourth round or earlier at The Championships every year between 2012 and 2017, it had seemed that the chances of his adding to his 2008 and 2010 titles might have gone for ever. Each year his exertions during the clay court season appeared to have taken their toll when he switched to grass.

However, he had gone desperately close to reaching the 2018 gentlemen's singles final, losing 10-8 in the fifth set of his semi-final against Novak Djokovic, and in 2019 he seemed to have put his injury issues behind him. Nadal had been runner-up at the Australian Open, won Roland-Garros (for the 12th time) and reached the semi-finals or better in seven of the eight tournaments he had played. By comparison, in his injury-stricken 2018 season he had completed just seven tournaments.

Above: Sam
Querrey gave every
last bead of sweat
but the man who
had beaten Novak
Djokovic and Andy
Murray at previous
Championships
found Rafael Nadal
(**left**) a champion
too far

Roger Federer continued to defy the years as he breezed into a 13th Wimbledon semi-final with victory over Kei Nishikori

Querrey had endured physical issues too. The latest, an abdominal injury, had kept the world No.65 out of Roland-Garros and his run to the final at Eastbourne in the week before The Championships had been his first appearance for more than two months.

The 6ft 6in American, who reached the Wimbledon semi-finals in 2017, was always a threat on grass. In his previous 72 service games at The Championships 2019 he had been broken only once. Nadal, nevertheless, broke at the second attempt and again at 5-5, after which the match was barely competitive. Querrey hit 22 aces but lost nearly three-quarters of the points when his first serve missed the target. Nadal was superior in almost every department and won 7-5, 6-2, 6-2, making only 12 unforced errors.

"I am playing with a very high intensity, playing aggressive, serving well and returning very well," Nadal said afterwards. "Today was a big, big challenge against a serve like Sam's. I broke him six times, which I think is a lot against a player like him. The victory means a lot to me."

At the end of the second set on No.1 Court the latest result from Centre Court flashed up on the screen: a 4-6, 6-1, 6-4, 6-4 victory for Federer over Nishikori. Despite a poor start against the world No.7, Federer had become the first man to win 100 singles matches at a single Grand Slam tournament. With Federer mistiming his shots and struggling on second serve, Nishikori had broken in the first game and had opportunities to break again at both 2-0 and 3-1. However, it did not take long for order to be restored as Federer promptly went 3-0 up in the second set. "I feel good on the court," he said afterwards. "Even if I'm down a set or down a break, no hurry there. I stay calm."

Above: *Kei Nishikori won the first set but Roger Federer (**left**) proved too good in their quarter-final as the Swiss landed his 100th Wimbledon win*

Looking ahead to his semi-final, Federer noted how much Nadal's grass court game had improved. "He's playing very different than he used to," Federer said. "He's serving way different. I remember back in the day how he used to serve, and now how much bigger he's serving, how much faster he finishes points."

Nadal agreed. "I am running less so I need to serve better," he said. "I probably cannot play 20 weeks per year any more, so I need to reschedule my planning to improve things to be very competitive every single time that I am on court. Of course, I am serving better. Of course, I am hitting the backhand better. Maybe volleying better, slicing better." The Spaniard said he and Federer had managed to stay at the top because they both "love the game and have big respect for this sport".

The day's Centre Court programme had begun with Djokovic making the semi-finals for the ninth time, a record bettered only by Federer and Jimmy Connors. Djokovic also made a slow start, but as soon as David Goffin had broken to lead 4-3 the defending champion took charge. Finding his range and striking the ball with relentless accuracy, Djokovic won the next 10 games and completed a 6-4, 6-0, 6-2 victory in less than two hours.

"I've been playing my best tennis in this tournament in the last two rounds," he said afterwards. "Especially today in the second and third sets against Goffin, who was in form, I felt like I managed to dismantle his game and always find the right shots. I was very pleased with the performance. This match could have gone a different way. I was a break down. He was the better player for most of the first set. But I managed to turn things around. I feel very good on the court, confident, going for the shots, trying to come to the net as well, being more aggressive."

Goffin, who had never appeared in the quarter-finals before, said that Djokovic had shown why he is world No.1. "You have to play the perfect point to win it against him," the Belgian said. "He puts you under pressure all the time."

Left: Novak Djokovic roared his delight after beating David Goffin to reach the Wimbledon semi-finals for a ninth time

Below: Goffin felt Djokovic was so good in their quarter-final that he had to play perfectly just to win a single point

Despite their domination in recent years, this was the first time since 2007 that Nadal, Federer and Djokovic had all reached the semi-finals at The Championships. Indeed they had not all reached the last four at any Grand Slam tournament for seven years until doing so at Roland-Garros the previous month.

The unlikely gatecrasher on the Big Three's semi-finals party would be Spain's Roberto Bautista Agut, who dropped his first set of the Fortnight in beating Argentina's Guido Pella 7-5, 6-4, 3-6, 6-3. In a tightly fought contest both players had plenty of opportunities to break serve, but Bautista Agut took more of his chances.

Bautista Agut's only previous appearance in a Grand Slam quarter-final had been at the Australian Open in January. The world No.22 had been an outstanding junior but took his time making his mark at senior level. He was 24 when he broke into the world's top 100 and did not win his first tour-level title until he was 26. "I did a lot of work during all these years to be a better player," he said.

Having never previously gone beyond the fourth round at Wimbledon, Bautista Agut had thought he would be safe to hold his bachelor party, ahead of his November wedding, in Ibiza towards the end of the second week of The Championships. Now he had some rearranging to do. "My friends, six of them, are all there [in Ibiza]," Bautista Agut said after securing his semi-final meeting with Djokovic. "Well, it feels better to be here in London. They are coming to London. I think they will fly on Friday."

Right: Spain's Roberto Bautista Agut beat Argentina's Guido Pella (above) to join the victorious 'Big Three' of Djokovic, Nadal and Federer in the semis

100 NOT OUT

—

Roger Federer sets new tennis landmarks practically each time he takes to the court these days but, even by his record-breaking standards, a historic 100th Wimbledon singles triumph made it a red letter day for the great Swiss.

Not that he actually realised what he had achieved following his four-set Centre Court victory over Kei Nishikori until a spectator reminded him as he was signing the customary autographs at courtside after the quarter-final.

"I didn't think of it while I was playing today. Actually not at all, not once," smiled Federer. "Then as I'm signing, the guy says, 'Congratulations for your 100!' Oh, yeah, I didn't know. I forgot.

"If I look back at the 100, some were so incredibly cool. Yeah, a hundred wins here at Wimbledon. Who would have thought? I didn't, for sure. It's special."

The first win came in 2001 when the soaring 19-year-old (*right*) defeated Christophe Rochus 6-2, 6-3, 6-2 in front of a few hundred fans on Court 13. Yes, so long ago the court doesn't even exist any more!

His century is currently unprecedented at any men's Grand Slam while Martina Navratilova remains Wimbledon's only other centurion on 120.

Yet while 100 was fantastic, Federer only had eyes for 101 after setting up an unmissable semi-final date with his greatest rival, Rafael Nadal.

Andy Murray and Serena Williams were back on court in the mixed doubles but met their match in the doubles specialists Bruno Soares and Nicole Melichar, who won 6-3, 4-6, 6-2. A packed No.2 Court enjoyed some spectacular shot-making by Murray and Williams, but the top seeds showed the benefit of their doubles experience.

Williams said afterwards that playing with Murray in front of his home crowd had been memorable. "We aren't ready for it to be over," she said. "I just love Andy's spirit. It's so fun to play with him. He's so calm and chilled. I loved having the support. It was amazing. Hopefully I can still have it. I think to play on this stage with Andy, who has done so well here for so many years, is literally just a lifetime experience."

Murray, who said he was impressed with Williams' competitiveness, was pleased with what he had achieved less than a month since beginning his comeback following hip surgery. "The most positive thing is that my body felt good," he said. "My hip anyway was feeling good, so that was positive. It's a lot of physical work now trying to get stronger."

It was fun while it lasted. Serena Williams and Andy Murray were all smiles as they reflected on the end of their mixed doubles campaign

Twenty-four hours after the first final set tie-break at The Championships there was another, this time in the mixed doubles, as Artem Sitak and Laura Siegemund beat Mate Pavic and Gabriela Dabrowski 5-7, 7-6(5), 13-12(5).

Britain's Anton Matusevich sprang the biggest surprise of the boys' singles so far when he beat the top seed, Holger Rune, 6-4, 7-5. "It's a great win," the 18-year-old from Kent said afterwards. "Last week he destroyed me 6-2, 6-2, so I knew what level he was coming in with." The No.2 seed, Jonas Forejtek, had been beaten in the opening round by Britain's James Story, who in turn lost next time out.

DAILY DIARY **DAY 9**

Jelena Ostapenko, the dynamic 2017 Roland-Garros champion, became an internet hit during the Fortnight thanks to the blows she accidentally and rather hilariously dished out to her doubles partners and opponents alike (*above*).

On Day Four, while partnering Veronika Kudermetova in their ladies' doubles match against Alize Cornet and Petra Martic, the Latvian smacked a wayward second serve to the wrong side of the court, striking Cornet. The Frenchwoman was left understandably miffed at the injustice of losing the point when she wasn't even the intended receiver.

Next, it was Ostapenko's mixed doubles partner, Robert Lindstedt, who felt her 94mph serving power as she hit him flush on the back of the head while he crouched at the net in not just one match, but two.

After another headache from Jelena in Wednesday's third round win over John Peers and Shuai Zhang, the 42-year-old Swede Lindstedt posted the painful video on Instagram with the message: "My biggest dream is to win @wimbledon but I am not sure I can handle three more..."

• Searching desperately for any British interest left in the singles, attention focused on Ukrainian semi-finalist Elina Svitolina, not just because she spends a lot of time in London and could at a stretch be considered an 'honorary Brit', but because her young coach, Andrew Bettles, was a former national junior champion from Somerset.

Bettles, 26, who's graduated from being her hitting partner to main coach, said he could hardly credit being in at the business end of Wimbledon when his only previous memory was a brief and painful one.

"It was a hot day, I was so nervous, I could barely hold the grip," he smiled, thinking of his defeat in the boys' event in 2011. "I hit about three double faults in the first game alone!"

• Johanna Konta's attempts to cheer herself up after her quarter-final defeat saw her take herself down to the cinema to watch *Toy Story 4*. Alas, her plan appeared to quickly backfire as she later tweeted ruefully: "Just cried 4 times during *Toy Story 4*... 1 of them before the film even started... during the trailers."

• Another junior with a famous tennis parent was in action on Court 7. "My biggest goal is to win Wimbledon because my mom never did," the 18-year-old Elizabeth Mandlik told wimbledon.com, as she talked about her mum Hana Mandlikova, the former world No.3. "I want to do it for her." Sadly, though, injury forced her to retire in the third round against Natsumi Kawaguchi.

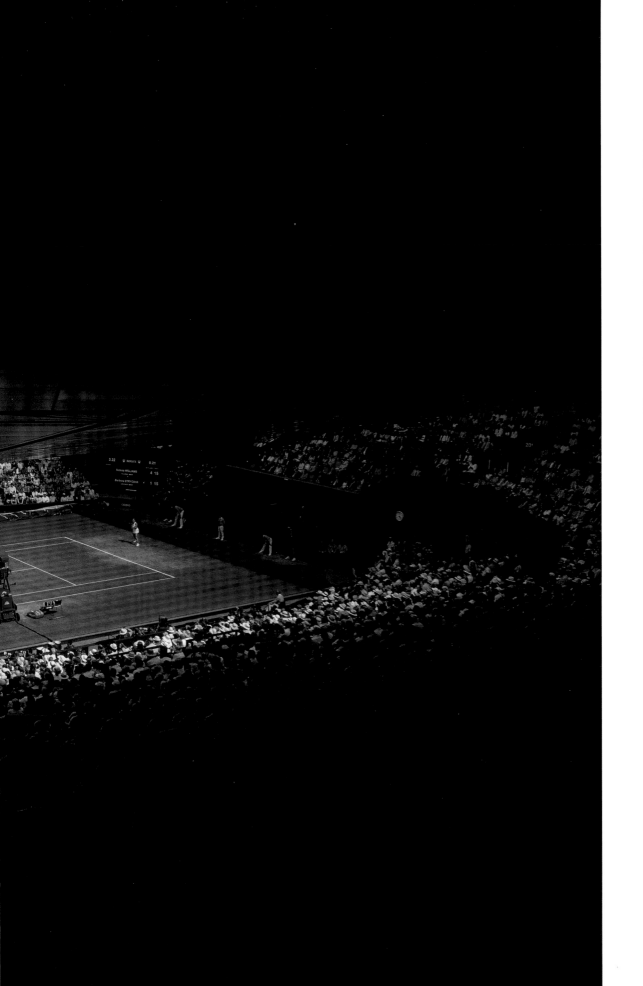

According to her coach, Patrick Mouratoglou, the reason why Serena Williams returned to tennis in 2018 after a 14-month maternity break was the chance to equal and then better Margaret Court's all-time record of 24 Grand Slam singles titles.

There had been times subsequently when the pressure of securing her place in history had seemed to get to Williams, but as she stood one win away from claiming that elusive 24th title the 37-year-old American insisted she was not obsessed by it. "I thought about it this morning," Williams said after her emphatic 6-1, 6-2 semi-final victory over Barbora Strycova. "I actually didn't think about it since, because it's really not about 24 or 23 or 25. It's really just about going out there and giving my best effort no matter what. No matter what I do, I will always have a great career. I just kind of let it go this morning. I feel really calm about it."

Williams' 'best effort' was way too much for Strycova, who at the age of 33 was playing in her first Grand Slam singles semi-final. The Czech's unpredictable mix of spins and slices had befuddled Johanna Konta in the previous round, but Williams eased past her in just 59 minutes with a relentless barrage of pounding serves and groundstrokes, hitting 28 winners to Strycova's eight. Williams, who dropped only three points when her first serve found the target, won five games in a row to take the first set and another five games in a row to take the second.

Although Strycova insisted it was not a reason for her defeat, the world No.54 said afterwards that she had suffered a muscle problem. "I felt my glutes," Strycova said. "At the beginning of the warm-up I felt it a little bit. On the second ball of the match I was running for a ball and I really, really felt it there. Since then it was getting worse and worse." Having paid credit to Williams for her "amazing" performance, Strycova said she was uncertain whether she would want to continue playing at her opponent's age. "I'm not sure if I want to reach 37," she said. "There are some other things I want to do in life rather

than just chasing a yellow ball." Williams, meanwhile, would be 37 years and 291 days old two days later, which would make her the oldest woman to play in a Grand Slam singles final in the Open era, overtaking Martina Navratilova, who had been 33 days younger when runner-up at The Championships 1994. Williams would be seeking her eighth Wimbledon singles title in her 11th final, 17 years after her first.

Winning the Australian Open in 2017, when she was already several weeks pregnant, had put the American within one title of matching Court's record, but in the five Grand Slam tournaments she had played since starting her comeback she had failed to add to her tally despite reaching two finals. At The Championships 2018 Williams had lost to Angelique Kerber and in the US Open two months later she had been beaten by Naomi Osaka. Her clash with umpire Carlos Ramos in the final at Flushing Meadows was perhaps an indication of the pressure she had been feeling.

"To even be in those two finals last year was unbelievable," Williams explained. "Now I'm in a different place. I just am more calm." Williams had clearly enjoyed playing in mixed

*Above: Ukraine's Elina Svitolina had battled through to her first-ever Grand Slam semi-final but Simona Halep (**opposite**) proved irresistible as she stormed into her maiden Wimbledon final for the loss of just four games*

doubles with Andy Murray, was pain-free after recovering from a knee injury and was serving like her old self. The one major doubt that lingered as she prepared for the final would be whether she would pay for her lack of matches.

Williams' opponent in the final would be Simona Halep, who beat Elina Svitolina 6-1, 6-3 in just 73 minutes. Nearly 20 minutes was taken up by the first two games and the outcome might have been very different if Svitolina had taken her chances in them. The 24-year-old Ukrainian, playing in her first Grand Slam semi-final, had three chances to break Halep's serve in the opening game and then three game points on her own serve, but did not take any of them. Although Svitolina broke back in the next game, Halep promptly won four in a row to take the first set.

Svitolina, who had won four of their previous seven meetings, held serve for the first time at the start of the second set, but by now Halep was striking the ball with great accuracy and winners flowed from her racket. The Romanian's default position was on the baseline, but she also won a number of points by attacking the net. Svitolina held on until 3-3, after which Halep made her fourth and fifth breaks of the match to seal her victory.

"I didn't take my chances," Svitolina said afterwards as she reflected on the opening two games. "That's what I think was disappointing. In the beginning, you want to play well, you want to make a statement that you are there for the fight."

Halep thought it was one of her best performances on grass and explained how she had improved on the surface. "I've changed my game a little bit," she said. "I play some drop shots. I use slice more.

The serve is helping me. Now when the ball is coming to me, now I know what to do with it. Maybe that's why. Maybe I feel confident and I'm not scared any more of how the ball bounces. I think I have the feeling. I also feel stable on my legs, which is very important on grass."

Having triumphed at Roland-Garros, where she had also lost two finals, and been runner-up at the Australian Open, Halep had now reached a Grand Slam final on clay, hard courts and grass. What did she think that said about her development as a player?

"As a player I have a better game these days," she said. "I can play everywhere, against anyone. It's good that I have more plans. When I go on court and face an opponent, I know how to play against her. Also I know how to change some things when it's not working very well. As a person, I'm trying just to be confident, to be positive. I'm working hard to do the best always when I step on the court."

Halep said that Darren Cahill, her former coach, had helped her to understand the importance of not over-thinking on court, as had Ion Tiriac, the former Romanian player, who had taken her under his wing. Cahill had also introduced Halep to a sports psychologist, Alexis Castorri, who had been very influential.

THE HISTORY MAKERS

—

Wheelchair tennis has quickly become an integral, important and much-savoured part of the Wimbledon Fortnight, with its leading players having become hugely popular figures at SW19. Three of the biggest names, all aiming to create history in 2019, were the early centre of attention as the tournament began on Courts 14, 15 and 17 in front of enthusiastic crowds on Day 10.

Argentina's Gustavo Fernandez (*left*), Dutchwoman Diede de Groot (*above*) and Australia's Dylan Alcott (*below, left*), all in line to achieve a calendar year Grand Slam having already prevailed at the Australian Open and Roland-Garros, launched their campaigns impressively. Fernandez, who had lost the previous two Wimbledon singles finals, defeated Britain's US Open champion Alfie Hewett to reach the semi-finals while de Groot, seeking a third straight crown at just 22, also made the last four, beating her compatriot Marjolein Buis.

It was a historic day as Wimbledon's inaugural Quad Wheelchair Championships were launched and Australian phenomenon Dylan Alcott, fresh from his Roland-Garros triumph, was inevitably at the heart of the action, beating Japan's Koji Sugeno in straight sets in his semi-final to set up a showdown with his friend and doubles partner Andy Lapthorne.

This was hardly a surprise. Alcott, at 28, had only ever lost one match in nine Grand Slams and a triumph at Wimbledon would mean he held all four majors at the same time – a veritable 'Dylan Slam'.

"I started to learn how to keep things simple because I overcomplicated everything in my head," Halep said. "I was thinking too much. Sometimes I had too many options how to play and I didn't pick the right one at the right moment. Darren helped me a lot with this. He always told me that I had to keep things simple. He showed me how to do that, which was great.

"I've also been working with a psychologist for almost two years now. She tried to make me understand myself and to accept everything I do wrong on court and to work on those things, which helped me a lot as well. Also Mr Tiriac, of course. He's been by my side since 2014. All the time he told me that I have just to play as it comes, by instinct, without thinking that much."

Halep said that her mother, Tania, had always dreamed of watching her play in a Wimbledon final in front of the Royal Box. "She said it would be an unbelievable moment," Halep said. "So today her dream came true as I will play a final. It's a very special moment. To be able to play in a Wimbledon final, it's pretty amazing." Asked if there was one person she would like to see watching her match from the Royal Box, Halep said: "Kate [HRH The Duchess of Cambridge]. I like her."

Asked how desperate she was to stop Williams equalling Court's record, Halep insisted: "I'm desperate to win Wimbledon more than to stop her. I will focus on myself. I'm not thinking about her record."

Three years after facing each other in a gentlemen's doubles final at The Championships, the Frenchmen Nicolas Mahut and Edouard Roger-Vasselin moved within one match of winning the title together by beating Ivan Dodig and Filip Polasek 6-2, 7-6(7), 7-6(2) in the semi-finals. In 2016 Mahut had partnered Pierre-Hugues Herbert to victory over Roger-Vasselin and Julien Benneteau in the final. This time Mahut and Roger-Vasselin would face the Colombians Juan Sebastian Cabal and Robert Farah, who beat Raven Klaasen and Michael Venus 6-4, 6-7(4), 7-6(2), 6-4.

A delightful shot of the Wheelchair tennis action on picturesque Court 17, with France's Stephane Houdet serving en route to a quarter-final victory over compatriot Nicolas Peifer

Right: Nicolas Mahut and Edouard Roger-Vasselin, who faced each other in the gentlemen's doubles final in 2016, teamed up to beat Ivan Dodig and Filip Polasek in the semi-finals

Below: Anton Matusevich was the last British junior in the boys' singles but lost out to Japan's Shintaro Mochizuki on No.3 Court

British interest in the mixed doubles ended when Evan Hoyt and Eden Silva, who were both making their senior debuts in The Championships, were beaten 5-7, 6-7(5) by Dodig and Latisha Chan in the quarter-finals. Anton Matusevich, Britain's last player in the boys' singles, also went out as Shintaro Mochizuki won their quarter-final 6-3, 6-3.

As the Wheelchair events got under way, Britain's Andy Lapthorne and Australia's Dylan Alcott secured places in the inaugural Quad Wheelchair Singles final with victories over David Wagner and Koji Sugeno respectively. Lapthorne was delighted to see Venus Williams in the crowd, 18 years after a chance meeting with the five-times Ladies' Singles Champion, her sister Serena and their father Richard in a lift at the All England Club had inspired him to take up the sport. "Ever since that day I've always wanted to play here," he said. "I had watched them so much on the TV. To see them in real life was just really inspiring, and to have a picture with their dad, it was crazy. For her to come out today and watch, it was surreal."

DAILY DIARY DAY 10

No wonder Claire Foy (*above, left*) seemed so at home in the Royal Box on ladies' semi-finals day. To the actress, who played the Queen in the award-winning series *The Crown*, this really did look like a home from home, and it turns out that Foy has a history at the All England Club, neither as a celluloid monarch nor a thespian but as a security officer.

"I used to work at Wimbledon, used to be one of the security people checking bags when I was 21," she told The Wimbledon Channel. "It feels a bit weird going into the Royal Box. I feel a bit duplicitous, a bit strange!"

• Simona Halep, having just roared into her first Wimbledon final, was happy to clear up one of the great mysteries of her career for reporters. Why exactly does she follow just two people on Twitter, one of them rather understandably being the coach who guided her to the top, Darren Cahill, but the other, quite puzzlingly, being the snooker player known as 'The Jester from Leicester'?

Yes, even former world snooker champion Mark Selby might have been surprised to learn that he's on Simona's list, especially as she admits to not knowing how even to play the game.

Yet the Romanian explained: "I appreciate him. He's been in Romania a few times. I met him. Also I have a snooker ball signed from him. That's why I follow him."

• Philip Brook, the outgoing Chairman, revealed the All England Club were working on plans to honour Sir

Andy Murray (*left*) with a statue after the two-times Gentlemen's Singles Champion calls time on his career.

Brook explained: "We want to recognise Andy's significant achievements here at Wimbledon in an appropriate way and at an appropriate time. We think an appropriate time is to unveil something when he retires.

"It is under consideration. What we don't want to do is retire him too early. We have done some work already on it and there is still more work to do."

• Serena Williams may have been knocked out of the mixed doubles with Andy Murray but she was still adamant that their partnership had helped her reach an 11th ladies' singles final.

"I promise you, when I hit a volley today, I was like 'would I have made that if I didn't play doubles?' I don't think so," she said, knowing exactly what her audience wanted to hear. "I kept telling you guys I thought the doubles would help me. I really think it did."

Of all the statistics relating to the rivalry between Roger Federer and Rafael Nadal over the past 15 years, perhaps the most striking was this: Federer had won only three of their 13 meetings in Grand Slam tournaments. Although the figures were coloured by Nadal's six wins out of six at Roland-Garros, he also led 3-1 in their Grand Slam head-to-head record on hard courts.

Above: Rafael Nadal, winner of the epic 2008 final, hit some stunning forehands (opposite) but the majestic Roger Federer claimed the spoils in the pair's 40th clash

Previous pages: Federer celebrates his epic semi-final triumph over Nadal in the incredible pair's first Wimbledon clash for 11 years

There was only one place where Federer bettered his great rival: Wimbledon. Federer had come out on top in their 2006 and 2007 finals before Nadal won arguably the finest match in history – and their most recent meeting on grass – in the 2008 gentlemen's singles final. Although returning to the greatest stage of all in this year's Championships was seen as a factor in Federer's favour, the majority of pundits thought that Nadal would win their second meeting in five weeks following his triumph the previous month at Roland-Garros.

Had there ever been a more eagerly awaited semi-final at Wimbledon than the 40th career meeting between the 37-year-old Swiss and the 33-year-old Spaniard? Not only was it a showdown between the most successful players in the 142-year history of Grand Slam competition but it also brought together the players who had won more tour-level matches than any other men in 2019.

With such a build-up the reality usually fails to live up to the hype, but not this time. For more than three hours on a sunlit afternoon Federer and Nadal entranced a rapt Centre Court crowd, and audiences around the world, with a wonderful exhibition of their magical talents.

It was a reminder of the contrast between the two men which has helped make their rivalry so captivating. Federer, the suave and sophisticated Swiss, danced across the court with apparently effortless ease, striking majestic forehands and elegant one-handed backhands or using his exquisite touch to hit winning volleys. Meanwhile Nadal thundered over the grass, turning heroic defence into deadly counter-attack with one sweep of his racket, his heavily top-spun forehands fizzing across the net before kicking off the turf. Although the match never quite reached the heady heights of 2008, it featured many breathtaking rallies and would live long in the memory.

Federer won 7-6(3), 1-6, 6-3, 6-4, passing another milestone along the way as he overtook Goran Ivanisevic's record of 1,397 aces struck at The Championships. A closely fought first set, which was dominated by serves and never quite caught fire, ended with Federer winning five points in a row to take the tie-break. Nadal upped his aggression and from 1-1 and 30-40 took the second set by winning 19 of the next 22 points. The third set turned on a moment of genius from Federer. Serving at 1-2 and 30-30, Nadal thundered what looked to be a winning forehand down the line only for Federer to reach the ball almost on the half-volley and hit a sensational forehand cross-court winner. The Swiss won the next point with a backhand volley and served out for the set.

Nadal, who struggled on occasions to find his rhythm on his backhands and returns, was broken again early in the fourth set, but his fighting spirit remained intact. Having saved two match points at 3-5 with bold serves, his last big chance evaporated when he netted a simple backhand on break point as Federer served at 5-4. Nadal saved two more match points in thrilling fashion, but on the fifth he hit a backhand beyond the baseline.

Following pages: The entire Centre Court crowd – and millions of viewers around the world – were on the edge of their seats throughout the match

A MATCH WORTH WAITING FOR

—

If you had suggested back in 2008, following what has since been dubbed the finest tennis match ever played (*above and left*), that it would be another 11 years before Rafael Nadal and Roger Federer would do battle again at Wimbledon, you would have been laughed off court.

Incredibly, there had been 22 more editions of Rafa v Roger staged all over the world in the intervening years – but never at Wimbledon, even though they reached another seven finals and lifted another four titles between them at SW19.

The year after Rafa's five-set triumph in 2008, a knee injury forced him to abandon his 2009 defence as Federer went on to win for a sixth time. In 2010, Nadal regained his crown, beating Federer's last-eight conqueror, Tomas Berdych, in the final, and in 2011 the Spaniard reached the final while the Swiss blew a two-set quarter-final lead against Jo-Wilfried Tsonga.

The next six years, though, were Nadal's leanest time at any Grand Slam as he never managed to get past the fourth round at Wimbledon, running into a series of inspired underdogs like Lukas Rosol (2012), Steve Darcis (2013), Dustin Brown (2015) and Nick Kyrgios (2014), before missing 2016 through injury. The more consistent Federer, meanwhile, won two further titles over that same stretch.

Yet now at long last, fate had brought them back together for 'Fedal 2019' – and it was absolutely worth the wait.

"It's always very, very cool to play against Rafa here, especially as we hadn't played in so long," Federer said afterwards. "It lived up to the hype, especially from coming out of the gates. We were both playing very well. Then the climax at the end, with the crazy last game, some tough rallies there. It had everything at the end, which was great. I'm just relieved it's all over. But it's definitely going to go down as one of my favourite matches to look back at – because it's Rafa, it's at Wimbledon, the crowds were into it, great weather."

He added: "I was able to stick to my game plan, stay aggressive, stay offensive. I guess I also started to serve a bit better after the second set. I think I won a lot of the important points in the third and fourth sets. There were some brutal rallies in key moments that went my way."

Nadal said he had had his chances. "He played a little bit better than me," the Spaniard said. "I probably didn't play as well as I did in the previous rounds and he played well. He deserves it."

Above: Roger Federer punched the air in delight after his victory over Rafael Nadal, also prompting scenes of delight among his team and family in the players' box (left) and his army of fans on The Hill (below, left)

THE GOLDEN TICKET

Who could say no? A Royal Box seat on Centre Court after a magnificent Wimbledon lunch with the great and the good. "Amazing, isn't it?" marvelled comedian Michael McIntyre, gazing at Friday's stellar list. "Alex Ferguson? Oh my God! David Attenborough? This is exciting! I'm slightly tense. I might not be on this list! I might have to go home!" He need not have worried. As Hugh Grant smiled: "The Royal Box? Is there anywhere else to sit? They're damned nice to us, I don't know why..."

For a gentlemen's semi-finals day featuring the sport's biggest hitters, it felt appropriate that the Royal Box should feature a heavyweight list of famous faces, including (from top left, clockwise) *Jude and Phillipa Law, Pat Cash with Sir David Attenborough, Damian Lewis, Gary Player with Fiona Ferguson and Sir Alex Ferguson, and Hugh Grant. David Beckham* (centre) *seemed to sum up all their thoughts when he rose to salute the end of the Federer-Nadal epic, exclaiming: "Unbelievable!"*

*Roberto Bautista Agut
in his first-ever Grand
Slam semi-final, gave
Novak Djokovic a real
test on Centre Court*

Asked what he appreciated most about Federer's game, Nadal said: "He is always able to do the most difficult things easily. He's able to move inside the court quicker than anyone. He puts pressure on the opponent all the time because he has the ability to take the ball earlier than anybody else."

Despite his disappointment Nadal remained positive. "I played a great event," he said. "At the same time today is sad because for me I know chances are not for ever. Last year I had chances here and today I had another one."

At 37 years and 340 days, Federer would be the oldest man to play in a Grand Slam singles final since 39-year-old Ken Rosewall at the 1974 US Open. The Swiss was the most senior of this year's semi-finalists, who with an average age of 33 years and six months were the oldest last four in a Grand Slam tournament in the Open era.

Roberto Bautista Agut, at 31, was the youngest of the semi-finalists. The world No.22 had never previously gone beyond the fourth round at The Championships and had reached his first Grand Slam quarter-final at the Australian Open in January. Nevertheless, there were reasons for optimism in the Spaniard's camp in that he had beaten his semi-final opponent, Novak Djokovic, in both their previous meetings in 2019.

Bautista Agut hit a scorching forehand return winner on the very first point, but Djokovic was soon 3-0 up and took the opening set with a second break of serve. The Spaniard served much better to take the second set, in which he made an early break, but in the third Djokovic made the early running.

With both players striking the ball with painstaking accuracy from the baseline there were some outstanding rallies, including a mesmerising 45-shot exchange – the longest ever recorded at The Championships – in which Djokovic successfully defended a break point. Both players later agreed it had been a key moment. Djokovic won five games in a row in the fourth set before closing out his 6-2, 4-6, 6-3, 6-2 victory.

Above: Novak Djokovic, who even had to endure one record-breaking 45-stroke rally before winning the point against his tough Spanish opponent, was pumped up after his four-set triumph (left)

Djokovic sometimes appeared irked when the crowd were cheering for Bautista Agut, but he insisted it had not affected him. "I've had enough support here over the years, so I don't complain," he said. "I focused on what I needed to do. At times they wanted him to come back in the match, maybe take the lead, because he was an underdog. I understand that."

The world No.1 was also confident that he would handle the situation if the majority of the crowd supported his opponent in the final. "I know what to expect," he said. "Regardless of who's across the net or what is happening, I'll definitely give it my all."

This was Djokovic's 11th win in his last 12 semi-finals in Grand Slam tournaments, his only loss over that run having been against Dominic Thiem at Roland-Garros the previous month. It was his fifth successive semi-final victory at The Championships and took him into his 25th Grand Slam final, with Federer (31 finals) and Nadal (26 finals) the only players above him on the all-time list.

Djokovic was asked what record he would most like to break. "My main motivation is really to be out on the court and enjoying what I do," he said. "Without that, magic cannot happen, good results cannot happen. I don't see this as my job or as my work. I've done enough in my career so I could stop playing professional tennis at any time, but I don't do it for those reasons. My first reason is because I really enjoy it. I still do. I have support from my family. Of course, I am looking to make history in this sport. Of course, I would love to have a shot at as many Grand Slam titles as possible. Those are probably the top goals and ambitions."

Barbora Strycova made up for her disappointment at losing in the ladies' singles semi-finals by reaching the final of the ladies' doubles. Strycova and Su-Wei Hsieh beat Timea Babos and Kristina Mladenovic, the No.1 seeds and champions of Roland-Garros, 7-6(5), 6-4 in the semi-finals. Their opponents in the final would be Gabriela Dabrowski and Yifan Xu, who beat the defending champions and No.2 seeds, Barbora Krejcikova and Katerina Siniakova, 6-1, 3-6, 6-3.

Britain's Andy Lapthorne and his Australian partner, Dylan Alcott, won the inaugural Quad Wheelchair Doubles title, beating David Wagner and Koji Sugeno 6-2, 7-6(4) in the final. Twenty-four hours later Lapthorne and Alcott would be on opposite sides of the net in the singles final.

Canada's Gabriela Dabrowski and China's Yifan Xu earned a shock win over the former world No.1 pairing of Barbora Krejcikova and Katerina Siniakova in the ladies' doubles semi-final on No.1 Court

DAILY DIARY DAY 11

They came, they saw and though they didn't quite see their pal conquer, the friends who arrived in London to cheer on Roberto Bautista Agut had the time of their lives on Centre Court watching his duel with Novak Djokovic.

As Roberto was unable to join them in Ibiza for his planned stag do celebrations since he happened to be otherwise occupied in the best tournament of his life, it seemed a better idea for them to all fly over to London instead to support him on this 'other' big day before his marriage in November.

For, as BBC commentator John Inverdale observed: "As stag dos go, being in the players' box at Wimbledon is right up there!"

This particular do, however, was shared with fiancée Ana, who was also cheering him on. "I think they really had a good plan. They spend Wednesday in Ibiza, and came to watch a good match, the semi-final of Wimbledon," smiled Bautista Agut.

And were there any plans to jet back and continue the party in Ibiza? "Maybe tomorrow," came the reply.

• Exactly a year on from the longest Centre Court match ever played, between Kevin Anderson and John Isner, The Championships 2019 witnessed the longest rally ever recorded at Wimbledon as Djokovic won a 45-stroke, minute-long battle of patience during his hard-earned victory over Bautista Agut.

It was a crucial point as Djokovic faced break-back point while 4-2 up and with the match locked at one set all. On the 45th shot of this war of attrition, Djokovic finally summoned an imperious backhand winner to rapturous applause.

The rally length beat the 42-stroke marathon between Jarkko Nieminen and Dmitry Tursunov, which had stood since 2006 as the longest recorded since IBM began recording statistics for The Championships in 2005.

• The day after England's Cricket World Cup win over Australia, the old rivals' sports fans joined forces on Court 14 to cheer Aussie Dylan Alcott and England's Andy Lapthorne to victory in the inaugural Quad Wheelchair Doubles final over Koji Sugeno and David Wagner. "A mix of Aussies and Londoners were cheering for the one team this time, it was great," beamed Lapthorne, who was also set to play Alcott in Sunday's singles final.

Court - South West Hall

As Simona Halep prepared to face Serena Williams in the ladies' singles final it was instructive to recall what the Romanian had said on the opening day of The Championships. "This is a chill year and I'm not putting pressure on myself," Halep explained. "I'm not analysing that much. I just want to go on court and see how good I can be this year. Next year maybe I will push a little bit more. Now I feel happy on court, I feel good. I just try to win every match I play. Nothing else in my mind."

Previous pages: Simona Halep held the Venus Rosewater Dish aloft in traditional fashion from the Centre Court balcony

Halep put her change of attitude down to winning her first Grand Slam title, at Roland-Garros in 2018, after losing in her first three finals. However, it might also have had something to do with her disappointment when Darren Cahill told her at the end of 2018 that he needed to take a break from coaching her to spend more time with his family. When Halep started the new year without a coach you had the sense that she knew the Australian would be all but impossible to replace.

Above: Simona Halep played the match of her life to sweep past the great Serena Williams in just 56 minutes and claim her first Wimbledon crown

Left: HRH The Duchess of Cambridge, who Halep had hoped would attend, and HRH The Duchess of Sussex, a good friend of Williams, enjoyed the action together in the Royal Box

In March Halep recruited her fellow Romanian, Daniel Dobre, who had worked with her previously, but even at The Championships she admitted to missing Cahill. "I feel his absence and I miss his person there in the box," she said. "I always had a great connection with him. He also gave me peace during matches and power to keep fighting."

Halep had arrived at the previous summer's Championships as world No.1, but over the following 12 months dropped to No.7 after losing to Kaia Kanepi in the first round of the US Open, to Williams in the fourth round of the Australian Open and to Amanda Anisimova at Roland-Garros.

At The Championships, nevertheless, she was running into some of her best form and had dropped only one set on her way to the final. Although Halep had a reasonable record at Wimbledon – one semi-final and two quarter-finals in her previous five appearances – the only problem was that Williams had won nine of their 10 previous completed meetings. Williams, however, faced pressures of her own, having lost in both her previous appearances in Grand Slam finals.

What transpired was one of the most remarkable finals of recent times as Halep played what she called the match of her life to win 6-2, 6-2 in just 56 minutes. The 27-year-old Romanian, who at 5ft 6in tall lacks the long levers of some of her rivals but is one of the game's best athletes, flew around the court, repeatedly retrieving Williams' booming groundstrokes before launching deadly counter-attacks. Halep made just three unforced errors while Williams, apparently feeling she had to hit even harder to win the points, made 26.

Halep went 4-0 up in 11 minutes, saved Williams' only break point of the match at 4-1 and served out for the opening set. Familiar roars of "C'mon!" bellowed around Centre Court as Williams raised her level at the start of the second set, but, serving at 2-2 and 15-40, the American put too much on what should have been a backhand winner down the line. Halep broke again two games later and then served out to love before sinking to her knees in apparent disbelief. "I never thought that I would be able to win on grass with all these players that are very tall and serving with a lot of power," she said later.

Halep said at the presentation ceremony that it felt "very special" to hold the Venus Rosewater Dish. "I will never forget this day," she added. "It was my mum's dream when I was about 10 or 12. She said that if I wanted to do something in tennis I had to play in the final at Wimbledon." Her parents were in the crowd and when they met afterwards her mother, Tania, was unable to speak through her tears. "I just hugged her and kissed her," Halep said.

Dobre, the new champion's coach, who was also crying at the end ("Every match," Halep said with a smile afterwards), had always believed she could win Wimbledon. "For me, her game is more for grass than for clay," he said. "She can stay down, her game is a little flatter, she can serve with slice, she's moving very well, passing very well. In my opinion it's more difficult for her to win Roland-Garros than here. I told her that five years ago – and this year she showed it."

Halep, meanwhile, said that she still talked to Cahill "all the time". She added: "He came to see my match again today. His heart is with us. That made me a little bit stronger today, honestly, to be able to believe that I had the chance to win."

In the past, Halep admitted, she had been "a little bit intimidated" when she faced Williams. "Today I decided before the match that I was going to focus on myself and on the final of a Grand Slam, not on her," she said. "That's why I was able to play my best, to be relaxed, and to be able to be positive and confident against her. I decided this morning how I had to play against her. I knew exactly what I had to do to put her in trouble, not to let her play her game. When she has time, she plays unbelievable."

Left: Victorious Simona Halep fell to her knees in joy, barely able to believe she had just won her second Grand Slam title and realised her long-held dream of becoming Wimbledon champion

Below: Serena Williams was graciousness personified after the match, waving to the Centre Court crowd before being presented with the runner-up prize

Previous pages:
One for the
family album.
Simona Halep
raised the Venus
Rosewater Dish
aloft for the
photographers
before parading
it to hearty cheers
around Centre
*Court (**above***
*and **right**)*

Williams, meanwhile, paid for her lack of matches, Halep having been the first top 10 opponent she had faced in six months. Williams admitted she had been "a little bit like a deer in the headlights" while Halep had "literally played out of her mind". The American added: "I just have to figure out a way to win a final. Maybe playing other finals outside of Grand Slams would be really helpful just to kind of get in the groove."

Theresa May, the outgoing Prime Minister, was among those in the Royal Box, while Halep said it had been an honour to play in front of HRH The Duchess of Cambridge, who sat next to HRH The Duchess of Sussex. "I had the chance to meet her after the match," Halep said. "She's very kind, very nice. It was an extra boost when I saw all of them there, the Royal family." Roger Federer's words of encouragement the previous day, when he said Halep needed to "back herself and also enjoy it", had also helped. "If you listen to him, you get the good things," she said.

Halep became the first Romanian to win a singles title at The Championships, Ilie Nastase having been runner-up in 1972 and 1976. She is from Constanta, on the country's Black Sea coast. "The champions are coming from Constanta," she said, pointing out that Andrei Pavel, a former world No.13, and Horia Tecau, a recent world No.2 in doubles, also hail from the city. "I think it's just the air from the beach. We train a lot on the beach when we are kids. I did a lot of training on the sand and in the sea." Halep said she had always loved representing her country and her next goal would be to win a medal at the 2020 Olympic Games.

Juan Sebastian Cabal and Robert Farah became the first Colombians to win a Grand Slam men's doubles title when they beat France's Nicolas Mahut and Edouard Roger-Vasselin 6-7(5), 7-6(5), 7-6(6), 6-7(5), 6-3 after four hours and 57 minutes. With the light fading, the Centre Court roof was closed for the final set. The win took the Colombians to the top of the world doubles rankings, while Mahut had a painful evening all round. He needed a medical time-out after being hit by a ball just above his left eye and was also struck in the neck and groin.

It took no time for the new champion's name to be engraved on the plinth of the Venus Rosewater Dish

THE DYLAN SLAM

Wimbledon saluted a charismatic new champion after Australian Dylan Alcott beat his British pal and doubles-winning partner Andy Lapthorne 6-0, 6-2 on Court 12 to win the inaugural Quad Wheelchair Singles title. It meant the 28-year-old from Melbourne, already hugely popular back home, now held all four Grand Slams simultaneously.

"Wimbledon just put out on their Instagram and Twitter 'The Dylan Slam'. That sounds all right, doesn't it?" he beamed. "It's a dream come true. Wearing the whites, strawberries and cream, everyone drinking Pimm's. It was so cool. Am I allowed to say Pimm's? I did anyway!"

Alcott, who was left a paraplegic after undergoing surgery as a baby to remove a tumour wrapped around his spinal cord, is delighted that he's helping change perceptions of people with a disability.

"In Australia, people used to stare at me because I was in a wheelchair. Now they stare because you're Dylan Alcott and they know who you are. That's like the coolest thing, because they could not care that I'm in a wheelchair."

Dylan's next dream? "I go boxing, training, doing everything every day because I want to repeat Rod Laver's calendar-year Grand Slam. One more to go, baby! Glad I didn't drop the bottle here!"

SIMONA JOINS THE CLUB

—

Simona Halep made no bones about it. Yes, it was wonderful to become Romania's first Wimbledon singles champion and, yes, winning the title was the culmination of a long-standing dream for her and her family.

But we were soon to learn what had tickled her most. "It feels good to become a member of the All England Club. I wanted this badly!" she said, laughing about how her victory had guaranteed her membership of one of sport's great clubs.

"When I started the tournament, I talked to the people from the locker room that my dream is to become a member here. So today it's real!"

Was there anything that she was particularly looking forward to doing at the venue where her name now shines on the honours board?

"Yes, I just want to come here and chill. Without pressure, without thinking I have a match tomorrow. I met Philip [Brook, All England Club Chairman] (*right*). He told me, 'Any time you want, you can come, have dinner, have lunch, play a little bit tennis.' I will come for sure!"

As it turned out, her All England Club membership was not the last honour Simona was to receive thanks to her Wimbledon triumph. When she returned home to a hero's reception, Romania's President Klaus Iohannis awarded her the country's highest distinction: the 'Steaua României', the Star of Romania.

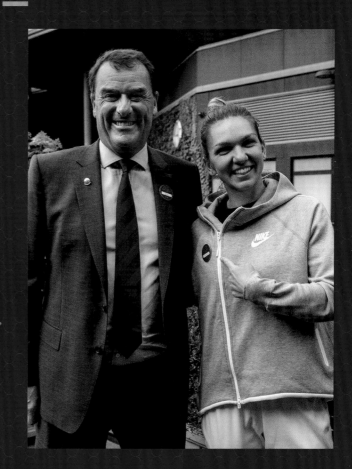

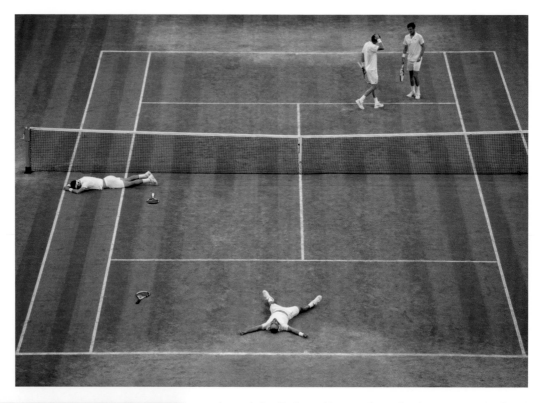

Right and below:
Exhausted but elated, Juan Sebastian Cabal and Robert Farah celebrate becoming Colombia's first Wimbledon champions after their near-five-hour gentlemen's doubles epic on Centre Court against France's Nicolas Mahut and Edouard Roger-Vasselin

Bottom:
Ukraine's Daria Snigur wheels away in delight at winning the girls' singles final

Australia's Dylan Alcott claimed the inaugural Quad Wheelchair Singles title with a 6-0, 6-2 victory over Britain's Andy Lapthorne, with whom he had won the doubles 24 hours earlier. Alcott had completed the same double earlier in the year at both the Australian Open and Roland-Garros. Britain's Alfie Hewett and Gordon Reid had been aiming to win the Gentlemen's Wheelchair Doubles title for the fourth time but were denied 4-6, 2-6 by Joachim Gerard and Stefan Olsson in the final.

Aniek van Koot pulled off a major surprise in the Ladies' Wheelchair Singles when she beat Diede de Groot, the champion of the previous two years, 6-4, 4-6, 7-5. De Groot had become the first player to hold all four wheelchair Grand Slam titles with her victory at Roland-Garros the previous month, while van Koot had been a runner-up at The Championships in both 2016 and 2018. It was her third Grand Slam singles title but her first for six years.

Daria Snigur, a 17-year-old Ukrainian, won the girls' singles title, beating Alexa Noel of the United States 6-4, 6-4. Snigur dropped only one set in the whole week. Having completed what she said would be her last junior Grand Slam competition, Snigur would now look forward to a career as a professional. If she needed encouragement she would need only to look down a list of recent girls' champions at the All England Club, Caroline Wozniacki, Ashleigh Barty and Jelena Ostapenko having all gone on to win senior Grand Slam titles in the last three years.

DAILY DIARY DAY 12

A story that was out of this world launched the weekend's singles finals on Centre Court, with the pre-match coin tosses performed by youngsters Marni Johnson and Omar Popal using bespoke gold coins that had travelled into outer space.

NASA astronaut Commander Drew Feustel (*above, second from left*) and Club Chairman Philip Brook had come up with the idea two years ago that special coins should be minted and given to Feustel to take on his six-month 'Mission 56' to the International Space Station. So, featuring the Mission 56 logo on one side and The Championships' crossed-rackets logo on the other, the coins went on their epic 197-day journey before returning to terra firma and then on to Centre Court, Wimbledon.

Ahead of the ladies' final, Feustel and his wife, Indira (*above, right*), presented one of the coins to 13-year-old Marni, who was representing the charity Regenerate. The pair returned again on Sunday before the gentlemen's final to hand over the coin to Omar, aged 14, representing the Prince's Trust.

• A Briton proud to play a small but significant part in Simona Halep's triumph was Tom Thelwall-Jones, a 19-year-old from Wrexham who landed the job as the Romanian's hitting partner during The Championships.

Thelwall-Jones, who'd just finished his first year on a tennis scholarship at the University of Tulsa, Oklahoma, studying finance and sports management, was designated to hit with Halep on the Saturday before The Championships.

Impressed, she requested him again before her first round match and, after reverting to a left-handed partner before her second round match, Halep asked Tom back to practise with her for the rest of the tournament.

Halep, who thought Tom was a "great guy", made sure he was rewarded with tickets for both her semi-final and final. "So it's been pretty cool," Tom said. "She's amazing. Her on-court interview really showed off who she is. She's very nice, very chilled out."

• Jordanne Whiley, Britain's 10-time wheelchair tennis Grand Slam champion (*below*), thought she was having a disappointing Fortnight until her boyfriend, Marc McCarroll, unveiled the loveliest surprise wedding proposal via their 18-month-old son, Jackson.

The toddler appeared in a T-shirt with the slogan

'Mummy will you marry my daddy?' "It was a total surprise," laughed Jordanne. "Marc's plan was to ask me if I made it to the final – he was going to come out onto the court – but because I didn't make it, he had to improvise." The couple plan to marry in 2020.

What a Fortnight it had been. In the ladies' singles, we had seen the emergence of a remarkable talent in 15-year-old Cori Gauff, confirmation that Serena Williams' powers remain undimmed, and the crowning of a worthy new champion after Simona Halep played the match of her life in the final.

Above: Roger Federer was magnificent but despite earning two match points could not overcome Novak Djokovic's amazing resilience to land that ninth Wimbledon title

Previous pages: HRH The Duchess of Cambridge presented a beaming Djokovic with the trophy on Centre Court

In the gentlemen's singles, Novak Djokovic, Roger Federer and Rafael Nadal had provided further demonstrations of their enduring brilliance. In doubles, the return of Andy Murray had lit up the men's and mixed competitions. Given that the two weeks had been blessed with superb weather, what more could we want? Yet, incredibly, the best was yet to come as Djokovic and Federer staged an unforgettable gentlemen's singles final on the last day that enthralled the Centre Court crowd for nearly five hours.

Where to start in describing such a momentous contest? The basic facts tell only part of the story. Djokovic, claiming his fifth Wimbledon title, won 7-6(5), 1-6, 7-6(4), 4-6, 13-12(3) after four hours and 57 minutes, which made it the longest singles final in the 142-year history of The Championships. The previous record had been set in 2008 when Nadal beat Federer in the match hailed as the greatest of all time, a verdict which might now have to be reconsidered. In the first final decided by a final set tie-break, Djokovic became the first man in 71 years to take the title after being match points down in the final, while Federer let slip his chance to become the oldest player in the Open era to win a Grand Slam singles title.

The head-to-head record between the two men had always suggested that it would be close. Djokovic had won 25 of their previous 47 matches (only Djokovic and Nadal, with 54, had played each other more often in the Open era), although the 32-year-old Serb had a clear edge in their Grand Slam record (nine wins to six, including the last four in a row) and in their most recent meetings, having won four in succession since Federer had last beaten him in 2015. It was their third meeting in the Wimbledon final, Djokovic having won in five sets in 2014 and in four sets 12 months later.

From the start the standard of play was exceptional. Djokovic chased balls down with the great athleticism that has become his trademark and struck the ball with relentless consistency. Perhaps most crucially, he played the key points superbly. While Federer won 218 points to Djokovic's 204 and was the better player for long periods, the fact that the world No.1 won all three tie-breaks told its own story.

Federer, ever the aggressor, cracked 94 winners (to Djokovic's 54), reaped a rich reward from his regular forays to the net and served brilliantly. The Swiss hit 25 aces and defended his first break point after two hours and 47 minutes. Perhaps most remarkably of all for a man one month short of his 38th birthday, he never showed any signs of fatigue.

While Djokovic has millions of fans around the world, the Wimbledon public adore Federer and there was a huge roar when the eight-times Gentlemen's Singles Champion hit an ace on the first point. The story of the opening set would become the script of the whole match as Federer failed to take the only break point and led 5-3 in the tie-break before losing four points in succession to hand the set to Djokovic. The Swiss nevertheless dominated the second set, dropping just 12 points as Djokovic's level dipped.

Federer continued to set the pace in the third set. A spectacular half-volley winner gave him set point at 4-5, but Djokovic served his way out of trouble and again capitalised on his opponent's mistakes in the tie-break. A missed backhand took Djokovic to 6-4 and a forehand into the net gave him the set.

Above: Novak Djokovic's unbelievable athleticism was on full display as he was forced to stretch himself to the limit to halt Roger Federer

Following pages: Many in the Centre Court crowd were desperate to see Federer make Wimbledon history but cheered both players to the rafters over the course of a fantastic match

THE HILL IS ALIVE

As an epic final between Novak Djokovic and Roger Federer see-sawed amid the highest drama, the enormous crowd on The Hill was utterly captivated. One spectator held aloft a banner saying 'I support both Novak and Roger – I can't decide' but it has to be said there weren't too many neutrals like her to be found. Federer, as ever, enjoyed enormous support but Novak had plenty of friends on hand too, as this young lad (*below*) with the Serbian flag demonstrated. And he had the last laugh...

Once again, however, Federer's response could not be faulted as two successive breaks gave him a 5-2 lead in the fourth set. Djokovic finally forced his first break point in the following game, only for Federer to save it with a backhand winner after a 35-stroke rally. Djokovic won the next two points to break for the first time, but Federer served out to love two games later to take the set. After three hours of breathtaking tennis the match was level at two sets apiece, but the greatest drama was yet to come.

At the start of the fifth set it was Djokovic who forced the issue. Federer saved two break points at 1-2 and another after going 15-40 down at 2-3, only to be beaten by a majestic backhand cross-court pass on the next point. Federer, nevertheless, broke back immediately and soon found himself in a similar position to his opponent in the 2009 final, Andy Roddick, who had kept serving to stay alive only to lose the final set 16-14 after dropping his serve for the first time following 37 successive holds.

Federer went within two points of defeat at 4-5 and 5-6, but at 7-7 it was Djokovic who cracked, beaten by a scintillating forehand cross-court pass on break point, to a thunderous roar from the crowd. Centre Court was at fever-pitch when Djokovic went two match points down at 8-7 as Federer hit two successive aces, but the Swiss missed what looked to be a routine forehand on the first and was beaten by a forehand cross-court pass on the second. When two more netted forehands handed back the break, both men might have started thinking back to the US Open semi-finals of 2010 and 2011, when Djokovic beat Federer after saving two match points on both occasions.

Djokovic saved two break points at 11-11 before the match went to a final set tie-break at 12-12. The All England Club had introduced tie-breaks in the final set for the first time for this year's Championships and this was the first singles match to be decided in such fashion. From the moment Federer made an unforced backhand error on the opening point Djokovic never trailed in the tie-break. A backhand winner down the line took him to 6-3, upon which Federer missed a forehand as Djokovic became the first Wimbledon Gentlemen's Singles Champion to win the final from match point down since Bob Falkenburg saved three in the fifth set against John Bromwich in 1948.

*Below: Novak Djokovic's understated celebration after nearly five hours of dazzling tennis saw him raise one hand to the skies (**left**) before crouching down for his favourite meal of Centre Court grass (**right**)*

INCREDIBLE SPORTING AFTERNOON

—

B ritish sport has never seen an afternoon quite as extraordinary as 14 July 2019, with its unique and nerve-shredding climaxes to two classic global showdowns happening simultaneously roughly 10 miles apart in London.

An afternoon which began with driving hero Lewis Hamilton winning the British Grand Prix (*below, left*) ended with the first-ever final set tie-break to decide a Wimbledon final between Novak Djokovic and Roger Federer coinciding with the first-ever 'Super Over' to settle a Cricket World Cup final between England and New Zealand at Lord's.

The sporting clash left millions posting photos of their double-screen set up, using their TV to watch one and another device to watch the other when the tennis was locked in a monumental final set and England were battling through a tense run chase.

When Federer served to save the match and England needed 15 off the final over, Wimbledon tweeted the International Cricket Council: "Hello @ICC – how are you coping your end?" only to be smilingly told: "Things are a bit hectic here right now, we'll get back to you."

It got more hectic, Djokovic eventually winning the tie-break at 7.08pm just as the Super Over was commencing after 100 overs of cricket had ended with the scores tied.

The Super Over couldn't separate the teams either but England won their first-ever men's World Cup by virtue of scoring more boundaries in the match. Inevitably, it was hailed the 'Champagne Super Over', while, at Wimbledon, 'C_____ _____' _____ ___ _ _ bubbly.

At the end, as is his wont, Djokovic bent down and ate some blades of Centre Court's hallowed grass. He said later that it tasted "better than ever". In another touch of history, the five-times champion was handed the trophy by HRH The Duchess of Cambridge, Patron of the All England Club, invited to present the trophy for the first time by HRH The Duke of Kent, President of the All England Club.

Djokovic later described the final as "probably the most demanding match mentally that I have ever been a part of" and admitted: "He was serving extremely well the entire match. I had a lot of difficulties reading his serve. But in these kind of moments, I just try to never lose self-belief, just stay calm, just focus on trying to get the ball back. In the most important moments, in all three tie-breaks, I found my best game."

The Serb said he had prepared for the match by visualising many scenarios, including how he would cope with Centre Court's inevitable support for his opponent. "When the crowd is chanting 'Roger' I hear 'Novak'," he said with a smile. "It sounds silly, but it is like that. I try to convince myself that it's like that."

Federer said he had been happy with his performance in "a great match with wonderful points played". Asked how he might recover from the defeat, he recalled his 2008 loss in the final to Nadal. "I will look back at it and think: 'Well, it's not that bad after all.' For now it hurts, and it should, like every loss does here at Wimbledon. I think it's a mindset. I'm very strong at being able to move on because I don't want to be depressed about what was actually an amazing tennis match."

It was the 12th successive men's Grand Slam singles title won by a player aged 30 or over and the 11th in a row won by Djokovic, Federer or Nadal. Since Lleyton Hewitt's victory in 2002, Andy Murray is the only other man to have been crowned singles champion on Centre Court.

Djokovic's fifth Wimbledon singles title put him level with Bjorn Borg and Laurie Doherty, leaving only Federer (eight titles), William Renshaw and Pete Sampras (seven each) with more. It was Djokovic's 16th Grand Slam singles title, leaving him two behind Nadal and four behind Federer at

*Opposite: HRH The Duchess of Cambridge (**top, right**) presented the trophy to Novak Djokovic (**bottom**) and commiserated with the defeated Roger Federer (**top, left**)*

Above: For the second year running and the fifth time in nine Championships, Djokovic showed off the Challenge Cup on the Centre Court balcony

DISTINGUISHED SERVICE

—

Andrew Jarrett – who had done such a superb job overseeing 14 editions – enjoyed his final day in the prestigious and demanding role of Wimbledon Championships Referee and was glad to see that, as so often under his stewardship, everything passed off efficiently and smoothly.

"A good tournament from a Referee's perspective is one where at the end of The Championships people are talking about tennis," smiled the 61-year-old from Belper. And this excellent rain-free edition, he reckoned, had been exactly that.

"The biggest challenge over the years has been to maintain Wimbledon's reputation for fairness, for treating players well and fairly and I've tried to maintain that," added the man who won widespread respect from the players, having won several matches himself as a professional at Wimbledon before becoming Referee in 2006.

"There are so many memories for me," said Jarrett, after receiving a special award for his outstanding service. "Every Championships in its own way has been special – lots of great rivalries, great players and some fantastic tennis. I'm incredibly proud and privileged to have served in the role."

Jarrett hands over to successor Gerry Armstrong next year and thinks it will feel "a little strange" wandering round the Grounds without any problems to solve nor having to gaze up at dark skies. "I'll enjoy that," he smiled.

the top of the all-time list. Asked about the possibility of eventually overtaking their totals, Djokovic said their continuing excellence motivated him. "Roger really inspires me with his effort at his age," he said. Did he hope to still be playing at 37? "I hope so," Djokovic said. "Hopefully in five years' time I can be hearing the same chants."

The Czech Republic's Barbora Strycova and Chinese Taipei's Su-Wei Hsieh won the ladies' doubles title, beating Gabriela Dabrowski and Yifan Xu 6-2, 6-4 after the final had been delayed 24 hours by the late-running men's doubles final the previous evening. They were the first team to win the title without dropping a set for 10 years.

For Hsieh it was a third Grand Slam doubles title after her victories alongside Shuai Peng at The Championships 2013 and at Roland-Garros the following year. Strycova, who had lost to Serena Williams in the singles semi-finals, went to the top of the world doubles rankings after claiming her first Grand Slam title. "It's a fairytale," she said. "It has been two weeks of amazing moments that I will never forget."

Another player from Chinese Taipei, Latisha Chan, joined forces with Croatia's Ivan Dodig to win the mixed doubles final, beating 22-year-old Jelena Ostapenko and 42-year-old Robert Lindstedt 6-2, 6-3 just a month after defending their title at Roland-Garros. "We have good chemistry and we've become good friends, which is very important in a team sport," Dodig said.

Argentina's Gustavo Fernandez, who had twice lost in the final of the Gentlemen's Wheelchair Singles, finally got his hands on the trophy when he beat Shingo Kunieda 4-6, 6-3, 6-2 to secure his third successive Grand Slam title. Kunieda had been aiming to win his 43rd Grand Slam title but has never won the singles at Wimbledon. The Dutch pair of Diede de Groot and Aniek van Koot beat Marjolein Buis and Giulia Capocci 6-1, 6-1 in the Ladies' Wheelchair Doubles final.

Gustavo Fernandez embraces his supporters both young and old after winning the Gentlemen's Wheelchair Singles title and keeping his dream of a calendar Grand Slam alive

Shintaro Mochizuki, aged 16, became the first Japanese player to win a Grand Slam junior boys' title when his bold serve-and-volley tactics helped secure a 6-3, 6-2 victory over Carlos Gimeno Valero. Mochizuki drew instant benefit from the All England Club's Junior Grass Court Strategy, drawn up in collaboration with the LTA, which had seen the launch of a new tournament in Nottingham, extending the junior grass court season to three weeks. Mochizuki, who is based at the IMG Academy in Florida, was the inaugural champion in Nottingham.

The Czechs Jonas Forejtek and Jiri Lehecka won the boys' doubles title, beating Liam Draxl and Govind Nanda 7-5, 6-4 in the final, while the Americans Savannah Broadus and Abigail Forbes beat Kamilla Bartone and Oksana Selekhmeteva 7-5, 5-7, 6-2 in the girls' doubles final.

Arnaud Clement and Michael Llodra won the Gentlemen's Invitation Doubles, beating Xavier Malisse and Max Mirnyi 6-3, 1-6, (10-7) in the final, while Jonas Bjorkman and Todd Woodbridge took the Gentlemen's Senior Invitation Doubles with a 4-6, 6-3, (10-6) victory over Jacco Eltingh and Paul Haarhuis. Cara Black and Martina Navratilova won the Ladies' Invitation Doubles, beating Marion Bartoli and Daniela Hantuchova 6-0, 3-6, (10-8) in the final.

A memorable Fortnight was celebrated that evening at the Champions' Dinner at the Guildhall in central London, with Djokovic only able to arrive after midnight had struck following his marathon final and ensuing media commitments. Philip Brook, the Chairman of the All England Club, congratulated all the champions, praised Halep's "extraordinary mental resilience that comes with learning how to rise to the occasion" and said that Djokovic's victory in the men's final would be remembered "for a very long time to come". For all who had been a part of the 133rd Championships, whether as players, coaches, officials, media or spectators, the only sorrow was that it was all over.

With the sun having set on another fabulous Championships, you could have sworn a silent, contemplative No.1 Court was reflecting proudly on its own unforgettable role

DAILY DIARY **DAY 13**

Shintaro Mochizuki (*above*), Japan's first-ever Wimbledon Boys' Singles Champion, paid thanks to the country's sporting hero for helping to inspire him and, in turn, was thrilled when he received congratulations from the man himself, Kei Nishikori.

The 16-year-old, who attends IMG's tennis academy in Bradenton, Florida, where former US Open finalist Nishikori also honed his game, smiled: "Kei's really nice. He gives me a lot of advices at the academy. Sometimes I practise with him. I learn from him a lot."

Even Nishikori hopes Mochizuki, who became world junior No.1 with his win, could go on to eclipse him. "Huge congrats to @ShintaroMOCHIZU! Such an amazing tournament," he tweeted.

• Su-Wei Hsieh had a problem as she waited and waited, along with partner Barbora Strycova, to play their delayed ladies' doubles final a day late on Sunday. It came in the shape of food, food, and more glorious food.

As Saturday's final had to be rescheduled and they had to remain patient again as the weekend's second five-hour gentlemen's final unfolded, Su-Wei just kept fuelling herself.

"All the stuff. I eat banana, chocolate cookie, gels. I eat two potatoes. One plate of vegetables. I was eating meat already," she explained, admitting it was a good job Wimbledon had introduced the 12-12 tie-break "otherwise I will keep eating and I will get fat!"

Fortunately, Su-Wei didn't seem the slightest weighed down as she and her fellow 33-year-old Strycova eventually took the title 6-2, 6-4.

• After an epic match to decide 'who's the daddy?', Novak Djokovic and Roger Federer were happy to be reminded that, actually, they both were. "They won't be excited with a plate. They'd rather take that golden thing," runner-up Roger smiled on court, as his two pairs of twins looked forlorn. "I love them and it's back to being Dad and husband. It's all good."

Meanwhile, Novak felt it was extra special that his four-year-old son Stefan was at courtside and he reckoned he couldn't wait to get home to see wife Jelena and baby daughter Tara too. "I love you and see you soon," he told them on TV. "Back to being Dad, I guess, as well."

• Whatever happened to American Bob Falkenburg, the last man before Djokovic to win from Championship points down? Well, the 1948 champion ended up introducing US fast food to Brazil, with his restaurant chain 'Bob's' becoming a South American household name. So, can we one day expect to dine at 'Novak's'?

THE END OF AN ERA

—

In his ninth and final Championships as AELTC Chairman, Philip Brook once again presided over a spellbinding edition and was able to look back proudly on overseeing an era of significant development in the history of his beloved Wimbledon.

The Yorkshireman, who has thrown himself into All England Club life ever since he was a student working as a scoreboard operator in the summer holidays, said on his appointment as Chairman in 2011 that, as a tennis-lover and former player, he might just have been given "the best job in the world".

Nothing subsequently made him think any differently as his "nine-year labour of love" at The Championships culminated in him watching the longest – and one of the greatest – gentlemen's singles finals of all.

It was not his favourite final, however. "I think for me the best tennis moment [as Chairman] would be when Andy [Murray] won the singles in 2013," he told reporters. "That was a really important moment for this Club to see a British man winning Wimbledon again after a 77-year gap, and just to be part of the occasion and the presentation party on that day was very special."

He felt his best achievements were fourfold; overseeing the completion of the refurbished, roofed No.1 Court on time and on budget; introducing the new, later start date for The Championships; the purchase of Wimbledon Park Golf Course to enable major developments of the site; and the appointment of a "superb" Chief Executive, Richard Lewis. Brook leaves a proud legacy.

Chairman 'Phil' Brook, illustrating just what a popular figurehead he had been for The Championships.

"I didn't know it was his last year. It's sad. He just really made my Wimbledon experience," said Serena. "I really love him, and his wife Gill is amazing too.

"I just love seeing him. Like, he'll pass my practice court and he has this great big smile on his face. He's always smiling. I just love it. I see him in Australia, I see him in New York, everywhere. I literally will be on the court and I swear I see him smiling. That is such a good moment and memory to have of Philip. He really makes me feel welcome every year."

The sentiments were echoed by Alison Riske, who explained that Phil and Gill had a knack of making all players, champions or not, feel good: "From the first Wimbledon I played, I met Phil. The next year, he remembered who I was. I was feeling like 'Oh, my gosh, does he do this with everyone? I feel so special. Do I get a membership right now, what happens?' He was amazing. Gill, the same thing.

"They always made every single player feel like they're awesome and doing a good job. I think it's really special that you can walk into a Grand Slam and someone says: 'Hey, Ali, good to see you. Great job in 's-Hertogenbosch.' I think that's really rare."

WIMBLEDON 2019

—

THE GENTLEMEN'S SINGLES
Novak DJOKOVIC

THE LADIES' SINGLES
Simona HALEP

THE GENTLEMEN'S DOUBLES
Juan Sebastian CABAL
Robert FARAH

THE LADIES' DOUBLES
Barbora STRYCOVA
Su-Wei HSIEH

THE MIXED DOUBLES
Ivan DODIG
Latisha CHAN

THE GENTLEMEN'S
WHEELCHAIR SINGLES
Gustavo FERNANDEZ

THE LADIES' WHEELCHAIR
SINGLES
Aniek VAN KOOT

THE GENTLEMEN'S
WHEELCHAIR DOUBLES
Stefan OLSSON
Joachim GERARD

THE CHAMPIONS

—

THE LADIES' WHEELCHAIR DOUBLES

Diede DE GROOT

Aniek VAN KOOT

THE QUAD WHEELCHAIR SINGLES

Dylan ALCOTT

THE QUAD WHEELCHAIR DOUBLES

Andy LAPTHORNE

Dylan ALCOTT

THE BOYS' SINGLES

Shintaro MOCHIZUKI

THE GIRLS' SINGLES

Daria SNIGUR

THE BOYS' DOUBLES

Jiri LEHECKA

Jonas FOREJTEK

THE GIRLS' DOUBLES

Savannah BROADUS

Abigail FORBES

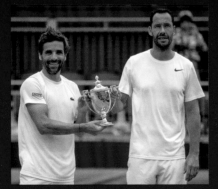

THE GENTLEMEN'S INVITATION DOUBLES

Arnaud CLEMENT

Michael LLODRA

THE LADIES' INVITATION DOUBLES

Martina NAVRATILOVA

Cara BLACK

THE GENTLEMEN'S SENIOR INVITATION DOUBLES

Todd WOODBRIDGE

Jonas BJORKMAN

THE GENTLEMEN'S SINGLES CHAMPIONSHIP 2019
Holder: NOVAK DJOKOVIC (SRB)

The Champion will become the holder, for the year only, of the CHALLENGE CUP. The Champion will receive a silver three-quarter size replica of the Challenge Cup. A Silver Salver will be presented to the Runner-up and a Bronze Medal to each defeated semi-finalist.
The matches will be the best of five sets. If the score should reach 12-12 in the final set, the match will be decided by a tie-break.

First Round	Second Round	Third Round	Fourth Round	Quarter-Finals	Semi-Finals	Final

First Round

1. Novak Djokovic [1] (1) (SRB)
2. Philipp Kohlschreiber (57) (GER)
3. Denis Kudla (113) (USA)
4. Malek Jaziri (98) (TUN)
5. Ernests Gulbis (90) (LAT)
6. Leonardo Mayer (56) (ARG)
7. Hubert Hurkacz (52) (POL)
8. Dusan Lajovic [32] (33) (SRB)
9. Felix Auger-Aliassime [19] (21) (CAN)
10. Vasek Pospisil (73) (CAN)
11. Grigor Dimitrov (48) (BUL)
(Q) 12. Corentin Moutet (85) (FRA)
13. Lorenzo Sonego (75) (ITA)
(Q) 14. Marcel Granollers (105) (ESP)
15. Ugo Humbert (64) (FRA)
16. Gael Monfils [16] (15) (FRA)
17. Daniil Medvedev [11] (13) (RUS)
18. Paolo Lorenzi (107) (ITA)
19. Pablo Carreno Busta (59) (ESP)
(Q) 20. Alexei Popyrin (99) (AUS)
21. Jeremy Chardy (81) (FRA)
22. Martin Klizan (54) (SVK)
23. Bradley Klahn (89) (USA)
24. David Goffin [21] (23) (BEL)
25. Kyle Edmund [30] (31) (GBR)
26. Jaume Munar (88) (ESP)
(Q) 27. Kamil Majchrzak (111) (POL)
28. Fernando Verdasco (36) (ESP)
(Q) 29. Andrea Arnaboldi (209) (ITA)
30. Ivo Karlovic (80) (CRO)
31. Thomas Fabbiano (102) (ITA)
32. Stefanos Tsitsipas [7] (6) (GRE)
33. Kevin Anderson [4] (8) (RSA)
34. Pierre-Hugues Herbert (38) (FRA)
35. Janko Tipsarevic (88) (SRB)
36. Yoshihito Nishioka (67) (JPN)
37. Andreas Seppi (71) (ITA)
38. Nicolas Jarry (55) (CHI)
39. Marius Copil (84) (ROU)
40. Guido Pella [26] (26) (ARG)
41. Stan Wawrinka [22] (19) (SUI)
42. Ruben Bemelmans (171) (BEL)
43. Cedrik-Marcel Stebe (95) (GER)
44. Reilly Opelka (61) (USA)
45. Jozef Kovalik (85) (SVK)
46. Robin Haase (73) (NED)
47. Prajnesh Gunneswaran (94) (IND)
48. Milos Raonic [15] (17) (CAN)
49. Karen Khachanov [10] (9) (RUS)
(Q) 50. Soonwoo Kwon (126) (KOR)
(Q) 51. Marcos Giron (158) (USA)
(WC) 52. Feliciano Lopez (53) (ESP)
53. Steve Darcis (90) (BEL)
54. Mischa Zverev (119) (GER)
55. Peter Gojowczyk (123) (GER)
56. Roberto Bautista Agut [23] (22) (ESP)
57. Benoit Paire [28] (32) (FRA)
58. Juan Ignacio Londero (62) (ARG)
59. Roberto Carballes Baena (72) (ESP)
60. Miomir Kecmanovic (82) (SRB)
61. Pablo Cuevas (URU)
62. Damir Dzumhur (63) (BIH)
(Q) 63. Jiri Vesely (108) (CZE)
64. Alexander Zverev [6] (5) (GER)
65. Dominic Thiem [5] (4) (AUT)
66. Sam Querrey (79) (USA)
67. Cristian Garin (35) (CHI)
68. Andrey Rublev (78) (RUS)
69. Hugo Dellien (93) (BOL)
70. John Millman (AUS)
71. Guido Andreozzi (116) (ARG)
72. Laslo Djere [31] (30) (SRB)
73. Gilles Simon [20] (25) (FRA)
(Q) 74. Salvatore Caruso (125) (ITA)
(Q) 75. Yasutaka Uchiyama (182) (JPN)
76. Tennys Sandgren (92) (USA)
77. Marton Fucsovics (50) (HUN)
(Q) 78. Dennis Novak (104) (AUT)
79. Frances Tiafoe (39) (USA)
80. Fabio Fognini [12] (10) (ITA)
81. Marin Cilic [13] (18) (CRO)
82. Adrian Mannarino (37) (FRA)
83. Joao Sousa (66) (POR)
(WC) 84. Paul Jubb (472) (GBR)
85. Federico Delbonis (76) (ARG)
86. Daniel Evans (65) (GBR)
(WC) 87. James Ward (205) (GBR)
88. Nikoloz Basilashvili [18] (16) (GEO)
89. Denis Shapovalov [29] (27) (CAN)
90. Ricardas Berankis (74) (LTU)
91. Bernard Tomic (101) (AUS)
92. Jo-Wilfried Tsonga (70) (FRA)
93. Nick Kyrgios (43) (AUS)
94. Jordan Thompson (45) (AUS)
(Q) 95. Yuichi Sugita (258) (JPN)
96. Rafael Nadal [3] (2) (ESP)
97. Kei Nishikori [8] (7) (JPN)
(Q) 98. Thiago Monteiro (115) (BRA)
99. Denis Istomin (109) (UZB)
100. Cameron Norrie (49) (GBR)
101. Steve Johnson (69) (USA)
102. Albert Ramos-Vinolas (97) (ESP)
103. Marco Cecchinato (40) (ITA)
104. Alex De Minaur [25] (29) (AUS)
105. Jan-Lennard Struff [33] (34) (GER)
106. Radu Albot (41) (MDA)
107. Taylor Fritz (42) (USA)
108. Tomas Berdych (57) (CZE)
109. Pablo Andujar (77) (ESP)
110. Mikhail Kukushkin (47) (KAZ)
111. Casper Ruud (60) (NOR)
112. John Isner [9] (12) (USA)
113. Matteo Berrettini [17] (20) (ITA)
114. Aljaz Bedene (86) (SLO)
(LL) 115. Brayden Schnur (114) (CAN)
(WC) 116. Marcos Baghdatis (138) (CYP)
(WC) 117. Dominik Koepfer (132) (GER)
118. Filip Krajinovic (51) (SRB)
119. Matthew Ebden (91) (AUS)
120. Diego Schwartzman [24] (24) (ARG)
121. Lucas Pouille [27] (28) (FRA)
122. Richard Gasquet (46) (FRA)
123. Alexander Bublik (83) (KAZ)
(Q) 124. Gregoire Barrere (117) (FRA)
(WC) 125. Jay Clarke (166) (GBR)
(Q) 126. Noah Rubin (183) (USA)
127. Lloyd Harris (87) (RSA)
128. Roger Federer [2] (3) (SUI)

Second Round

Novak Djokovic [1] — 6/3 7/5 6/3
Denis Kudla
Leonardo Mayer — 6/1 7/6(12) 6/2
Hubert Hurkacz — 6/3 4/6 6/4 6/4
Felix Auger-Aliassime [19] — 5/7 6/2 6/4 6/3
Corentin Moutet — 2/6 3/6 7/6(4) 6/3 6/1
Marcel Granollers — 7/6(4) 6/4 6/4
Ugo Humbert — 6/7(6) 3/6 6/4 7/5 3/0 Ret'd
Daniil Medvedev [11] — 6/3 7/6(2) 7/6(2)
Alexei Popyrin — 7/6(2) 7/5 6/2
Jeremy Chardy — 3/6 6/0 6/3 6/4
David Goffin [21] — 6/2 6/4 6/3
Kyle Edmund [30] — 6/4 6/4 6/4
Fernando Verdasco — 6/4 6/4 6/4
Ivo Karlovic — 6/4 6/4 7/6(4)
Thomas Fabbiano — 6/4 3/6 6/4 6/7(8) 6/3
Kevin Anderson [4] — 6/3 6/4 6/4
Janko Tipsarevic — 6/4 6/7(2) 6/2 5/7 6/2
Andreas Seppi — 6/3 6/7(8) 6/1 6/2
Guido Pella [26] — 7/6(11) 5/7 6/3 6/4
Stan Wawrinka [22] — 6/3 6/2 6/2
Reilly Opelka — 6/3 7/6(4) 6/1
Robin Haase
Milos Raonic [15] — 7/6(1) 6/6 6/4
Karen Khachanov [10] — 7/6(6) 6/4 4/6 7/5
Feliciano Lopez — 6/4 6/2 6/4
Steve Darcis — 6/2 6/4 6/4
Roberto Bautista Agut [23] — 6/3 6/2 6/3
Benoit Paire [28] — 4/6 6/4 6/4 7/6(4)
Miomir Kecmanovic — 2/6 6/3 6/3 6/1
Pablo Cuevas — 4/6 7/6(8) 2/6 6/4 6/2
Jiri Vesely — 4/6 6/3 6/2 7/5
Sam Querrey — 6/7(4) 7/6(1) 6/3 6/0
Andrey Rublev — 4/6 4/6 7/5 6/4
John Millman — 6/2 6/3 6/4
Laslo Djere [31] — 3/6 7/6(3) 7/6(3) 6/3
Gilles Simon [20] — 7/6(7) 6/3 6/3
Tennys Sandgren — 3/6 6/2 6/4 6/4
Marton Fucsovics — 3/6 6/4 7/6(2) 6/2
Fabio Fognini [12] — 5/7 6/4 6/3 4/6 6/4
Marin Cilic [13] — 7/6(6) 7/6(4) 6/3
Joao Sousa — 6/0 6/3 6/7(8) 6/1
Daniel Evans — 6/3 7/6(5) 6/3
Nikoloz Basilashvili [18] — 2/6 4/6 6/4 6/4 8/6
Ricardas Berankis — 7/6(0) 6/4 6/4
Jo-Wilfried Tsonga — 6/2 6/1 6/4
Nick Kyrgios — 7/6(4) 3/6 7/6(10) 0/6 6/1
Rafael Nadal [3] — 6/3 6/3 6/2
Kei Nishikori [8] — 6/4 7/6(3) 6/4
Cameron Norrie — 6/2 6/4 6/4
Steve Johnson — 6/4 6/2 6/3
Alex De Minaur [25] — 6/0 6/4 7/6(5)
Jan-Lennard Struff [33] — 6/4 6/3 6/2
Taylor Fritz — 6/4 6/4 6/3
Mikhail Kukushkin — 6/3 6/2 6/3
John Isner [9] — 6/3 6/4 7/6(9)
Matteo Berrettini [17] — 3/6 6/3 6/2 7/6(3)
Marcos Baghdatis — 6/1 7/6(4) 6/3
Dominik Koepfer — 6/3 4/6 7/6(9) 6/1
Diego Schwartzman [24] — 6/4 3/6 7/6(2)
Lucas Pouille [27] — 6/1 6/3 6/4
Gregoire Barrere — 3/6 6/4 6/4
Jay Clarke — 4/6 7/5 6/4 6/4
Roger Federer [2] — 3/6 6/1 6/2 6/2

Third Round

Novak Djokovic [1] — 6/3 6/2 6/2
Hubert Hurkacz — 6/7(4) 6/1 7/6(7) 6/3
Felix Auger-Aliassime [19] — 6/3 4/6 6/4 6/3
Ugo Humbert — 6/4 7/6(3) 7/5
Daniil Medvedev [11] — 6/7(6) 6/1 6/4 6/4
David Goffin [21] — 4/6 6/2 3/6 6/3 7/5
Fernando Verdasco — 4/6 4/6 7/6(3) 6/3 6/4
Thomas Fabbiano — 6/4 7/6(1) 6/4
Kevin Anderson [4] — 6/4 7/6(5) 6/1 6/4
Guido Pella [26] — 6/4 4/6 4/6 7/5 6/1
Milos Raonic [15] — 7/5 3/6 4/6 6/4 8/6
Karen Khachanov [10] — 4/6 6/4 7/5 6/4
Roberto Bautista Agut [23] — 6/3 4/2 Ret'd
Benoit Paire [28] — 7/6(5) 6/4 0/0 Ret'd
Jiri Vesely — 4/6 7/6(5) 6/4 6/4
Sam Querrey — 6/3 6/2 6/3
John Millman — 6/3 6/2 6/1
Tennys Sandgren — 6/2 6/3 4/6 3/6 8/6
Fabio Fognini [12] — 6/7(6) 6/4 7/6(3) 2/6 6/3
Joao Sousa — 6/4 6/4 6/4
Daniel Evans — 6/3 6/2 7/6(2)
Jo-Wilfried Tsonga — 7/6(4) 6/3 6/3
Rafael Nadal [3] — 6/3 3/6 6/7(5) 7/6(3)
Kei Nishikori [8] — 6/4 6/4 6/0
Steve Johnson — 3/6 7/6(4) 6/3 3/6 6/2
Jan-Lennard Struff [33] — 6/4 6/3 5/7 7/6(2)
Mikhail Kukushkin — 6/4 6/7(3) 4/6 6/1 6/4
Matteo Berrettini [17] — 6/1 7/6(4) 6/3
Diego Schwartzman [24] — 6/0 6/3 7/6(9)
Lucas Pouille [27] — 6/1 7/6(0) 6/4
Roger Federer [2] — 6/1 7/6(3) 6/2

Fourth Round

Novak Djokovic [1] — 7/5 6/7(5) 6/1 6/4
Ugo Humbert
David Goffin [21] — 4/6 6/2 3/6 6/3 7/5
Fernando Verdasco — 6/4 7/6(1) 6/4
Guido Pella [26] — 4/6 4/6 4/6 7/5 6/1
Milos Raonic [15] — 7/6(1) 6/2 6/1
Roberto Bautista Agut [23] — 6/3 7/6(3) 6/1
Benoit Paire [28] — 5/7 7/6(5) 6/3 7/6(2)
Sam Querrey — 7/6(3) 7/6(8) 6/3
Tennys Sandgren — 6/3 7/6(12) 6/3
Joao Sousa — 4/6 4/7 4/5 4/6 6/4
Rafael Nadal [3] — 6/2 6/3 6/2
Kei Nishikori [8] — 6/4 6/3 6/2
Mikhail Kukushkin — 6/3 7/6(5) 4/6 7/6
Matteo Berrettini [17] — 6/7(5) 7/6(2) 4/6 7/6(5) 6/3
Roger Federer [2] — 7/5 6/2 7/6(4)

Quarter-Finals

Novak Djokovic [1] — 6/4 6/0 6/2
David Goffin [21] — 7/6(9) 2/6 6/3 6/4
Guido Pella [26] — 3/6 4/6 6/3 7/6(3) 8/6
Roberto Bautista Agut [23] — 6/3 7/5 6/2
Sam Querrey — 6/4 6/7(7) 7/6(3) 7/6(5)
Rafael Nadal [3] — 6/2 6/2 6/2
Kei Nishikori [8] — 6/3 3/6 6/3 6/4
Roger Federer [2] — 6/1 6/2 6/2

Semi-Finals

Novak Djokovic [1] — 6/2 4/6 6/3 6/2
Roberto Bautista Agut [23] — 7/5 6/4 3/6 6/3
Rafael Nadal [3] — 7/5 6/2 6/2
Roger Federer [2] — 4/6 6/1 6/4 6/4

Final

Novak Djokovic [1] — 7/6(5) 1/6 7/6(4) 4/6 13/12(3)
Roger Federer [2] — 7/6(3) 1/6 6/3 6/4

Heavy type denotes seeded players. The figure in brackets against names denotes the order in which they have been seeded. The figure in italics denotes ATP World Tour Ranking – 01.07.2019.
(WC)=Wild card. (Q)=Qualifier. (LL)=Lucky loser.

THE GENTLEMEN'S DOUBLES CHAMPIONSHIP 2019
Holders: MIKE BRYAN (USA) & JACK SOCK (USA)

The Champions will become the holders, for the year only, of the CHALLENGE CUPS presented by the OXFORD UNIVERSITY LAWN TENNIS CLUB in 1884 and the late SIR HERBERT WILBERFORCE in 1937. The Champions will each receive a silver three-quarter size replica of the Challenge Cup.
A Silver Salver will be presented to each of the Runners-up, and a Bronze Medal to each defeated semi-finalist. The matches will be the best of five sets. If the score should reach 12-12 in the final set, the match will be decided by a tie-break.

First Round	Second Round	Third Round	Quarter-Finals	Semi-Finals	Final

1. **Lukasz Kubot** (POL) & **Marcelo Melo** (BRA) .... [1]
   - Lukasz Kubot & Marcelo Melo [1]
2. Ben McLachlan (JPN) & Jan-Lennard Struff (GER) 4/6 6/3 7/5 7/5
   - Lukasz Kubot & Marcelo Melo [1]
3. Alex De Minaur (AUS) & Matt Reid (AUS) ....
   - Alex De Minaur & Matt Reid ... 6/7(11) 6/4 6/3 7/6(10)
4. Federico Delbonis (ARG) & Andres Molteni (ARG)...... 6/4 6/4 6/4
   - Lukasz Kubot & Marcelo Melo [1]
5. Sander Gille (BEL) & Joran Vliegen (BEL) .... 7/5 6/7(8) 7/6(6) 6/3
   - Sander Gille & Joran Vliegen
6. Guillermo Duran (ARG) & Juan Ignacio Londero (ARG).... 6/2 7/6(4) 4/6 6/2
   - Marcelo Demoliner & Divij Sharan
7. Marcelo Demoliner (BRA) & Divij Sharan (IND) ....
   - Marcelo Demoliner & Divij Sharan ... 7/6(1) 5/7 7/6(6) 6/4
8. **Kevin Krawietz** (GER) & **Andreas Mies** (GER) .... [13]
   - 7/5 6/4 7/5
9. **Nicolas Mahut** (FRA) & **Edouard Roger-Vasselin** (FRA)..... [11]
   - Nicolas Mahut & Edouard Roger-Vasselin [11]
   (WC) 10. Liam Broady (GBR) & Scott Clayton (GBR).............. 6/1 6/4 6/2
   - Nicolas Mahut & Edouard Roger-Vasselin [11]
   (WC) 11. Daniel Evans (GBR) & Lloyd Glasspool (GBR)...........
   - Leonardo Mayer & Joao Sousa ... 6/1 5/7 6/4 7/5
12. Leonardo Mayer (ARG) & Joao Sousa (POR)........... 7/6(3) 4/6 7/5 6/3
   - Nicolas Mahut & Edouard Roger-Vasselin [11]
13. Lloyd Harris (RSA) & Casper Ruud (NOR)..............
   - Marcelo Arevalo & Miguel Angel Reyes-Varela ... 7/6(3) 6/2 4/6 7/6(5)
14. Marcelo Arevalo (ESA) & Miguel Angel Reyes-Varela (MEX)....
   - Marcelo Arevalo & Miguel Angel Reyes-Varela ... 6/7(3) 6/1 6/3 6/4
15. Denys Molchanov (UKR) & Igor Zelenay (SVK)..........
   - Bob Bryan & Mike Bryan [7]
16. **Bob Bryan** (USA) & **Mike Bryan** (USA).............. [7]
   - Bob Bryan & Mike Bryan [7] ... 7/6(3) 6/4 6/4
   - Bob Bryan & Mike Bryan [7] ... 6/7(13) 6/3 6/4 6/1

17. **Mate Pavic** (CRO) & **Bruno Soares** (BRA)............ [4]
   - Mate Pavic & Bruno Soares [4]
18. Sander Arends (NED) & Matwe Middelkoop (NED) ...... 4/6 6/3 6/2 6/7(5) 6/3
   - Santiago Gonzalez & Aisam-Ul-Haq Qureshi
19. Laslo Djere (SRB) & Janko Tipsarevic (SRB)............
   - Santiago Gonzalez & Aisam-Ul-Haq Qureshi ... 4/6 4/6 7/6(5) 6/4 6/4
20. Santiago Gonzalez (MEX) & Aisam-Ul-Haq Qureshi (PAK)..... 4/6 6/3 6/4 7/6(4)
   - Marcus Daniell & Wesley Koolhof
21. Marcus Daniell (NZL) & Wesley Koolhof (NED) ....
   - Marcus Daniell & Wesley Koolhof ... 7/5 6/7(6) 6/4 6/4
22. Rohan Bopanna (IND) & Pablo Cuevas (URU) .... 6/4 6/4 4/6 7/6(7)
   - Marcus Daniell & Wesley Koolhof
23. Jaume Munar (ESP) & Cameron Norrie (GBR) ....
   - Jaume Munar & Cameron Norrie ... 1/6 4/6 7/6(2) 6/2 6/2
24. **Dominic Inglot** (GBR) & **Austin Krajicek** (USA).... [15]
   - 4/6 6/3 6/4 6/7(11) 6/3
25. **Jamie Murray** (GBR) & **Neal Skupski** (GBR).......... [10]
   - Ivan Dodig & Filip Polasek
26. Ivan Dodig (CRO) & Filip Polasek (SVK).............. 2/6 7/6(2) 3/6 6/1 6/4
   - Ivan Dodig & Filip Polasek
   (A) 27. Nicholas Monroe (USA) & Mischa Zverev (GER).........
   - Nicholas Monroe & Mischa Zverev ... 7/6(5) 6/4 6/4
   (WC) 28. Evan Hoyt (GBR) & Luke Johnson (GBR)................ 6/4 6/4 7/5
   - Ivan Dodig & Filip Polasek
29. Marius Copil (ROU) & Ugo Humbert (FRA).............
   - Pierre-Hugues Herbert & Andy Murray
30. Pierre-Hugues Herbert (FRA) & Andy Murray (GBR).... 4/6 6/1 6/4 6/0
   - Nikola Mektic & Franko Skugor [6]
31. Ricardas Berankis (LTU) & Marton Fucsovics (HUN)....
   - Nikola Mektic & Franko Skugor [6] ... 6/7(4) 6/4 6/2 6/3
32. **Nikola Mektic** (CRO) & **Franko Skugor** (CRO)........... [6]
   - 6/2 6/2 6/2

33. **Henri Kontinen** (FIN) & **John Peers** (AUS)............ [8]
   - Henri Kontinen & John Peers [8]
34. Gerard Granollers (ESP) & Marcel Granollers (ESP)...... 6/3 6/4 6/3
   - Henri Kontinen & John Peers [8]
35. Robert Lindstedt (SWE) & Tim Puetz (GER)...........
   - Robert Lindstedt & Tim Puetz ... 4/6 6/7(1) 7/6(9) 6/3 6/4
   (A) 36. Max Purcell (AUS) & Luke Saville (AUS)................ 6/7(2) 6/4 6/2 6/4
   - Henri Kontinen & John Peers [8]
37. Filip Krajinovic (SRB) & Dusan Lajovic (SRB)...........
   - Matthew Ebden & Vasek Pospisil
38. Matthew Ebden (AUS) & Vasek Pospisil (CAN)........... 6/3 6/2 6/2
   - Rajeev Ram & Joe Salisbury [12]
39. Radu Albot (MDA) & Malek Jaziri (TUN)...............
   - Rajeev Ram & Joe Salisbury [12] ... 7/5 6/4 7/6(3)
40. **Rajeev Ram** (USA) & **Joe Salisbury** (GBR)............. [12]
   - 6/3 6/4 6/2
41. **Robin Haase** (NED) & **Frederik Nielsen** (DEN) .... [16]
   - Robin Haase & Frederik Nielsen [16]
42. Romain Arneodo (MON) & Damir Dzumhur (BIH)....... 6/2 6/2 6/3
   - Robin Haase & Frederik Nielsen [16]
43. Ken Skupski (GBR) & John-Patrick Smith (AUS).........
   - Ken Skupski & John-Patrick Smith ... 7/6(14) 7/6(7) 7/6(2)
   (WC) 44. Jay Clarke (GBR) & James Ward (GBR)................ 6/2 6/4 6/2
   - Raven Klaasen & Michael Venus [3]
45. Jeevan Nedunchezhiyan (IND) & Purav Raja (IND)......
   - Lleyton Hewitt & Jordan Thompson
   (WC) 46. Lleyton Hewitt (AUS) & Jordan Thompson (AUS)....... 6/2 6/3 6/2
   - Raven Klaasen & Michael Venus [3]
47. Luke Bambridge (GBR) & Jonny O'Mara (GBR)..........
   - Raven Klaasen & Michael Venus [3] ... 6/3 7/6(3) 6/2
48. **Raven Klaasen** (RSA) & **Michael Venus** (NZL)........ [3]
   - 7/5 7/6(3) 6/4

49. **Jean-Julien Rojer** (NED) & **Horia Tecau** (ROU)....... [5]
   - Jean-Julien Rojer & Horia Tecau [5]
50. Marco Cecchinato (ITA) & Andreas Seppi (ITA)........ 6/4 6/3 6/1
   - Jean-Julien Rojer & Horia Tecau [5]
51. Roberto Carballes Baena (ESP) & Lorenzo Sonego (ITA)....
   - Fabrice Martin & Hugo Nys ... 6/1 6/4 6/4
52. Fabrice Martin (FRA) & Hugo Nys (MON).............. 6/3 6/4 6/3
   - Jean-Julien Rojer & Horia Tecau [5]
53. Pablo Carreno Busta (ESP) & Feliciano Lopez (ESP).....
   - Pablo Carreno Busta & Feliciano Lopez ... 7/6(1) 3/6 7/5 4/3 Ret'd
54. Cristian Garin (CHI) & Nicolas Jarry (CHI)........... 4/6 6/3 6/4 7/6(4)
   - Maximo Gonzalez & Horacio Zeballos [9]
55. Jonathan Erlich (ISR) & Artem Sitak (NZL).............
   - Maximo Gonzalez & Horacio Zeballos [9] ... 7/5 7/6(3) 6/3
56. **Maximo Gonzalez** (ARG) & **Horacio Zeballos** (ARG)..... [9]
   - 7/5 7/6(5) 6/3
57. **Oliver Marach** (AUT) & **Jurgen Melzer** (AUT)......... [14]
   - Oliver Marach & Jurgen Melzer [14]
58. Cheng-Peng Hsieh (TPE) & Christopher Rungkat (INA)..... 6/3 6/4 1/6 2/6 11/9
   - Roman Jebavy & Philipp Oswald
59. Roman Jebavy (CZE) & Philipp Oswald (AUT)...........
   - Roman Jebavy & Philipp Oswald ... 7/5 6/4 5/7 7/6(6)
60. Hugo Dellien (BOL) & Guido Pella (ARG)............. 6/4 5/2 Ret'd
   - Juan Sebastian Cabal & Robert Farah [2]
61. Leander Paes (IND) & Benoit Paire (FRA)..............
   - Alexander Bublik & Mikhail Kukushkin
62. Alexander Bublik (KAZ) & Mikhail Kukushkin (KAZ)..... 4/6 6/7(1) 6/3 7/6(3) 9/7
   - Juan Sebastian Cabal & Robert Farah [2]
   (WC) 63. Jack Draper (GBR) & Paul Jubb (GBR) ....
   - Juan Sebastian Cabal & Robert Farah [2] ... 4/6 6/2 6/2 6/1
64. **Juan Sebastian Cabal** (COL) & **Robert Farah** (COL).... [2]
   - 6/1 6/4 6/2

Quarter-Finals / Semi-Finals / Final:

- Lukasz Kubot & Marcelo Melo [1] ... 6/7(11) 6/4 6/3 7/6(10)
- Marcelo Demoliner & Divij Sharan
- Nicolas Mahut & Edouard Roger-Vasselin [11] ... 7/6(3) 6/2 4/6 7/6(5)
- Bob Bryan & Mike Bryan [7]
- Santiago Gonzalez & Aisam-Ul-Haq Qureshi
- Marcus Daniell & Wesley Koolhof ... 7/5 6/7(6) 6/4 6/4
- Ivan Dodig & Filip Polasek ... 7/6(5) 6/4 7/6(3)
- Nikola Mektic & Franko Skugor [6]
- Henri Kontinen & John Peers [8] ... 7/6(2) 6/4 3/6 4/6 13/12(2)
- Rajeev Ram & Joe Salisbury [12]
- Robin Haase & Frederik Nielsen [16]
- Raven Klaasen & Michael Venus [3] ... 6/2 6/3 7/6(0)
- Jean-Julien Rojer & Horia Tecau [5] ... 7/6(1) 3/6 7/5 4/3 Ret'd
- Maximo Gonzalez & Horacio Zeballos [9]
- Roman Jebavy & Philipp Oswald
- Juan Sebastian Cabal & Robert Farah [2] ... 7/6(6) 7/6(5) 7/5

- Nicolas Mahut & Edouard Roger-Vasselin [11] ... 7/6(3) 6/7(5) 6/3 6/3
- Ivan Dodig & Filip Polasek ... 6/2 7/6(1) 6/3
- Henri Kontinen & John Peers [8] ... 7/6(2) 6/4 3/6 4/6 13/12(2)
- Raven Klaasen & Michael Venus [3] ... 4/6 6/3 6/7(5) 6/4 6/3
- Jean-Julien Rojer & Horia Tecau [5] ... 6/4 3/6 6/7(8) 6/4 11/9
- Juan Sebastian Cabal & Robert Farah [2] ... 7/6(6) 7/6(5) 7/5

Semi-Finals:
- Nicolas Mahut & Edouard Roger-Vasselin [11] ... 6/2 7/6(7) 7/6(2)
- Juan Sebastian Cabal & Robert Farah [2] ... 6/7(5) 7/6(5) 7/6(6) 6/7(5) 6/3

Final:
- Juan Sebastian Cabal & Robert Farah [2] ... 6/7(5) 7/6(5) 7/6(6) 6/7(5) 6/3

Heavy type denotes seeded players. The figure in brackets against names denotes the order in which they have been seeded.
(WC)=Wild cards. (Q)=Qualifiers. (LL)=Lucky losers.

THE LADIES' SINGLES CHAMPIONSHIP 2019
Holder: ANGELIQUE KERBER (GER)

The Champion will become the holder, for the year only, of the CHALLENGE TROPHY presented by The All England Lawn Tennis and Croquet Club in 1886. The Champion will receive a silver three-quarter size replica of the Challenge Trophy. A Silver Salver will be presented to the Runner-up and a Bronze Medal to each defeated semi-finalist. The matches will be the best of three sets. If the score should reach 12-12 in the final set, the match will be decided by a tie-break.

	First Round	Second Round	Third Round	Fourth Round	Quarter-Finals	Semi-Finals	Final
	1. **Ashleigh Barty [1]** *(1)* (AUS)	Ashleigh Barty [1] ... 6/4 6/2	Ashleigh Barty [1] ... 6/1 6/3	Ashleigh Barty [1] ... 6/1 6/1			
	2. Saisai Zheng *(43)* (CHN)						
	3. Svetlana Kuznetsova *(102)* (RUS)	Alison Van Uytvanck ... 6/4 4/6 6/2					
	4. Alison Van Uytvanck *(57)* (BEL)						
(WC)	5. Harriet Dart *(170)* (GBR)	Harriet Dart ... 4/6 6/4 6/4	Harriet Dart ... 7/6(4) 3/6 6/1		Alison Riske ... 3/6 6/2 6/3		
(LL)	6. Christina McHale *(109)* (USA)						
(Q)	7. Beatriz Haddad Maia *(121)* (BRA)	Beatriz Haddad Maia ... 6/4 6/4					
	8. **Garbiñe Muguruza [26]** *(27)* (ESP)						
	9. Donna Vekic *(22)* (CRO)	Alison Riske ... 3/6 6/3 7/5	Alison Riske ... 6/2 6/7(3) 9/7				
	10. Alison Riske *(54)* (USA)						
(Q)	11. Lesley Kerkhove *(203)* (NED)	Ivana Jorovic ... 7/6(5) 6/4		Alison Riske ... 4/6 6/4 6/4			
	12. Ivana Jorovic *(101)* (SRB)						
	13. Stefanie Voegele *(100)* (SUI)	Kaia Kanepi ... 5/7 7/5 6/4	Belinda Bencic [13] ... 6/3 6/1				
	14. Kaia Kanepi *(72)* (EST)						
	15. Anastasia Pavlyuchenkova *(45)* (RUS)	Belinda Bencic [13] ... 6/2 6/3				Serena Williams [11] ... 6/4 4/6 6/3	
	16. **Belinda Bencic [13]** *(13)* (SUI)						
	17. **Serena Williams [11]** *(11)* (USA)	Serena Williams [11] ... 6/2 6/2	Serena Williams [11] ... 2/6 6/2 6/4				
(Q)	18. Giulia Gatto-Monticone *(762)* (ITA)						
(Q)	19. Kaja Juvan *(125)* (SLO)	Kaja Juvan ... 6/4 2/6 6/4		Serena Williams [11] ... 6/3 6/4			
	20. Kristyna Pliskova *(95)* (CZE)						
(Q)	21. Paula Badosa *(126)* (ESP)	Varvara Flink ... 6/4 6/2	Julia Goerges [18] ... 6/1 6/4				
(Q)	22. Varvara Flink *(140)* (RUS)						
(Q)	23. Elena-Gabriela Ruse *(177)* (ROU)	Julia Goerges [18] ... 7/5 6/1			Serena Williams [11] ... 6/2 6/2		
	24. **Julia Goerges [18]** *(18)* (GER)						
	25. **Carla Suarez Navarro [30]** *(31)* (ESP)	Carla Suarez Navarro [30] ... 6/3 6/2	Carla Suarez Navarro [30] ... 7/6(2) 7/6(4)				
	26. Samantha Stosur *(132)* (AUS)						
	27. Maria Sharapova *(80)* (RUS)	Pauline Parmentier ... 4/6 7/6(4) 5/0 Ret'd		Carla Suarez Navarro [30] ... 6/3 6/3			
	28. Pauline Parmentier *(82)* (FRA)						
	29. Kateryna Kozlova *(67)* (UKR)	Lauren Davis ... 6/3 6/2	Lauren Davis ... 2/6 6/2 6/1				
(LL)	30. Lauren Davis *(96)* (USA)						
	31. Tatjana Maria *(65)* (GER)	Angelique Kerber [5] ... 6/2 6/2					
	32. **Angelique Kerber [5]** *(5)* (GER)						
	33. **Kiki Bertens [4]** *(4)* (NED)	Kiki Bertens [4] ... 6/3 6/2	Kiki Bertens [4] ... 3/6 7/6(5) 6/2				
	34. Mandy Minella *(98)* (LUX)						
(Q)	35. Arina Rodionova *(212)* (AUS)	Taylor Townsend ... 6/2 6/3		Barbora Strycova ... 7/5 6/1			
	36. Taylor Townsend *(120)* (USA)						
	37. Laura Siegemund *(84)* (GER)	Laura Siegemund ... 6/2 6/4	Barbora Strycova ... 6/3 7/5				
(WC)	38. Katie Swan *(207)* (GBR)						
	39. Barbora Strycova *(50)* (CZE)	Barbora Strycova ... 6/3 6/2			Barbora Strycova ... 4/6 7/5 6/2		
	40. **Lesia Tsurenko [32]** *(33)* (UKR)						
	41. **Elise Mertens [21]** *(21)* (BEL)	Elise Mertens [21] ... 6/2 6/0	Elise Mertens [21] ... 7/5 6/0				
	42. Fiona Ferro *(99)* (FRA)						
	43. Andrea Petkovic *(70)* (GER)	Monica Niculescu ... 2/6 6/2 7/5		Elise Mertens [21] ... 6/2 6/7(9) 6/4			
(WC)	44. Monica Niculescu *(113)* (ROU)						
	45. Tamara Zidansek *(59)* (SLO)	Tamara Zidansek ... 6/3 5/7 8/6	Qiang Wang [15] ... 6/1 6/2				
	46. Eugenie Bouchard *(79)* (CAN)						
	47. Vera Lapko *(105)* (BLR)	Qiang Wang [15] ... 6/2 6/2			Barbora Strycova ... 7/6(5) 6/1		
	48. **Qiang Wang [15]** *(15)* (CHN)						
	49. **Sloane Stephens [9]** *(9)* (USA)	Sloane Stephens [9] ... 6/2 6/4	Sloane Stephens [9] ... 6/0 6/2				
	50. Timea Bacsinszky *(93)* (SUI)						
	51. Yafan Wang *(56)* (CHN)	Yafan Wang ... 6/2 7/5		Johanna Konta [19] ... 3/6 6/4 6/1			
(Q)	52. Tereza Martincova *(139)* (CZE)						
	53. Ekaterina Alexandrova *(52)* (RUS)	Katerina Siniakova ... 2/6 6/1 6/1	Johanna Konta [19] ... 6/3 6/4				
	54. Katerina Siniakova *(38)* (CZE)						
(Q)	55. Ana Bogdan *(134)* (ROU)	Johanna Konta [19] ... 7/5 6/2			Johanna Konta [19] ... 4/6 6/2 6/4		
	56. **Johanna Konta [19]** *(19)* (GBR)						
	57. **Amanda Anisimova [25]** *(26)* (USA)	Amanda Anisimova [25] ... 6/3 6/3	Magda Linette ... 6/4 7/5				
	58. Sorana Cirstea *(76)* (ROU)						
	59. Magda Linette *(75)* (POL)	Magda Linette ... 6/0 7/6(9)		Petra Kvitova [6] ... 6/3 6/2			
(Q)	60. Anna Kalinskaya *(144)* (RUS)						
	61. Vitalia Diatchenko *(186)* (RUS)	Kristina Mladenovic ... 7/5 6/7(4) 6/2	Petra Kvitova [6] ... 7/5 6/2				
	62. Kristina Mladenovic *(48)* (FRA)						
	63. Ons Jabeur *(62)* (TUN)	Petra Kvitova [6] ... 6/4 6/2				Barbora Strycova ... 7/6(4) 6/1	
	64. **Petra Kvitova [6]** *(6)* (CZE)						
	65. **Elina Svitolina [8]** *(8)* (UKR)	Elina Svitolina [8] ... 7/5 6/0	Elina Svitolina [8] ... 5/7 6/5 Ret'd				
	66. Daria Gavrilova *(78)* (AUS)						
	67. Margarita Gasparyan *(61)* (RUS)	Margarita Gasparyan ... 6/4 6/4		Elina Svitolina [8] ... 6/3 6/7(1) 6/2			
	68. Anna-Lena Friedsam *(50)* (GER)						
(LL)	69. Marie Bouzkova *(116)* (CZE)	Marie Bouzkova ... 6/3 6/3	Maria Sakkari [31] ... 6/4 6/1				
	70. Mona Barthel *(97)* (GER)						
	71. Bernarda Pera *(92)* (USA)	Maria Sakkari [31] ... 7/6(4) 6/3			Elina Svitolina [8] ... 6/4 6/2		
	72. **Maria Sakkari [31]** *(32)* (GRE)						
	73. **Petra Martic [24]** *(24)* (CRO)	Petra Martic [24] ... 3/6 6/3 6/4	Petra Martic [24] ... 6/3 6/3 6/4				
	74. Jennifer Brady *(64)* (USA)						
	75. Anastasia Potapova *(71)* (RUS)	Anastasia Potapova ... 2/6 6/4 6/1		Petra Martic [24] ... 6/4 3/6 6/4			
	76. Jil Teichmann *(91)* (SUI)						
	77. Danielle Collins *(34)* (USA)	Danielle Collins ... 6/3 7/5	Danielle Collins ... 4/6 6/4 6/3				
	78. Zarina Diyas *(89)* (KAZ)						
(Q)	79. Kristie Ahn *(191)* (USA)	Anastasija Sevastova [12] ... 6/3 6/4			Elina Svitolina [8] ... 7/5 6/4		
	80. **Anastasija Sevastova [12]** *(12)* (LAT)						
	81. **Marketa Vondrousova [16]** *(16)* (CZE)	Madison Brengle ... 6/4 6/4	Karolina Muchova ... 6/3 6/4				
	82. Madison Brengle *(88)* (USA)						
	83. Karolina Muchova *(68)* (CZE)	Karolina Muchova ... 7/5 6/2		Karolina Muchova ... 7/6(7) 6/3			
	84. Aleksandra Krunic *(108)* (SRB)						
(Q)	85. Caty McNally *(164)* (USA)	Heather Watson ... 7/6(3) 6/4	Anett Kontaveit [20] ... 7/5 6/1				
	86. Heather Watson *(122)* (GBR)						
	87. Shelby Rogers *(81)* (USA)	Anett Kontaveit [20] ... 6/0 3/6 6/4		Karolina Muchova ... 4/6 7/5 13/11			
	88. **Anett Kontaveit [20]** *(20)* (EST)						
	89. **Su-Wei Hsieh [28]** *(29)* (TPE)	Su-Wei Hsieh [28] ... 6/2 6/2	Su-Wei Hsieh [28] ... 7/6(3) 6/3				
	90. Jelena Ostapenko *(35)* (LAT)						
	91. Dalila Jakupovic *(143)* (SLO)	Kirsten Flipkens ... 6/1 6/3		Karolina Pliskova [3] ... 6/3 2/6 6/4			
	92. Kirsten Flipkens *(81)* (BEL)						
	93. Anna Karolina Schmiedlova *(90)* (SVK)	Monica Puig ... 5/7 6/4 7/5	Karolina Pliskova [3] ... 6/0 6/4				
	94. Monica Puig *(53)* (PUR)						
	95. Lin Zhu *(103)* (CHN)	Karolina Pliskova [3] ... 6/2 7/6(4)			Simona Halep [7] ... 6/1 6/3		
	96. **Karolina Pliskova [3]** *(3)* (CZE)						
	97. **Simona Halep [7]** *(7)* (ROU)	Simona Halep [7] ... 6/4 7/5	Simona Halep [7] ... 6/3 4/6 6/2				
	98. Aliaksandra Sasnovich *(37)* (BLR)						
	99. Mihaela Buzarnescu *(47)* (ROU)	Mihaela Buzarnescu ... 6/4 6/4		Simona Halep [7] ... 6/3 6/3			
	100. Jessica Pegula *(74)* (USA)						
	101. Alize Cornet *(55)* (FRA)	Victoria Azarenka ... 6/4 6/4	Victoria Azarenka ... 6/2 6/0				
	102. Victoria Azarenka *(42)* (BLR)						
	103. Ajla Tomljanovic *(49)* (AUS)	Ajla Tomljanovic ... 6/3 6/1			Simona Halep [7] ... 6/3 6/3		
	104. **Daria Kasatkina [29]** *(30)* (RUS)						
	105. **Madison Keys [17]** *(17)* (USA)	Madison Keys [17] ... 6/3 6/3	Polona Hercog ... 6/2 6/4				
	106. Luksika Kumkhum *(107)* (THA)						
	107. Polona Hercog *(60)* (SLO)	Polona Hercog ... 4/6 7/6(5) 7/5		Cori Gauff ... 3/6 7/6(7) 7/5			
	108. Viktoria Kuzmova *(46)* (SVK)						
	109. Venus Williams *(44)* (USA)	Cori Gauff ... 6/4 6/4	Cori Gauff ... 6/3 6/3				
(Q)	110. Cori Gauff *(301)* (USA)						
	111. Magdalena Rybarikova *(141)* (SVK)	Magdalena Rybarikova ... 6/2 6/4			Simona Halep [7] ... 6/3 6/3		
	112. **Aryna Sabalenka [10]** *(10)* (BLR)						
	113. **Caroline Wozniacki [14]** *(14)* (DEN)	Caroline Wozniacki [14] ... 5/4 Ret'd	Caroline Wozniacki [14] ... 7/6(5) 6/3				
	114. Sara Sorribes Tormo *(69)* (ESP)						
	115. Veronika Kudermetova *(58)* (RUS)	Veronika Kudermetova ... 6/2 6/4		Shuai Zhang ... 6/4 6/2			
(Q)	116. Ysaline Bonaventure *(115)* (BEL)						
	117. Rebecca Peterson *(66)* (SWE)	Yanina Wickmayer ... 6/4 6/3	Shuai Zhang ... 6/3 6/2				
(Q)	118. Yanina Wickmayer *(148)* (BEL)						
	119. Shuai Zhang *(51)* (CHN)	Shuai Zhang ... 6/4 6/0			Shuai Zhang ... 6/4 1/6 6/2		
	120. **Caroline Garcia [23]** *(23)* (FRA)						
	121. **Sofia Kenin [27]** *(28)* (USA)	Sofia Kenin [27] ... 6/4 6/2	Dayana Yastremska ... 7/5 4/6 6/3				
	122. Astra Sharma *(85)* (AUS)						
	123. Dayana Yastremska *(36)* (UKR)	Dayana Yastremska ... 6/3 6/3		Dayana Yastremska ... 7/5 6/3			
	124. Camila Giorgi *(41)* (ITA)						
	125. Iga Swiatek *(63)* (POL)	Viktorija Golubic ... 6/2 7/6(3)	Viktorija Golubic ... 6/4 7/6(3)				
	126. Viktorija Golubic *(83)* (SUI)						
	127. Yulia Putintseva *(39)* (KAZ)	Yulia Putintseva ... 7/6(4) 6/2					
	128. **Naomi Osaka [2]** *(2)* (JPN)						

Serena Williams [11] 6/1 6/2
Barbora Strycova 7/6(5) 6/1
Simona Halep [7] 6/2 6/2
Elina Svitolina [8] 6/1 6/3
Simona Halep [7] 7/6(4) 6/1
Serena Williams [11] 6/2 6/2
Simona Halep [7] 6/2 6/4

Heavy type denotes seeded players. The figure in brackets against names denotes the order in which they have been seeded. The figure in italics denotes WTA Ranking – 01.07.2019.
(WC)=Wild card. (Q)=Qualifier. (LL)=Lucky loser.

THE LADIES' DOUBLES CHAMPIONSHIP 2019
Holders: BARBORA KREJCIKOVA (CZE) & KATERINA SINIAKOVA (CZE)

The Champions will become the holders, for the year only, of the CHALLENGE CUPS presented by H.R.H. PRINCESS MARINA, DUCHESS OF KENT, the late President of The All England Lawn Tennis and Croquet Club in 1949 and The All England Lawn Tennis and Croquet Club in 2001. The Champions will each receive a silver three-quarter size replica of the Challenge Cup. A Silver Salver will be presented to each of the Runners-up and a Bronze Medal to each defeated semi-finalist. The matches will be the best of three sets. If the score should reach 12-12 in the final set, the match will be decided by a tie-break.

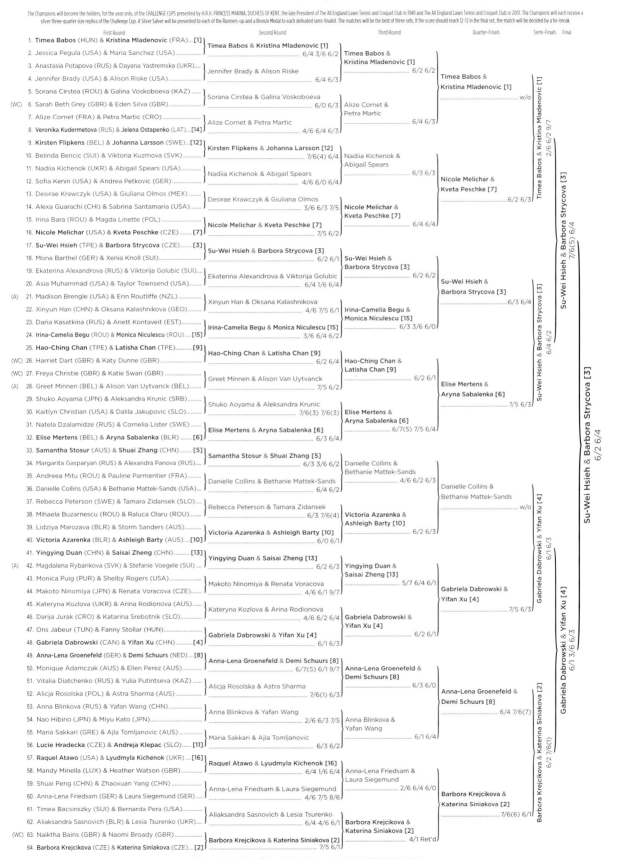

First Round

1. **Timea Babos** (HUN) & **Kristina Mladenovic** (FRA)... [1]
2. Jessica Pegula (USA) & Maria Sanchez (USA)
3. Anastasia Potapova (RUS) & Dayana Yastremska (UKR)
4. Jennifer Brady (USA) & Alison Riske (USA)
5. Sorana Cirstea (ROU) & Galina Voskoboeva (KAZ)
(WC) 6. Sarah Beth Grey (GBR) & Eden Silva (GBR)
7. Alize Cornet (FRA) & Petra Martic (CRO)
8. Veronika Kudermetova (RUS) & Jelena Ostapenko (LAT)... [14]
9. Kirsten Flipkens (BEL) & Johanna Larsson (SWE)... [12]
10. Belinda Bencic (SUI) & Viktoria Kuzmova (SVK)
11. Nadiia Kichenok (UKR) & Abigail Spears (USA)
12. Sofia Kenin (USA) & Andrea Petkovic (GER)
13. Desirae Krawczyk (USA) & Giuliana Olmos (MEX)
14. Alexa Guarachi (CHI) & Sabrina Santamaria (USA)
15. Irina Bara (ROU) & Magda Linette (POL)
16. **Nicole Melichar** (USA) & **Kveta Peschke** (CZE)... [7]
17. **Su-Wei Hsieh** (TPE) & **Barbora Strycova** (CZE)... [3]
18. Mona Barthel (GER) & Xenia Knoll (SUI)
19. Ekaterina Alexandrova (RUS) & Viktorija Golubic (SUI)
20. Asia Muhammad (USA) & Taylor Townsend (USA)
(A) 21. Madison Brengle (USA) & Erin Routliffe (NZL)
22. Xinyun Han (CHN) & Oksana Kalashnikova (GEO)
23. Daria Kasatkina (RUS) & Anett Kontaveit (EST)
24. Irina-Camelia Begu (ROU) & Monica Niculescu (ROU)... [15]
25. Hao-Ching Chan (TPE) & Latisha Chan (TPE)... [9]
(WC) 26. Harriet Dart (GBR) & Katy Dunne (GBR)
(WC) 27. Freya Christie (GBR) & Katie Swan (GBR)
(A) 28. Greet Minnen (BEL) & Alison Van Uytvanck (BEL)
29. Shuko Aoyama (JPN) & Aleksandra Krunic (SRB)
30. Kaitlyn Christian (USA) & Dalila Jakupovic (SLO)
31. Natela Dzalamidze (RUS) & Cornelia Lister (SWE)
32. **Elise Mertens** (BEL) & **Aryna Sabalenka** (BLR)... [6]
33. **Samantha Stosur** (AUS) & **Shuai Zhang** (CHN)... [5]
34. Margarita Gasparyan (RUS) & Alexandra Panova (RUS)
35. Andreea Mitu (ROU) & Pauline Parmentier (FRA)
36. Danielle Collins (USA) & Bethanie Mattek-Sands (USA)
37. Rebecca Peterson (SWE) & Tamara Zidansek (SLO)
38. Mihaela Buzarnescu (ROU) & Raluca Olaru (ROU)
39. Lidziya Marozava (BLR) & Storm Sanders (AUS)
40. **Victoria Azarenka** (BLR) & **Ashleigh Barty** (AUS)... [10]
41. **Yingying Duan** (CHN) & **Saisai Zheng** (CHN)... [13]
(A) 42. Magdalena Rybarikova (SVK) & Stefanie Voegele (SUI)
43. Monica Puig (PUR) & Shelby Rogers (USA)
44. Makoto Ninomiya (JPN) & Renata Voracova (CZE)
45. Kateryna Kozlova (UKR) & Arina Rodionova (AUS)
46. Darija Jurak (CRO) & Katarina Srebotnik (SLO)
47. Ons Jabeur (TUN) & Fanny Stollar (HUN)
48. **Gabriela Dabrowski** (CAN) & **Yifan Xu** (CHN)... [4]
49. **Anna-Lena Groenefeld** (GER) & **Demi Schuurs** (NED)... [8]
50. Monique Adamczak (AUS) & Ellen Perez (AUS)
51. Vitalia Diatchenko (RUS) & Yulia Putintseva (KAZ)
52. Alicja Rosolska (POL) & Astra Sharma (AUS)
53. Anna Blinkova (RUS) & Yafan Wang (CHN)
54. Nao Hibino (JPN) & Miyu Kato (JPN)
55. Maria Sakkari (GRE) & Ajla Tomljanovic (AUS)
56. **Lucie Hradecka** (CZE) & **Andreja Klepac** (SLO)... [11]
57. **Raquel Atawo** (USA) & **Lyudmyla Kichenok** (UKR)... [16]
58. Mandy Minella (LUX) & Heather Watson (GBR)
59. Shuai Peng (CHN) & Zhaoxuan Yang (CHN)
60. Anna-Lena Friedsam (GER) & Laura Siegemund (GER)
61. Timea Bacsinszky (SUI) & Bernarda Pera (USA)
62. Aliaksandra Sasnovich (BLR) & Lesia Tsurenko (UKR)
(WC) 63. Naiktha Bains (GBR) & Naomi Broady (GBR)
64. **Barbora Krejcikova** (CZE) & **Katerina Siniakova** (CZE)... [2]

Second Round

Timea Babos & Kristina Mladenovic [1]
 6/4 3/6 6/2
Jennifer Brady & Alison Riske
 6/4 6/3
Sorana Cirstea & Galina Voskoboeva
 6/0 6/3
Alize Cornet & Petra Martic
 4/6 6/4 6/3
Kirsten Flipkens & Johanna Larsson [12]
 7/6(4) 6/4
Nadiia Kichenok & Abigail Spears
 4/6 6/0 6/4
Desirae Krawczyk & Giuliana Olmos
 3/6 6/3 7/5
Nicole Melichar & Kveta Peschke [7]
 7/5 6/2
Su-Wei Hsieh & Barbora Strycova [3]
 6/2 6/1
Ekaterina Alexandrova & Viktorija Golubic
 6/4 1/6 6/4
Xinyun Han & Oksana Kalashnikova
 4/6 7/5 6/1
Irina-Camelia Begu & Monica Niculescu [15]
 3/6 6/4
Hao-Ching Chan & Latisha Chan [9]
 6/2 6/4
Greet Minnen & Alison Van Uytvanck
 7/5 6/2
Shuko Aoyama & Aleksandra Krunic
 7/6(3) 7/6(3)
Elise Mertens & Aryna Sabalenka [6]
 6/3 6/4
Samantha Stosur & Shuai Zhang [5]
 6/3 3/6 6/2
Danielle Collins & Bethanie Mattek-Sands
Rebecca Peterson & Tamara Zidansek
 6/3 7/6(4)
Victoria Azarenka & Ashleigh Barty [10]
 6/0 6/1
Yingying Duan & Saisai Zheng [13]
 6/2 6/3
Makoto Ninomiya & Renata Voracova
 4/6 6/1 9/7
Kateryna Kozlova & Arina Rodionova
 4/6 6/2 6/4
Gabriela Dabrowski & Yifan Xu [4]
 6/1 6/3
Anna-Lena Groenefeld & Demi Schuurs [8]
 6/7(5) 6/1 9/7
Alicja Rosolska & Astra Sharma
 7/6(1) 6/3
Anna Blinkova & Yafan Wang
 2/6 6/3 7/5
Maria Sakkari & Ajla Tomljanovic
 6/3 6/2
Raquel Atawo & Lyudmyla Kichenok [16]
 6/4 1/6 6/4
Anna-Lena Friedsam & Laura Siegemund
 4/6 7/5 8/6
Aliaksandra Sasnovich & Lesia Tsurenko
 6/4 4/6 6/1
Barbora Krejcikova & Katerina Siniakova [2]
 7/5 6/1

Third Round

Timea Babos & Kristina Mladenovic [1]
 6/2 6/2
Alize Cornet & Petra Martic
 6/4 6/3
Nadiia Kichenok & Abigail Spears
 6/3 6/3
Nicole Melichar & Kveta Peschke [7]
 6/4 6/4
Su-Wei Hsieh & Barbora Strycova [3]
 6/2 6/2
Irina-Camelia Begu & Monica Niculescu [15]
 6/3 6/0
Hao-Ching Chan & Latisha Chan [9]
 6/2 6/1
Elise Mertens & Aryna Sabalenka [6]
 6/7(5) 7/5 6/4
Danielle Collins & Bethanie Mattek-Sands
 4/6 6/2 6/2
Victoria Azarenka & Ashleigh Barty [10]
 6/2 6/3
Yingying Duan & Saisai Zheng [13]
 5/7 6/4 6/1
Gabriela Dabrowski & Yifan Xu [4]
 6/2 6/1
Anna-Lena Groenefeld & Demi Schuurs [8]
 6/3 6/0
Anna Blinkova & Yafan Wang
 6/1 6/4
Anna-Lena Friedsam & Laura Siegemund
 2/6 6/4 6/0
Barbora Krejcikova & Katerina Siniakova [2]
 4/1 Ret'd

Quarter-Finals

Timea Babos & Kristina Mladenovic [1]
 6/2 6/2
Nicole Melichar & Kveta Peschke [7]
 6/2 6/3
Su-Wei Hsieh & Barbora Strycova [3]
 6/3 6/4
Elise Mertens & Aryna Sabalenka [6]
 7/5 6/3
Danielle Collins & Bethanie Mattek-Sands
 w/o
Gabriela Dabrowski & Yifan Xu [4]
 7/5 6/3
Anna-Lena Groenefeld & Demi Schuurs [8]
 6/4 7/6(7)
Barbora Krejcikova & Katerina Siniakova [2]
 7/6(6) 6/1

Semi-Finals

Timea Babos & Kristina Mladenovic [1]
 2/6 6/2 9/7
Su-Wei Hsieh & Barbora Strycova [3]
 6/4 6/2
Gabriela Dabrowski & Yifan Xu [4]
 6/1 3/6 6/3
Barbora Krejcikova & Katerina Siniakova [2]
 6/2 7/6(1)

Final

Su-Wei Hsieh & Barbora Strycova [3]
 7/6(5) 6/4
Su-Wei Hsieh & Barbora Strycova [3]
 6/2 6/4

Heavy type denotes seeded players. The figure in brackets against names denotes the order in which they have been seeded.
(WC)=Wild cards. (Q)=Qualifiers. (LL)=Lucky losers.

THE MIXED DOUBLES CHAMPIONSHIP 2019
Holders: ALEXANDER PEYA (AUT) & NICOLE MELICHAR (USA)

The Champions will become the holders, for the year only, of the CHALLENGE CUPS presented by members of the family of the late Mr. S. H. SMITH in 1949 and The All England Lawn Tennis and Croquet Club in 2001. The Champions will each receive a silver three-quarter size replica of the Challenge Cup. A Silver Salver will be presented to each of the Runners-up and a Bronze Medal to each defeated semi-finalist. The matches will be the best of three sets. If the score should reach 12-12 in the final set, the match will be decided by a tie-break.

First Round | **Second Round** | **Third Round** | **Quarter-Finals** | **Semi-Finals** | **Final**

1. **Bruno Soares** (BRA) & **Nicole Melichar** (USA)............[1]
2. Bye
  — **Bruno Soares & Nicole Melichar [1]**
3. Denys Molchanov (UKR) & Galina Voskoboeva (KAZ)
4. Jurgen Melzer (AUT) & Anastasia Pavlyuchenkova (RUS)
  — Denys Molchanov & Galina Voskoboeva 7/6(6) 1/6 6/4
  — **Bruno Soares & Nicole Melichar [1]** .... 7/6(4) 3/6 6/3
5. Andy Murray (GBR) & Serena Williams (USA)
6. Andreas Mies (GER) & Alexa Guarachi (CHI)
  — Andy Murray & Serena Williams 6/4 6/1
  — Andy Murray & Serena Williams 7/5 6/3
7. Bye
8. **Fabrice Martin** (FRA) & **Raquel Atawo** (USA)............[14]
  — **Fabrice Martin & Raquel Atawo [14]**
  — **Bruno Soares & Nicole Melichar [1]** 6/3 4/6 6/2

9. **Neal Skupski** (GBR) & **Hao-Ching Chan** (TPE)............[9]
10. Bye
  — **Neal Skupski & Hao-Ching Chan [9]**
11. (WC) Jonny O'Mara (GBR) & Naomi Broady (GBR)
12. Matwe Middelkoop (NED) & Zhaoxuan Yang (CHN)
  — Matwe Middelkoop & Zhaoxuan Yang 7/6(4) 6/3
  — Matwe Middelkoop & Zhaoxuan Yang 7/6(1) 6/2
13. Nick Kyrgios (AUS) & Desirae Krawczyk (USA)
14. Marcus Daniell (NZL) & Jennifer Brady (USA)
  — Marcus Daniell & Jennifer Brady 6/7(4) 7/6(4) 7/5
  — Marcus Daniell & Jennifer Brady w/o
15. Bye
16. **Maximo Gonzalez** (ARG) & **Yifan Xu** (CHN)............[7]
  — **Maximo Gonzalez & Yifan Xu [7]**
  — Matwe Middelkoop & Zhaoxuan Yang 6/2 6/7(5) 6/4

17. **John Peers** (AUS) & **Shuai Zhang** (CHN)............[4]
18. Bye
  — **John Peers & Shuai Zhang [4]**
19. Marcelo Demoliner (BRA) & Abigail Spears (USA)
20. Henri Kontinen (FIN) & Heather Watson (GBR)
  — Henri Kontinen & Heather Watson 6/3 6/2
  — **John Peers & Shuai Zhang [4]** 4/6 6/3 6/4
21. Robert Lindstedt (SWE) & Jelena Ostapenko (LAT)
22. (WC) Jay Clarke (GBR) & Cori Gauff (USA)
  — Robert Lindstedt & Jelena Ostapenko 6/1 6/4
  — Robert Lindstedt & Jelena Ostapenko 6/3 6/1
23. Bye
24. (A) Andres Molteni (ARG) & Makoto Ninomiya (JPN)
  — Andres Molteni & Makoto Ninomiya
  — Robert Lindstedt & Jelena Ostapenko 2/6 7/5 6/4

25. **Franko Skugor** (CRO) & **Raluca Olaru** (ROU)............[12]
26. Bye
  — **Franko Skugor & Raluca Olaru [12]**
27. (WC) Scott Clayton (GBR) & Sarah Beth Grey (GBR)
28. Frances Tiafoe (USA) & Venus Williams (USA)
  — Frances Tiafoe & Venus Williams 6/2 6/3
  — **Franko Skugor & Raluca Olaru [12]** 6/3 6/1
29. Christopher Rungkat (INA) & Shuko Aoyama (JPN)
30. Nicolas Mahut (FRA) & Alize Cornet (FRA)
  — Christopher Rungkat & Shuko Aoyama 1/6 6/4 6/4
  — Nikola Mektic & Alicja Rosolska [6] 7/5 6/4
31. Bye
32. **Nikola Mektic** (CRO) & **Alicja Rosolska** (POL)............[6]
  — **Nikola Mektic & Alicja Rosolska [6]**
  — **Franko Skugor & Raluca Olaru [12]** 6/2 6/2

33. **Wesley Koolhof** (NED) & **Kveta Peschke** (CZE)............[5]
34. Bye
  — **Wesley Koolhof & Kveta Peschke [5]**
35. Kevin Krawietz (GER) & Sabrina Santamaria (USA)
36. (A) Philipp Oswald (AUT) & Monique Adamczak (AUS)
  — Philipp Oswald & Monique Adamczak 7/5 6/2
  — **Wesley Koolhof & Kveta Peschke [5]** 6/1 6/4
37. Santiago Gonzalez (MEX) & Xinyun Han (CHN)
38. Aisam-Ul-Haq Qureshi (PAK) & Nadiia Kichenok (UKR)
  — Aisam-Ul-Haq Qureshi & Nadiia Kichenok 7/6(2) 6/4
  — Aisam-Ul-Haq Qureshi & Nadiia Kichenok 6/4 7/6(9)
39. Bye
40. **Michael Venus** (NZL) & **Katarina Srebotnik** (SLO)............[10]
  — **Michael Venus & Katarina Srebotnik [10]**
  — **Wesley Koolhof & Kveta Peschke [5]** 7/6(5) 6/4

41. **Rohan Bopanna** (IND) & **Aryna Sabalenka** (BLR)............[13]
42. Bye
  — **Rohan Bopanna & Aryna Sabalenka [13]**
43. Artem Sitak (NZL) & Laura Siegemund (GER)
44. Ken Skupski (GBR) & Darija Jurak (CRO)
  — Artem Sitak & Laura Siegemund 3/6 6/3 6/4
  — Artem Sitak & Laura Siegemund 6/4 6/4
45. Jamie Murray (GBR) & Bethanie Mattek-Sands (USA)
46. (WC) Joe Salisbury (GBR) & Katy Dunne (GBR)
  — Jamie Murray & Bethanie Mattek-Sands 7/5 7/6(8)
  — Mate Pavic & Gabriela Dabrowski [3] 6/4 3/6 6/3
47. Bye
48. **Mate Pavic** (CRO) & **Gabriela Dabrowski** (CAN)............[3]
  — **Mate Pavic & Gabriela Dabrowski [3]**
  — Artem Sitak & Laura Siegemund 5/7 7/6(5) 13/12(5)

49. **Ivan Dodig** (CRO) & **Latisha Chan** (TPE)............[8]
50. Bye
  — **Ivan Dodig & Latisha Chan [8]**
51. Ben McLachlan (JPN) & Miyu Kato (JPN)
52. Cheng-Peng Hsieh (TPE) & Su-Wei Hsieh (TPE)
  — Cheng-Peng Hsieh & Su-Wei Hsieh 6/4 6/4
  — **Ivan Dodig & Latisha Chan [8]** 6/3 6/2
53. Rajeev Ram (USA) & Alison Riske (USA)
54. Luke Bambridge (GBR) & Asia Muhammad (USA)
  — Luke Bambridge & Asia Muhammad 6/3 6/4
  — Edouard Roger-Vasselin & Andreja Klepac [11] 6/4 6/4
55. Bye
56. **Edouard Roger-Vasselin** (FRA) & **Andreja Klepac** (SLO)............[11]
  — **Edouard Roger-Vasselin & Andreja Klepac [11]**
  — **Ivan Dodig & Latisha Chan [8]** 2/6 6/3 6/4

57. **Divij Sharan** (IND) & **Yingying Duan** (CHN)............[16]
58. Bye
  — **Divij Sharan & Yingying Duan [16]**
59. Leander Paes (IND) & Samantha Stosur (AUS)
60. (WC) Evan Hoyt (GBR) & Eden Silva (GBR)
  — Evan Hoyt & Eden Silva 6/4 2/6 6/4
  — Evan Hoyt & Eden Silva 6/3 6/4
61. Frederik Nielsen (DEN) & Kaitlyn Christian (USA)
62. Joran Vliegen (BEL) & Saisai Zheng (CHN)
  — Joran Vliegen & Saisai Zheng 6/3 7/5
  — Joran Vliegen & Saisai Zheng 6/4 7/5
63. Bye
64. **Jean-Julien Rojer** (NED) & **Demi Schuurs** (NED)............[2]
  — **Jean-Julien Rojer & Demi Schuurs [2]**
  — Evan Hoyt & Eden Silva 5/7 7/6(5) 6/4

Quarter-Finals / Semi-Finals / Final:

Matwe Middelkoop & Zhaoxuan Yang 6/4 6/3
Robert Lindstedt & Jelena Ostapenko 6/7(6) 6/3 7/5
— Robert Lindstedt & Jelena Ostapenko 7/5 6/2

Wesley Koolhof & Kveta Peschke [5] 6/1 6/2
Ivan Dodig & Latisha Chan [8] 7/5 7/6(5)
— Ivan Dodig & Latisha Chan [8] 7/5 6/4

— Robert Lindstedt & Jelena Ostapenko 2/6 7/5 6/4

Final: Ivan Dodig & Latisha Chan [8] 6/2 6/3

Heavy type denotes seeded players. The figure in brackets against names denotes the order in which they have been seeded.
(WC)=Wild cards. (A)=Alternates.

THE GENTLEMEN'S WHEELCHAIR SINGLES 2019
Holder: STEFAN OLSSON (SWE)

The Champion will become the holder, for the year only, of a Cup presented by The All England Lawn Tennis and Croquet Club. The Champion will receive a three-quarter size replica of the Cup. A Silver Salver will be presented to the Runner-up.
The matches will be the best of three tie-break sets.

First Round	Semi-final	Final

1. **Shingo Kunieda** (JPN) .... **[1]**

(WC) 2. Gordon Reid (GBR) ....

    Shingo Kunieda [1] 6/1 6/1

3. Joachim Gerard (BEL) ....

4. Stefan Olsson (SWE) ....

    Stefan Olsson 2/6 6/4 6/3

      Shingo Kunieda [1] 4/6 6/2 6/3

5. Stephane Houdet (FRA) ....

6. Nicolas Peifer (FRA) ....

    Stephane Houdet .... 6/7(5) 6/3 6/3

7. Alfie Hewett (GBR) ....

8. **Gustavo Fernandez** (ARG) .... **[2]**

    Gustavo Fernandez [2] 6/1 6/3

      Gustavo Fernandez [2] 6/0 6/4

Gustavo Fernandez [2] — 4/6 6/3 6/2

Heavy type denotes seeded players. The figure in brackets against names denotes the order in which they have been seeded. The Committee reserves the right to alter the seeding order in the event of withdrawals.
(WC)=Wild cards. (A)=Alternates.

THE GENTLEMEN'S WHEELCHAIR DOUBLES 2019
Holders: ALFIE HEWETT (GBR) & GORDON REID (GBR)

The Champions will become the holders, for the year only, of a Cup presented by The All England Lawn Tennis and Croquet Club. The Champions will receive a three-quarter size replica of the Cup. A Silver Salver will be presented to each of the Runners-up.
The matches will be the best of three tie-break sets.

First Round	Final

1. **Stephane Houdet** (FRA) & **Nicolas Peifer** (FRA) .... **[1]**

2. Alfie Hewett (GBR) & Gordon Reid (GBR) ....

    Alfie Hewett & Gordon Reid .... 6/3 2/6 7/6(4)

3. Gustavo Fernandez (ARG) & Shingo Kunieda (JPN) ....

4. **Joachim Gerard** (BEL) & **Stefan Olsson** (SWE) .... **[2]**

    Joachim Gerard & Stefan Olsson [2] .... 6/3 5/7 7/6(5)

Joachim Gerard & Stefan Olsson [2] — 6/4 6/2

Heavy type denotes seeded players. The figure in brackets against names denotes the order in which they have been seeded. The Committee reserves the right to alter the seeding order in the event of withdrawals.
(WC)=Wild cards. (A)=Alternates.

THE LADIES' WHEELCHAIR SINGLES 2019
Holder: DIEDE DE GROOT (NED)

The Champion will become the holder, for the year only, of a Cup presented by The All England Lawn Tennis and Croquet Club. The Champion will receive a three-quarter size replica of the Cup. A Silver Salver will be presented to the Runner-up.
The matches will be the best of three tie-break sets.

First Round	Semi-final	Final

1. **Diede De Groot** (NED) .... **[1]**

2. Marjolein Buis (NED) ....

    Diede De Groot [1] .... 7/6(3) 4/6 6/1

3. Kgothatso Montjane (RSA) ....

4. Sabine Ellerbrock (GER) ....

    Kgothatso Montjane .... 6/7(3) 6/1 6/2

      Diede De Groot [1] 6/3 6/2

5. Aniek Van Koot (NED) ....

6. Giulia Capocci (ITA) ....

    Aniek Van Koot 6/3 6/2

(WC) 7. Jordanne Whiley (GBR) ....

8. **Yui Kamiji** (JPN) .... **[2]**

    Yui Kamiji [2] 6/4 6/1

      Aniek Van Koot 6/3 6/4

Aniek Van Koot — 6/4 4/6 7/5

Heavy type denotes seeded players. The figure in brackets against names denotes the order in which they have been seeded. The Committee reserves the right to alter the seeding order in the event of withdrawals.
(WC)=Wild cards. (A)=Alternates.

THE LADIES' WHEELCHAIR DOUBLES 2019
Holders: DIEDE DE GROOT (NED) & YUI KAMIJI (JPN)

The Champions will become the holders, for the year only, of a Cup presented by The All England Lawn Tennis and Croquet Club. The Champions will receive a three-quarter size replica of the Cup. A Silver Salver will be presented to each of the Runners-up.
The matches will be the best of three tie-break sets.

First Round	Final

1. **Diede De Groot** (NED) & **Aniek Van Koot** (NED) .... **[1]**

2. Yui Kamiji (JPN) & Jordanne Whiley (GBR) ....

    Diede De Groot & Aniek Van Koot [1] .... 3/6 7/6(2) 6/1

3. Sabine Ellerbrock (GER) & Kgothatso Montjane (RSA) ....

4. **Marjolein Buis** (NED) & **Giulia Capocci** (ITA) .... **[2]**

    Marjolein Buis & Giulia Capocci [2] 7/5 6/2

Diede De Groot & Aniek Van Koot [1] — 6/1 6/1

Heavy type denotes seeded players. The figure in brackets against names denotes the order in which they have been seeded. The Committee reserves the right to alter the seeding order in the event of withdrawals.
(WC)=Wild cards. (A)=Alternates.

QUAD WHEELCHAIR SINGLES 2019
INAUGURAL EVENT

The Champion will become the holder, for the year only, of a Cup presented by The All England Lawn Tennis and Croquet Club. The Champion will receive a three-quarter size replica of the Cup. A Silver Salver will be presented to the Runner-up.
The matches will be the best of three sets. If the score should reach 6-6 in the final set, the match will be decided by a tie-break.

Third & Fourth Place Play-off	Semi-final	Final

1. Dylan Alcott [1] .... (AUS)

Koji Sugeno

    Dylan Alcott [1]

2. Koji Sugeno .... (JPN) 6/3 6/4

David Wagner [2] 6/2 7/5

Dylan Alcott [1] 6/0 6/2

3. Andy Lapthorne .... (GBR)

David Wagner [2]

    Andy Lapthorne

4. **David Wagner [2]** .... (USA) 7/5 6/4

Heavy type denotes seeded players. The figure in brackets against names denotes the order in which they have been seeded. The Committee reserves the right to alter the seeding order in the event of withdrawals.
(WC)=Wild cards. (A)=Alternates.

QUAD WHEELCHAIR DOUBLES 2019
INAUGURAL EVENT

The Champions will become the holder, for the year only, of a Cup presented by The All England Lawn Tennis and Croquet Club. The Champions will receive a three-quarter size replica of the Cup. A Silver Salver will be presented to each of the Runners-up.
The matches will be the best of three sets. If the score should reach 6-6 in the final set, the match will be decided by a tie-break.

Final

1. Dylan Alcott (AUS) & Andy Lapthorne (GBR) ....

    Dylan Alcott & Andy Lapthorne .... 6/2 7/6(4)

2. Koji Sugeno (JPN) & David Wagner (USA) ....

Heavy type denotes seeded players. The figure in brackets against names denotes the order in which they have been seeded. The Committee reserves the right to alter the seeding order in the event of withdrawals.
(WC)=Wild cards. (A)=Alternates.

*Eventual champions Dylan Alcott (**right**) and Andy Lapthorne in action in the final of the Quad Wheelchair Doubles on Court 14*

THE BOYS' SINGLES CHAMPIONSHIP 2019

Holder: CHUN-HSIN TSENG (TPE)

The Champion will become the holder, for the year only, of a Cup presented by The All England Lawn Tennis and Croquet Club.
The Champion will receive a three-quarter size Cup and the Runner-up will receive a Silver Salver. The matches will be the best of three sets. If the score should reach 12-12 in the final set, the match will be decided by a tie-break.

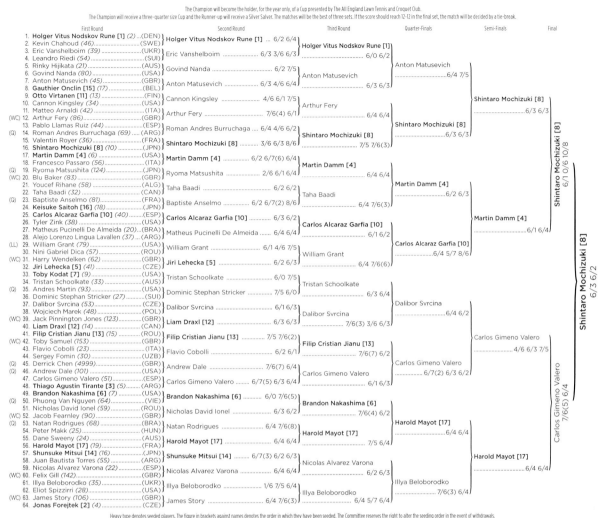

First Round	Second Round	Third Round	Quarter-Finals	Semi-Finals	Final
1. **Holger Vitus Nodskov Rune [1]** *(2)* ...(DEN)	Holger Vitus Nodskov Rune [1] 6/2 6/4	Holger Vitus Nodskov Rune [1] 6/0 6/2	Anton Matusevich 6/4 7/5	Shintaro Mochizuki [8] 6/3 6/3	Shintaro Mochizuki [8] 6/1 0/6 10/8
2. Kevin Chahoud *(46)*......................(SWE)					
3. Eric Vanshelboim *(39)*..................(UKR)	Eric Vanshelboim 6/3 3/6 6/3				
4. Leandro Riedi *(54)*........................(SUI)					
5. Rinky Hijikata *(21)*.......................(AUS)	Govind Nanda 6/2 7/5	Anton Matusevich 6/3 6/3			
6. Govind Nanda *(80)*........................(USA)					
7. Anton Matusevich *(45)*.................(GBR)	Anton Matusevich 6/3 4/6 6/3				
8. **Gauthier Onclin [15]** *(17)*..............(BEL)					
9. **Otto Virtanen [11]** *(13)*................(FIN)	Cannon Kingsley 4/6 6/1 7/5	Arthur Fery 6/4 6/4	Shintaro Mochizuki [8] 6/3 6/3		
10. Cannon Kingsley *(34)*....................(USA)					
11. Matteo Arnaldi *(42)*......................(ITA)	Arthur Fery .... 7/6(4) 6/1				
(WC) 12. Arthur Fery *(86)*...........................(GBR)					
13. Pablo Llamas Ruiz *(44)*...............(ESP)	Roman Andres Burruchaga ... 6/4 4/6 6/2	Shintaro Mochizuki [8] 7/5 7/6(3)			
(Q) 14. Roman Andres Burruchaga *(69)* .....(ARG)					
15. Valentin Royer *(36)*.....................(FRA)	Shintaro Mochizuki [8] ... 3/6 6/3 8/6				
16. **Shintaro Mochizuki [8]** *(10)*..........(JPN)					
17. **Martin Damm [4]** *(6)*....................(USA)	Martin Damm [4] ... 6/2 6/7(6) 6/4	Martin Damm [4] 6/4 6/4	Martin Damm [4] 6/2 6/3	Martin Damm [4] 6/1 6/4	
18. Francesco Passaro *(56)*..................(ITA)					
(Q) 19. Ryoma Matsushita *(124)*................(JPN)	Ryoma Matsushita 2/6 6/1 6/4				
(WC) 20. Blu Baker *(83)*...........................(GBR)					
21. Youcef Rihane *(58)*.....................(ALG)	Taha Baadi 6/2 6/2	Taha Baadi 6/4 7/6(3)			
22. Taha Baadi *(32)*...........................(CAN)					
(Q) 23. Baptiste Anselmo *(81)*..................(FRA)	Baptiste Anselmo ... 6/2 6/7(2) 8/6				
24. **Keisuke Saitoh [16]** *(18)*...............(JPN)					
25. **Carlos Alcaraz Garfia [10]** *(40)*.....(ESP)	Carlos Alcaraz Garfia [10] ... 6/3 6/2	Carlos Alcaraz Garfia [10] 6/1 6/2	Carlos Alcaraz Garfia [10] 6/4 5/7 8/6		
26. Tyler Zink *(38)*............................(USA)					
27. Matheus Pucinelli De Almeida *(20)*...(BRA)	Matheus Pucinelli De Almeida ... 6/4 6/4				
28. Alejo Lorenzo Lingua Lavallen *(37)* ...(ARG)					
(LL) 29. William Grant *(79)*.....................(USA)	William Grant 6/1 4/6 7/5	William Grant 6/4 7/6(6)			
30. Nini Gabriel Dica *(57)*..................(ROU)					
(WC) 31. Harry Wendelken *(62)*..................(GBR)	Jiri Lehecka [5] 6/2 6/3				
32. **Jiri Lehecka [5]** *(41)*.....................(CZE)					
33. **Toby Kodat [7]** *(9)*.......................(USA)	Tristan Schoolkate 6/0 7/5	Tristan Schoolkate 6/3 6/4	Dalibor Svrcina 6/4 6/2		Shintaro Mochizuki [8] 6/3 6/2
34. Tristan Schoolkate *(33)*................(AUS)					
(Q) 35. Andres Martin *(93)*....................(USA)	Dominic Stephan Stricker 7/5 6/0				
36. Dominic Stephan Stricker *(27)*........(SUI)					
37. Dalibor Svrcina *(53)*....................(CZE)	Dalibor Svrcina 6/1 6/3	Dalibor Svrcina 7/6(3) 3/6 6/3			
38. Wojciech Marek *(48)*....................(POL)					
(WC) 39. Jack Pinnington Jones *(123)*...........(GBR)	Liam Draxl [12] 6/3 6/3				
40. **Liam Draxl [12]** *(14)*....................(CAN)					
41. **Filip Cristian Jianu [13]** *(15)*.........(ROU)	Filip Cristian Jianu [13] .... 7/5 7/6(2)	Filip Cristian Jianu [13] 7/6(7) 6/4	Carlos Gimeno Valero 6/7(2) 6/3 6/2	Carlos Gimeno Valero 4/6 6/3 7/5	Carlos Gimeno Valero 7/6(5) 6/4
(WC) 42. Toby Samuel *(153)*....................(GBR)					
43. Flavio Cobolli *(23)*.......................(ITA)	Flavio Cobolli 6/2 6/1				
44. Sergey Fomin *(30)*........................(UZB)					
(Q) 45. Derrick Chen *(4999)*...................(USA)	Andrew Dale .... 7/6(7) 6/4	Carlos Gimeno Valero 6/1 6/3			
(Q) 46. Andrew Dale *(101)*.......................(USA)					
47. Carlos Gimeno Valero *(51)*............(ESP)	Carlos Gimeno Valero ... 6/7(5) 6/3 6/4				
48. **Thiago Agustin Tirante [3]** *(5)*.........(ARG)					
49. **Brandon Nakashima [6]** *(7)*............(USA)	Brandon Nakashima [6] .... 6/0 7/6(5)	Brandon Nakashima [6] 7/6(4) 6/4	Harold Mayot [17] 6/4 6/4	Harold Mayot [17] 6/4 6/4	
50. Phuong Van Nguyen *(64)*..............(VIE)					
(Q) 51. Nicholas David Ionel *(59)*...........(ROU)	Nicholas David Ionel				
(WC) 52. Jacob Fearnley *(90)*....................(GBR)					
(Q) 53. Natan Rodrigues *(68)*..................(BRA)	Natan Rodrigues .... 6/4 7/6(8)	Harold Mayot [17] 7/5 6/4			
54. Peter Makk *(25)*..........................(HUN)					
55. Dane Sweeny *(24)*.......................(AUS)	Harold Mayot [17] 6/3 6/4				
56. **Harold Mayot [17]** *(19)*................(FRA)					
57. **Shunsuke Mitsui [14]** *(16)*............(JPN)	Shunsuke Mitsui [14] ... 6/7(3) 6/2 6/3	Nicolas Alvarez Varona 6/2 6/3	Illya Beloborodko 7/6(3) 6/4		
58. Juan Bautista Torres *(55)*..............(ARG)					
59. Nicolas Alvarez Varona *(22)*..........(ESP)	Nicolas Alvarez Varona 6/4 6/4				
(WC) 60. Felix Gill *(142)*...........................(GBR)					
61. Illya Beloborodko *(35)*..................(UKR)	Illya Beloborodko 1/6 7/5 6/4	Illya Beloborodko 6/4 5/7 6/4			
62. Eliot Spizzirri *(28)*.......................(USA)					
(WC) 63. James Story *(106)*......................(GBR)	James Story .... 6/4 7/6(3)				
64. **Jonas Forejtek [2]** *(4)*...................(CZE)					

Heavy type denotes seeded players. The figure in brackets against names denotes the order in which they have been seeded. The Committee reserves the right to alter the seeding order in the event of withdrawals.
(WC)=Wild card. (Q)=Qualifier. (LL)=Lucky loser.

THE BOYS' DOUBLES CHAMPIONSHIP 2019

Holders: YANKI EREL (TUR) & OTTO VIRTANEN (FIN)

The Champions will become the holders, for the year only, of a Cup presented by The All England Lawn Tennis and Croquet Club.
The Champions will receive a three-quarter size Cup and the Runners-up will receive Silver Salvers. The matches will be the best of three sets. If the score should reach 12-12 in the final set, the match will be decided by a tie-break.

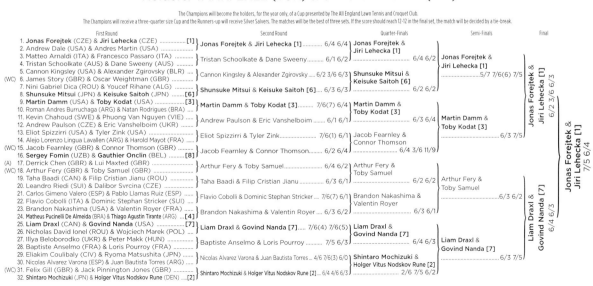

First Round	Second Round	Quarter-Finals	Semi-Finals	Final
1. **Jonas Forejtek (CZE) & Jiri Lehecka (CZE)** ....[1]	Jonas Forejtek & Jiri Lehecka [1] ... 6/4 6/4	Jonas Forejtek & Jiri Lehecka [1] 6/4 6/2	Jonas Forejtek & Jiri Lehecka [1] 5/7 7/6(6) 7/5	Jonas Forejtek & Jiri Lehecka [1] 6/2 3/6 6/3
2. Andrew Dale (USA) & Andres Martin (USA)				
3. Matteo Arnaldi (ITA) & Francesco Passaro (ITA)	Tristan Schoolkate & Dane Sweeny ... 6/1 6/2			
4. Tristan Schoolkate (AUS) & Dane Sweeny (AUS)				
5. Cannon Kingsley (USA) & Alexander Zgirovsky (BLR)	Cannon Kingsley & Alexander Zgirovsky 6/2 3/6 6/3	Shunsuke Mitsui & Keisuke Saitoh [6] 6/2 6/2		
(WC) 6. James Story (GBR) & Oscar Weightman (GBR)				
7. Nini Gabriel Dica (ROU) & Youcef Rihane (ALG)	Shunsuke Mitsui & Keisuke Saitoh [6] 6/3 6/3			
8. **Shunsuke Mitsui (JPN) & Keisuke Saitoh (JPN)** ....[6]				
9. **Martin Damm (USA) & Toby Kodat (USA)** ....[3]	Martin Damm & Toby Kodat [3] .... 7/6(7) 6/4	Martin Damm & Toby Kodat [3] 6/3 6/4	Martin Damm & Toby Kodat [3] 6/3 7/5	
10. Roman Andres Burruchaga (ARG) & Natan Rodrigues (BRA)				
11. Kevin Chahoud (SWE) & Phuong Van Nguyen (VIE)	Andrew Paulson & Eric Vanshelboim ... 6/1 6/1			
12. Andrew Paulson (CZE) & Eric Vanshelboim (UKR)				
13. Eliot Spizzirri (USA) & Tyler Zink (USA)	Eliot Spizzirri & Tyler Zink .... 7/6(1) 6/1	Jacob Fearnley & Connor Thomson 6/4 3/6 11/9		
14. Alejo Lorenzo Lingua Lavallen (ARG) & Harold Mayot (FRA)				
(WC) 15. Jacob Fearnley (GBR) & Connor Thomson (GBR)	Jacob Fearnley & Connor Thomson ... 6/2 6/4			
16. **Sergey Fomin (UZB) & Gauthier Onclin (BEL)** ....[8]				
(A) 17. Derrick Chen (GBR) & Lui Maxted (GBR)	Arthur Fery & Toby Samuel 6/4 6/2	Arthur Fery & Toby Samuel 6/2 6/2	Arthur Fery & Toby Samuel 6/3 6/2	Liam Draxl & Govind Nanda [7] 4/6 6/3
(WC) 18. Arthur Fery (GBR) & Toby Samuel (GBR)				
19. Taha Baadi (CAN) & Filip Cristian Jianu (ROU)	Taha Baadi & Filip Cristian Jianu ... 6/3 6/1			
20. Leandro Riedi (SUI) & Dalibor Svrcina (CZE)				
21. Carlos Gimeno Valero (ESP) & Pablo Llamas Ruiz (ESP)	Flavio Cobolli & Dominic Stephan Stricker ... 7/6(7) 6/1	Brandon Nakashima & Valentin Royer 6/3 6/1		
22. Flavio Cobolli (ITA) & Dominic Stephan Stricker (SUI)				
23. Brandon Nakashima (USA) & Valentin Royer (FRA)	Brandon Nakashima & Valentin Royer ... 6/3 6/2			
24. **Matheus Pucinelli De Almeida (BRA) & Thiago Agustin Tirante (ARG)** ...[4]				
25. **Liam Draxl (CAN) & Govind Nanda (USA)** ....[7]	Liam Draxl & Govind Nanda [7] .... 7/6(4) 7/6(5)	Liam Draxl & Govind Nanda [7] 6/4 6/3	Liam Draxl & Govind Nanda [7] 6/3 7/5	
26. Nicholas David Ionel (ROU) & Wojciech Marek (POL)				
27. Illya Beloborodko (UKR) & Peter Makk (HUN)	Baptiste Anselmo & Loris Pourroy ... 7/5 6/3			
28. Baptiste Anselmo (FRA) & Loris Pourroy (FRA)				
29. Eliakim Coulibaly (CIV) & Ryoma Matsushita (JPN)	Nicolas Alvarez Varona & Juan Bautista Torres ... 4/6 7/6(3) 6/0	Shintaro Mochizuki & Holger Vitus Nodskov Rune [2] 6/3 7/5		
30. Nicolas Alvarez Varona (ESP) & Juan Bautista Torres (ARG)				
(WC) 31. Felix Gill (GBR) & Jack Pinnington Jones (GBR)	Shintaro Mochizuki & Holger Vitus Nodskov Rune [2] ... 6/4 4/6 6/3			
32. **Shintaro Mochizuki (JPN) & Holger Vitus Nodskov Rune (DEN)** .....[2]				

Heavy type denotes seeded players. The figure in brackets against names denotes the order in which they have been seeded. The Committee reserves the right to alter the seeding order in the event of withdrawals.
(WC)=Wild cards. (A)=Alternates.

THE GIRLS' SINGLES CHAMPIONSHIP 2019

Holder: IGA SWIATEK (POL)

The Champion will become the holder, for the year only, of a Cup presented by The All England Lawn Tennis and Croquet Club.
The Champion will receive a three-quarter size Cup and the Runner-up will receive a Silver Salver. The matches will be the best of three sets. If the score should reach 12-12 in the final set, the match will be decided by a tie-break.

First Round

1. **Emma Navarro [1]** *(16)* .... (USA)
2. Diana Shnaider *(37)* .... (RUS)
3. Antonia Samudio *(52)* .... (COL)
4. Selena Janicijevic *(32)* .... (FRA)
5. (WC) Sonay Kartal *(135)* .... (GBR)
6. Annerly Poulos *(56)* .... (AUS)
7. (Q) Katrina Scott *(97)* .... (USA)
8. **Adrienn Nagy [16]** *(26)* .... (HUN)
9. **Mananchaya Sawangkaew [9]** *(15)* .... (THA)
10. Elizabeth Mandlik *(22)* .... (USA)
11. Elina Avanesyan *(68)* .... (RUS)
12. Carlota Martinez Cirez *(48)* .... (ESP)
13. (WC) Emma Raducanu *(85)* .... (GBR)
14. (Q) Martyna Kubka *(115)* .... (POL)
15. Alexandra Vecic *(38)* .... (GER)
16. **Natsumi Kawaguchi [6]** *(13)* .... (JPN)
17. **Qinwen Zheng [3]** *(10)* .... (CHN)
18. Thasaporn Naklo *(51)* .... (THA)
19. Savannah Broadus *(42)* .... (USA)
20. Carole Monnet *(44)* .... (FRA)
21. (Q) Polina Kudermetova *(80)* .... (RUS)
22. (WC) Amarni Banks *(108)* .... (GBR)
23. (Q) Alexandra Yepifanova *(104)* .... (USA)
24. **Helene Pellicano [15]** *(25)* .... (MLT)
25. **Kamilla Bartone [11]** *(17)* .... (LAT)
26. Daria Snigur *(50)* .... (UKR)
27. Kristyna Lavickova *(54)* .... (CZE)
28. (WC) Erin Richardson *(192)* .... (GBR)
29. Marta Custic *(40)* .... (ESP)
30. Robin Montgomery *(55)* .... (USA)
31. (Q) Funa Kozaki *(101)* .... (JPN)
32. **Alina Charaeva [8]** *(19)* .... (RUS)
33. **Hurricane Tyra Black [5]** *(12)* .... (USA)
34. Elsa Jacquemot *(58)* .... (FRA)
35. (Q) Weronika Baszak *(99)* .... (POL)
36. Oksana Selekhmeteva *(27)* .... (RUS)
37. Mai Napatt Nirundorn *(66)* .... (THA)
38. (WC) Holly Fischer *(276)* .... (GBR)
39. Valentina Ryser *(61)* .... (SUI)
40. **Sohyun Park [12]** *(23)* .... (KOR)
41. **Anastasia Tikhonova [13]** *(21)* .... (RUS)
42. Hong Yi Cody Wong *(33)* .... (HKG)
43. Ane Mintegi Del Olmo *(41)* .... (ESP)
44. (WC) Victoria Allen *(105)* .... (GBR)
45. Abigail Forbes *(53)* .... (USA)
46. Liubov Kostenko *(35)* .... (UKR)
47. Darja Semenistaja *(43)* .... (LAT)
48. **Diane Parry [4]** *(8)* .... (FRA)
49. **Sada Nahimana [7]** *(20)* .... (BDI)
50. (WC) Matilda Mutavdzic *(98)* .... (GBR)
51. Daria Frayman *(49)* .... (RUS)
52. Pia Lovric *(63)* .... (SLO)
53. (Q) Charlotte Owensby *(92)* .... (USA)
54. Shavit Kimchi *(46)* .... (ISR)
55. (Q) Amarissa Kiara Toth *(76)* .... (HUN)
56. **Alexa Noel [10]** *(14)* .... (USA)
57. **Joanna Garland [14]** *(18)* .... (TPE)
58. Aubane Droguet *(59)* .... (FRA)
59. Priska Madelyn Nugroho *(57)* .... (INA)
60. Chloe Beck *(62)* .... (USA)
61. Linda Fruhvirtova *(31)* .... (CZE)
62. (WC) Destinee Martins *(139)* .... (GBR)
63. Mell Elizabeth Reasco Gonzalez *(34)* .... (ECU)
64. **Maria Camila Osorio Serrano [2]** *(9)* .... (COL)

Second Round

- **Emma Navarro [1]** 6/0 6/2
- Selena Janicijevic 6/3 6/2
- Sonay Kartal .... 7/6(1) 7/6(3)
- Katrina Scott 6/3 6/4
- Elizabeth Mandlik .... 6/7(2) 7/5 11/9
- Elina Avanesyan 6/3 6/0
- Martyna Kubka 0/6 6/1 7/5
- **Natsumi Kawaguchi [6]** 6/1 5/7 6/4
- **Qinwen Zheng [3]** 6/0 6/2
- Carole Monnet 2/6 7/5 6/2
- Polina Kudermetova 6/1 6/0
- **Helene Pellicano [15]** 1/6 6/3 6/4
- Daria Snigur 6/1 6/4
- Erin Richardson .... 6/2 6/7(5) 6/1
- Robin Montgomery .... 6/4 7/6(5)
- Funa Kozaki 6/2 6/3
- Elsa Jacquemot 6/2 6/0
- Oksana Selekhmeteva 6/2 7/5
- Mai Napatt Nirundorn 7/5 4/6 6/1
- **Sohyun Park [12]** 7/5 4/6 8/6
- Hong Yi Cody Wong 6/4 6/2
- Ane Mintegi Del Olmo 6/3 6/3
- Abigail Forbes .... 6/2 6/7(8) 6/3
- **Diane Parry [4]** 6/3 6/3
- Matilda Mutavdzic 6/3 3/6 6/3
- Daria Frayman 7/5 2/6 8/6
- Charlotte Owensby 6/2 6/2
- **Alexa Noel [10]** 6/4 6/4
- Aubane Droguet 6/2 6/2
- Priska Madelyn Nugroho ... 6/7(7) 6/2 6/4
- Linda Fruhvirtova 6/4 5/7 6/1
- **Maria Camila Osorio Serrano [2]** 6/1 6/2

Third Round

- **Emma Navarro [1]** 4/6 6/4 7/5
- Katrina Scott 6/1 6/4
- Elizabeth Mandlik 6/0 6/0
- **Natsumi Kawaguchi [6]** .... 6/1 7/6(5)
- **Qinwen Zheng [3]** 6/3 4/6 6/2
- Polina Kudermetova .... 6/2 0/0 Ret'd
- Daria Snigur 6/0 6/1
- Robin Montgomery .... 7/6(1) 6/2
- Elsa Jacquemot 7/5 6/1
- Mai Napatt Nirundorn 6/4 3/6 6/3
- Hong Yi Cody Wong 6/1 6/3
- **Diane Parry [4]** .... 7/6(5) 6/4
- Matilda Mutavdzic 4/6 6/3 6/3
- **Alexa Noel [10]** 6/2 6/1
- Priska Madelyn Nugroho 3/6 6/4 6/0
- Linda Fruhvirtova 6/4 6/3

Quarter-Finals

- **Emma Navarro [1]** 0/6 6/1 6/1
- **Natsumi Kawaguchi [6]** .... 3/6 6/4 0/0 Ret'd
- Polina Kudermetova 6/2 6/1
- Daria Snigur .... 6/7(4) 6/1 6/2
- Elsa Jacquemot 7/5 6/0
- **Diane Parry [4]** 6/2 6/3
- **Alexa Noel [10]** 6/4 6/4
- Priska Madelyn Nugroho 4/6 6/3 6/3

Semi-Finals

- **Emma Navarro [1]** 4/6 6/1 6/1
- Daria Snigur 6/2 6/4
- **Diane Parry [4]** 6/1 6/4
- **Alexa Noel [10]** .... 7/6(4) 6/2

Final

- Daria Snigur 6/3 6/0
- **Alexa Noel [10]** 6/2 6/1

Winner: Daria Snigur 6/4 6/4

Heavy type denotes seeded players. The figure in brackets against names denotes the order in which they have been seeded. The Committee reserves the right to alter the seeding order in the event of withdrawals.
(WC)=Wild card. (Q)=Qualifier. LL=Lucky loser.

THE GIRLS' DOUBLES CHAMPIONSHIP 2019

Holders: XINYU WANG (CHN) & XIYU WANG (CHN)

The Champions will become the holders, for the year only, of a Cup presented by The All England Lawn Tennis and Croquet Club. The Champions will receive a three-quarter size Cup and the Runners-up will receive Silver Salvers.
The matches will be the best of three sets. If the score should reach 12-12 in the final set, the match will be decided by a tie-break.

First Round

1. **Diane Parry** (FRA) & **Qinwen Zheng** (CHN) .... [1]
2. Kamilla Bartone (LAT) & Oksana Selekhmeteva (RUS) ...
3. Elina Avanesyan (RUS) & Elsa Jacquemot (FRA) ....
4. Robin Montgomery (USA) & Maria Camila Osorio Serrano (COL) ....
5. Daria Frayman (RUS) & Darja Semenistaja (LAT) ....
6. (WC) Holly Fischer (GBR) & Matilda Mutavdzic (GBR) ....
7. Pia Lovric (SLO) & Mai Napatt Nirundorn (THA) ....
8. **Chloe Beck** (USA) & **Emma Navarro** (USA) .... [7]
9. **Natsumi Kawaguchi** (JPN) & **Adrienn Nagy** (HUN) ... [3]
10. Carole Monnet (FRA) & Hong Yi Cody Wong (HKG) .....
11. Polina Kudermetova (RUS) & Giulia Morlet (FRA) ....
12. (WC) Sonay Kartal (GBR) & Erin Richardson (GBR) ....
13. Funa Kozaki (JPN) & Amarissa Kiara Toth (HUN) ....
14. Mell Elizabeth Reasco Gonzalez (ECU) & Antonia Samudio (COL) ....
15. Carlota Martinez Cirez (ESP) & Ane Mintegi Del Olmo (ESP) ....
16. (A) Michaela Kadleckova (SVK) & Katrina Scott (USA) ....
17. **Hurricane Tyra Black** (USA) & **Shavit Kimchi** (ISR) ..... [8]
18. Romana Cisovska (SVK) & Diana Shnaider (RUS) ....
19. Aubane Droguet (FRA) & Selena Janicijevic (FRA) ....
20. Priska Madelyn Nugroho (INA) & Annerly Poulos (AUS) ....
21. Valentina Ryser (SUI) & Alexandra Vecic (GER) ....
22. (WC) Victoria Allen (GBR) & Destinee Martins (GBR) ....
23. Charlotte Owensby (USA) & Alexandra Yepifanova (USA) ...
24. **Joanna Garland** (TPE) & **Sohyun Park** (KOR) .... [4]
25. **Liubov Kostenko** (UKR) & **Sada Nahimana** (BDI) ..... [6]
26. Savannah Broadus (USA) & Abigail Forbes (USA) ....
27. Weronika Baszak (POL) & Martyna Kubka (POL) ....
28. (WC) Amelia Bissett (GBR) & Morgan Cross (GBR) ....
29. Thasaporn Naklo (THA) & Mananchaya Sawangkaew (THA) ....
30. Linda Fruhvirtova (CZE) & Kristyna Lavickova (CZE) ....
31. Marta Custic (ESP) & Elizabeth Mandlik (USA) ....
32. **Alina Charaeva** (RUS) & **Anastasia Tikhonova** (RUS) ... [2]

Second Round

- Kamilla Bartone & Oksana Selekhmeteva..... 7/5 6/4
- Robin Montgomery & Maria Camila Osorio Serrano.... 6/2 6/4
- Holly Fischer & Matilda Mutavdzic ..... 7/6(5) 6/4
- **Chloe Beck** & **Emma Navarro [7]**....... 7/6(5) 6/3
- **Natsumi Kawaguchi** & **Adrienn Nagy [3]**.... 2/6 6/3 6/4
- Polina Kudermetova & Giulia Morlet......... 6/1 6/4
- Funa Kozaki & Amarissa Kiara Toth......... 6/3 6/2
- Carlota Martinez Cirez & Ane Mintegi Del Olmo... 3/6 7/6(4) 6/3
- **Hurricane Tyra Black** & **Shavit Kimchi [8]**.... 6/4 6/4
- Aubane Droguet & Selena Janicijevic..... 6/2 6/4
- Valentina Ryser & Alexandra Vecic.... 3/6 7/5 6/4
- **Joanna Garland** & **Sohyun Park [4]**......... 6/3 6/2
- Savannah Broadus & Abigail Forbes........ 6/1 6/4
- Weronika Baszak & Martyna Kubka... 4/6 6/4 6/2
- Linda Fruhvirtova & Kristyna Lavickova.... 6/3 3/6 5/3 Ret'd
- **Alina Charaeva** & **Anastasia Tikhonova [2]**.... 7/6(4) 4/6 6/4

Quarter-Finals

- Kamilla Bartone & Oksana Selekhmeteva 6/4 6/4
- **Chloe Beck** & **Emma Navarro [7]** 6/3 5/7 6/4
- Polina Kudermetova & Giulia Morlet 4/6 6/4 7/5
- Funa Kozaki & Amarissa Kiara Toth 6/4 6/1
- Aubane Droguet & Selena Janicijevic 7/5 6/0
- **Joanna Garland** & **Sohyun Park [4]** 6/4 6/4
- Savannah Broadus & Abigail Forbes 6/4 7/5
- **Alina Charaeva** & **Anastasia Tikhonova [2]** .... 4/6 7/6(4) 6/3

Semi-Finals

- Kamilla Bartone & Oksana Selekhmeteva 6/4 6/3
- Polina Kudermetova & Giulia Morlet .... 7/6(9) 6/4
- Aubane Droguet & Selena Janicijevic 6/2 6/3
- Savannah Broadus & Abigail Forbes .... 6/7(3) 6/3 9/7

Final

- Kamilla Bartone & Oksana Selekhmeteva 7/6(6) 7/5
- Savannah Broadus & Abigail Forbes 6/1 6/1

Winners: Savannah Broadus & Abigail Forbes 7/5 5/7 6/2

Heavy type denotes seeded players. The figure in brackets against names denotes the order in which they have been seeded. The Committee reserves the right to alter the seeding order in the event of withdrawals.
(WC)=Wild cards. (A)=Alternates.

THE GENTLEMEN'S INVITATION DOUBLES 2019
Holders: TOMMY HAAS (GER) & MARK PHILIPPOUSSIS (AUS)

The Champions will become the holders, for the year only, of a Cup presented by The All England Lawn Tennis and Croquet Club. The Champions will receive a silver three-quarter size Cup. A Silver Medal will be presented to each of the Runners-up.
The matches will be the best of three sets. If a match should reach one set all a 10-point tie-break will replace the third set.

GROUP A	Arnaud Clement (FRA) & Michael Llodra (FRA)	Colin Fleming (GBR) & Ross Hutchins (GBR)	Fernando Gonzalez (CHI) & Sebastien Grosjean (FRA)	Tommy Haas (GER) & Mark Philippoussis (AUS)	Wins	Losses
Arnaud Clement (FRA) & Michael Llodra (FRA)		7/6(4) 7/6(3) W	6/3 3/6 [11-9] W	6/3 6/4 W	3	0
Colin Fleming (GBR) & Ross Hutchins (GBR)	6/7(4) 6/7(3) L		7/5 6/4 W	3/6 7/6(6) [10-7] W	2	1
Fernando Gonzalez (CHI) & Sebastien Grosjean (FRA)	3/6 6/3 [9-11] L	5/7 4/6 L		3/6 7/6(3) [7-10] L	0	3
Tommy Haas (GER) & Mark Philippoussis (AUS)	3/6 4/6 L	6/3 6/7(6) [7-10] L	6/3 6/7(3) [10-7] W		1	2

Final: Arnaud Clement & Michael Llodra

GROUP B	Mario Ancic (CRO) & Wayne Black (ZIM)	Jamie Delgado (GBR) & Jonathan Marray (GBR)	Thomas Enqvist (SWE) & Thomas Johansson (SWE)	Xavier Malisse (BEL) & Max Mirnyi (BLR)	Wins	Losses
Mario Ancic (CRO) & Wayne Black (ZIM)		7/6(6) 6/4 W	7/6(6) 7/5 W	3/6 4/6 L	2	1
Jamie Delgado (GBR) & Jonathan Marray (GBR)	6/7(6) 4/6 L		6/2 6/7(7) [8-10] L	6/7(5) 2/6 L	0	3
Thomas Enqvist (SWE) & Thomas Johansson (SWE)	6/7(6) 5/7 L	2/6 7/6(7) [10-8] W		2/6 7/6(4) [7-10] L	1	2
Xavier Malisse (BEL) & Max Mirnyi (BLR)	6/3 6/4 W	7/6(5) 6/2 W	6/2 6/7(4) [10-7] W		3	0

Final: Xavier Malisse & Max Mirnyi

Champions: Arnaud Clement & Michael Llodra 6/3 1/6 [10-7]

This event consists of eight invited pairs divided into two groups, playing each other within their group on a 'round robin' basis. The group winner is the pair with the highest number of wins.
In the case of a tie the winning pair may be determined by head to head results or a formula based on percentage of sets/games won to those played.

THE GENTLEMEN'S SENIOR INVITATION DOUBLES 2019
Holders: JONAS BJORKMAN (SWE) & TODD WOODBRIDGE (AUS)

The Champions will become the holders, for the year only, of a Cup presented by The All England Lawn Tennis and Croquet Club. The Champions will receive a silver half-size Cup. A Silver Medal will be presented to each of the Runners-up.
The matches will be the best of three sets. If a match should reach one set all a 10-point tie-break will replace the third set.

GROUP A	Mansour Bahrami (FRA) & Chris Wilkinson (GBR)	Jeremy Bates (GBR) & Andrew Castle (GBR)	Jonas Bjorkman (SWE) & Todd Woodbridge (AUS)	Wayne Ferreira (RSA) & Mark Woodforde (AUS)	Wins	Losses
Mansour Bahrami (FRA) & Chris Wilkinson (GBR)		4/6 6/3 [4-10] L	4/6 3/6 L	3/6 5/7 L	0	3
Jeremy Bates (GBR) & Andrew Castle (GBR)	6/4 3/6 [10-4] W		4/6 2/6 L	5/7 6/7(3) L	1	2
Jonas Bjorkman (SWE) & Todd Woodbridge (AUS)	6/4 6/3 W	6/4 6/2 W		6/3 6/3 W	3	0
Wayne Ferreira (RSA) & Mark Woodforde (AUS)	6/3 7/5 W	7/5 7/6(3) W	3/6 3/6 L		2	1

Final: Jonas Bjorkman & Todd Woodbridge

GROUP B	Jacco Eltingh (NED) & Paul Haarhuis (NED)	Richard Krajicek (NED) & Mark Petchey (GBR)	Henri Leconte (FRA) & Patrick McEnroe (USA)	Greg Rusedski (GBR) & Fabrice Santoro (FRA)	Wins	Losses
Jacco Eltingh (NED) & Paul Haarhuis (NED)		5/7 6/1 [10-7] W	6/3 7/5 W	3/6 1/1 Ret'd W	3	0
Richard Krajicek (NED) & Mark Petchey (GBR)	7/5 1/6 [7-10] L		6/3 6/4 W	5/7 3/6 L	1	2
Henri Leconte (FRA) & Patrick McEnroe (USA)	3/6 5/7 L	3/6 4/6 L		4/6 2/6 L	0	3
Greg Rusedski (GBR) & Fabrice Santoro (FRA)	6/3 1/1 Ret'd L	7/5 6/3 W	6/4 6/2 W		2	1

Final: Jacco Eltingh & Paul Haarhuis

Champions: Jonas Bjorkman & Todd Woodbridge 4/6 6/3 [10-6]

This event consists of eight invited pairs divided into two groups, playing each other within their group on a 'round robin' basis. The group winner is the pair with the highest number of wins.
In the case of a tie the winning pair may be determined by head to head results or a formula based on percentage of sets/games won to those played.

THE LADIES' INVITATION DOUBLES 2019
Holders: KIM CLIJSTERS (BEL) & RENNAE STUBBS (AUS)

The Champions will become the holders, for the year only, of a Cup presented by The All England Lawn Tennis and Croquet Club. The Champions will receive a silver three-quarter size Cup. A Silver Medal will be presented to each of the Runners-up.
The matches will be the best of three sets. If a match should reach one set all a 10-point tie-break will replace the third set.

GROUP A	Tracy Austin (USA) & Andrea Jaeger (USA)	Marion Bartoli (FRA) & Daniela Hantuchova (SVK)	Kim Clijsters (BEL) & Rennae Stubbs (AUS)	Conchita Martinez (ESP) & Barbara Schett (AUT)	Results Wins	Results Losses	Final
Tracy Austin (USA) & Andrea Jaeger (USA)		3/6 2/6 L	Walk Over W	2/6 3/6 L	1	2	
Marion Bartoli (FRA) & Daniela Hantuchova (SVK)	6/3 6/2 W		3/6 4/6 L	6/3 2/6 [11-9] W	2	1	Marion Bartoli & Daniela Hantuchova
Kim Clijsters (BEL) & Rennae Stubbs (AUS)	Walk Over L	6/3 6/4 W		6/3 6/2 W	2	1	
Conchita Martinez (ESP) & Barbara Schett (AUT)	6/2 6/3 W	3/6 6/2 [9-11] L	3/6 2/6 L		1	2	

GROUP B	Cara Black (ZIM) & Martina Navratilova (USA)	Mary Joe Fernandez (USA) & Ai Sugiyama (JPN)	Anne Keothavong (GBR) & Arantxa Sanchez Vicario (ESP)	Iva Majoli (CRO) & Magdalena Maleeva (BUL)	Results Wins	Results Losses	
Cara Black (ZIM) & Martina Navratilova (USA)		6/3 6/3 W	6/3 6/2 W	6/3 6/4 W	3	0	Cara Black & Martina Navratilova
Mary Joe Fernandez (USA) & Ai Sugiyama (JPN)	3/6 3/6 L		6/2 7/6(6) W	6/3 0/6 [10-4] W	2	1	
Anne Keothavong (GBR) & Arantxa Sanchez Vicario (ESP)	3/6 2/6 L	2/6 6/7(6) L		4/6 4/6 L	0	3	
Iva Majoli (CRO) & Magdalena Maleeva (BUL)	3/6 4/6 L	3/6 6/0 [4-10] L	6/4 6/4 W		1	2	

Final: Cara Black & Martina Navratilova 6/0 3/6 [10-8]

This event consists of eight invited pairs divided into two groups, playing each other within their group on a 'round robin' basis. The group winner is the pair with the highest number of wins.
In the case of a tie the winning pair may be determined by head to head results or a formula based on percentage of sets/games won to those played.

COUNTRIES IN THE CHAMPIONSHIPS 2019 – ABBREVIATIONS

ALG	Algeria	CZE	Czech Republic
ARG	Argentina	DEN	Denmark
AUS	Australia	ECU	Ecuador
AUT	Austria	ESA	El Salvador
BDI	Burundi	ESP	Spain
BEL	Belgium	EST	Estonia
BIH	Bosnia-Herzegovina	FIN	Finland
BLR	Belarus	FRA	France
BOL	Bolivia	GBR	Great Britain
BRA	Brazil	GEO	Georgia
BUL	Bulgaria	GER	Germany
CAN	Canada	GRE	Greece
CHI	Chile	HKG	Hong Kong
CHN	China	HUN	Hungary
CIV	Ivory Coast	INA	Indonesia
COL	Colombia	IND	India
CRO	Croatia	ISR	Israel
CYP	Cyprus		

ITA	Italy	PUR	Puerto Rico
JPN	Japan	ROU	Romania
KAZ	Kazakhstan	RSA	South Africa
KOR	South Korea	RUS	Russia
LAT	Latvia	SLO	Slovenia
LTU	Lithuania	SRB	Serbia
LUX	Luxembourg	SUI	Switzerland
MDA	Moldova	SVK	Slovakia
MEX	Mexico	SWE	Sweden
MLT	Malta	THA	Thailand
MON	Monaco	TPE	Chinese Taipei
NED	Netherlands	TUN	Tunisia
NOR	Norway	UKR	Ukraine
NZL	New Zealand	URU	Uruguay
PAK	Pakistan	USA	USA
POL	Poland	UZB	Uzbekistan
POR	Portugal	VIE	Vietnam
		ZIM	Zimbabwe

THE ROLLS OF HONOUR
GENTLEMEN'S SINGLES CHAMPIONS & RUNNERS-UP

1877 S.W.Gore *W.C.Marshall*	1904 H.L.Doherty *F.L.Riseley*	1935 F.J.Perry *G.von Cramm*	1968 R.G.Laver *A.D.Roche*	1995 P.Sampras *B.F.Becker*	
1878 P.F.Hadow *S.W.Gore*	1905 H.L.Doherty *N.E.Brookes*	1936 F.J.Perry *G.von Cramm*	1969 R.G.Laver *J.D.Newcombe*	1996 R.P.S.Krajicek *M.O.Washington*	
*1879 J.T.Hartley *V.T.St.L.Goold*	1906 H.L.Doherty *F.L.Riseley*	*1937 J.D.Budge *G.von Cramm*	1970 J.D.Newcombe *K.R.Rosewall*	1997 P.Sampras *C.A.Pioline*	
1880 J.T.Hartley *H.F.Lawford*	*1907 N.E.Brookes *A.W.Gore*	1938 J.D.Budge *H.W.Austin*	1971 J.D.Newcombe *S.R.Smith*	1998 P.Sampras *G.S.Ivanisevic*	
1881 W.C.Renshaw *J.T.Hartley*	*1908 A.W.Gore *H.R.Barrett*	*1939 R.L.Riggs *E.T.Cooke*	*1972 S.R.Smith *I.Nastase*	1999 P.Sampras *A.K.Agassi*	
1882 W.C.Renshaw *J.E.Renshaw*	1909 A.W.Gore *M.J.G.Ritchie*	*1946 Y.F.M.Petra *G.E.Brown*	*1973 J.Kodes *A.Metreveli*	2000 P.Sampras *P.M.Rafter*	
1883 W.C.Renshaw *J.E.Renshaw*	1910 A.F.Wilding *A.W.Gore*	1947 J.A.Kramer *T.P.Brown*	1974 J.S.Connors *K.R.Rosewall*	2001 G.Ivanisevic *P.M.Rafter*	
1884 W.C.Renshaw *H.F.Lawford*	1911 A.F.Wilding *H.R.Barrett*	*1948 R.Falkenburg *J.E.Bromwich*	1975 A.R.Ashe *J.S.Connors*	2002 L.G.Hewitt *D.P.Nalbandian*	
1885 W.C.Renshaw *H.F.Lawford*	1912 A.F.Wilding *A.W.Gore*	1949 F.R.Schroeder *J.Drobny*	1976 B.R.Borg *I.Nastase*	2003 R.Federer *M.A.Philippoussis*	
1886 W.C.Renshaw *H.F.Lawford*	1913 A.F.Wilding *M.E.McLoughlin*	*1950 J.E.Patty *F.A.Sedgman*	1977 B.R.Borg *J.S.Connors*	2004 R.Federer *A.S.Roddick*	
*1887 H.F.Lawford *J.E.Renshaw*	1914 N.E.Brookes *A.F.Wilding*	1951 R.Savitt *K.B.McGregor*	1978 B.R.Borg *J.S.Connors*	2005 R.Federer *A.S.Roddick*	
1888 J.E.Renshaw *H.F.Lawford*	1919 G.L.Patterson *N.E.Brookes*	1952 F.A.Sedgman *J.Drobny*	1979 B.R.Borg *L.R.Tanner*	2006 R.Federer *R.Nadal*	
1889 W.C.Renshaw *J.E.Renshaw*	1920 W.T.Tilden *G.L.Patterson*	*1953 E.V.Seixas *K.Nielsen*	1980 B.Borg *J.P.McEnroe*	2007 R.Federer *R.Nadal*	
1890 W.J.Hamilton *W.C.Renshaw*	1921 W.T.Tilden *B.I.C.Norton*	1954 J.Drobny *K.R.Rosewall*	1981 J.P.McEnroe *B.R.Borg*	2008 R.Nadal *R.Federer*	
*1891 W.Baddeley *J.Pim*	*†1922 G.L.Patterson *R.Lycett*	1955 M.A.Trabert *K.Nielsen*	1982 J.S.Connors *J.P.McEnroe*	2009 R.Federer *A.S.Roddick*	
1892 W.Baddeley *J.Pim*	*1923 W.M.Johnston *F.T.Hunter*	*1956 L.A.Hoad *K.R.Rosewall*	1983 J.P.McEnroe *C.J.Lewis*	2010 R.Nadal *T.Berdych*	
1893 J.Pim *W.Baddeley*	*1924 J.R.Borotra *J.R.Lacoste*	1957 L.A.Hoad *A.J.Cooper*	1984 J.P.McEnroe *J.S.Connors*	2011 N.Djokovic *R.Nadal*	
1894 J.Pim *W.Baddeley*	1925 J.R.Lacoste *J.R.Borotra*	*1958 A.J.Cooper *N.A.Fraser*	1985 B.F.Becker *K.M.Curren*	2012 R.Federer *A.B.Murray*	
*1895 W.Baddeley *W.V.Eaves*	*1926 J.R.Borotra *H.O.Kinsey*	*1959 A.R.Olmedo *R.G.Laver*	1986 B.F.Becker *I.Lendl*	2013 A.B.Murray *N.Djokovic*	
1896 H.S.Mahony *W.Baddeley*	1927 H.J.Cochet *J.R.Borotra*	*1960 N.A.Fraser *R.G.Laver*	1987 P.H.Cash *I.Lendl*	2014 N.Djokovic *R.Federer*	
1897 R.F.Doherty *H.S.Mahony*	1928 J.R.Lacoste *H.J.Cochet*	1961 R.G.Laver *C.R.McKinley*	1988 S.B.Edberg *B.F.Becker*	2015 N.Djokovic *R.Federer*	
1898 R.F.Doherty *H.L.Doherty*	*1929 H.J.Cochet *J.R.Borotra*	1962 R.G.Laver *M.F.Mulligan*	1989 B.F.Becker *S.B.Edberg*	2016 A.B.Murray *M.Raonic*	
1899 R.F.Doherty *A.W.Gore*	1930 W.T.Tilden *W.L.Allison*	*1963 C.R.McKinley *F.S.Stolle*	1990 S.B.Edberg *B.F.Becker*	2017 R.Federer *M.Cilic*	
1900 R.F.Doherty *S.H.Smith*	*1931 S.B.B.Wood *F.X.Shields*	1964 R.S.Emerson *F.S.Stolle*	1991 M.D.Stich *B.F.Becker*	2018 N.Djokovic *K.Anderson*	
1901 A.W.Gore *R.F.Doherty*	1932 H.E.Vines *H.W.Austin*	1965 R.S.Emerson *F.S.Stolle*	1992 A.K.Agassi *G.S.Ivanisevic*	2019 N.Djokovic *R.Federer*	
1902 H.L.Doherty *A.W.Gore*	1933 J.H.Crawford *H.E.Vines*	1966 M.M.Santana *R.D.Ralston*	1993 P.Sampras *J.S.Courier*		
1903 H.L.Doherty *F.L.Riseley*	1934 F.J.Perry *J.H.Crawford*	1967 J.D.Newcombe *W.P.Bungert*	1994 P.Sampras *G.S.Ivanisevic*		

For the years 1913, 1914 and 1919-1923 inclusive the above records include the "World's Championships on Grass" granted to The Lawn Tennis Association by The International Lawn Tennis Federation. This title was then abolished and commencing in 1924 they became The Official Lawn Tennis Championships recognised by The International Lawn Tennis Federation.
Prior to 1922 the holders in the Singles Events and Gentlemen's Doubles did not compete in The Championships but met the winners of these events in the Challenge Rounds.
† Challenge Round abolished: holders subsequently played through.
* The holder did not defend the title.

LADIES' SINGLES CHAMPIONS & RUNNERS-UP

1884 Miss M.E.E.Watson *Miss L.M.Watson*	1910 Mrs.R.L.Chambers *Miss P.D.H.Boothby*	*1946 Miss P.M.Betz *Miss A.L.Brough*	1972 Mrs.L.W.King *Miss E.F.Goolagong*	*1997 Miss M.Hingis *Miss J.Novotna*
1885 Miss M.E.E.Watson *Miss B.Bingley*	1911 Mrs.R.L.Chambers *Miss P.D.H.Boothby*	*1947 Miss M.E.Osborne *Miss D.J.Hart*	1973 Mrs.L.W.King *Miss C.M.Evert*	1998 Miss J.Novotna *Miss N.Tauziat*
1886 Miss B.Bingley *Miss M.E.E.Watson*	*1912 Mrs.D.T.R.Larcombe *Mrs.A.Sterry*	1948 Miss A.L.Brough *Miss D.J.Hart*	1974 Miss C.M.Evert *Mrs.O.V.Morozova*	1999 Miss L.A.Davenport *Miss S.M.Graf*
1887 Miss C.Dod *Miss B.Bingley*	*1913 Mrs.R.L.Chambers *Mrs.R.J.McNair*	1949 Miss A.L.Brough *Mrs.W.du Pont*	1975 Mrs.L.W.King *Mrs.R.A.Cawley*	2000 Miss V.E.S.Williams *Miss L.A.Davenport*
1888 Miss C.Dod *Mrs.G.W.Hillyard*	1914 Mrs.R.L.Chambers *Mrs.D.T.R.Larcombe*	1950 Miss A.L.Brough *Mrs.W.du Pont*	*1976 Miss C.M.Evert *Mrs.R.A.Cawley*	2001 Miss V.E.S.Williams *Miss J.Henin*
*1889 Mrs.G.W.Hillyard *Miss H.G.B.Rice*	1919 Miss S.R.F.Lenglen *Mrs.R.L.Chambers*	1951 Miss D.J.Hart *Miss S.J.Fry*	1977 Miss S.V.Wade *Miss B.F.Stove*	2002 Miss S.J.Williams *Miss V.E.S.Williams*
*1890 Miss H.G.B.Rice *Miss M.Jacks*	1920 Miss S.R.F.Lenglen *Mrs.R.L.Chambers*	1952 Miss M.C.Connolly *Miss A.L.Brough*	1978 Miss M.Navratilova *Miss C.M.Evert*	2003 Miss S.J.Williams *Miss V.E.S.Williams*
*1891 Miss C.Dod *Mrs.G.W.Hillyard*	1921 Miss S.R.F.Lenglen *Miss E.M.Ryan*	1953 Miss M.C.Connolly *Miss D.J.Hart*	1979 Miss M.Navratilova *Mrs.J.M.Lloyd*	2004 Miss M.Sharapova *Miss S.J.Williams*
1892 Miss C.Dod *Mrs.G.W.Hillyard*	†1922 Miss S.R.F.Lenglen *Mrs.F.I.Mallory*	1954 Miss M.C.Connolly *Miss A.L.Brough*	1980 Mrs.R.A.Cawley *Mrs.J.M.Lloyd*	2005 Miss V.E.S.Williams *Miss L.A.Davenport*
1893 Miss C.Dod *Mrs.G.W.Hillyard*	1923 Miss S.R.F.Lenglen *Miss K.McKane*	*1955 Miss A.L.Brough *Mrs.J.G.Fleitz*	*1981 Mrs.J.M.Lloyd *Miss H.Mandlikova*	2006 Miss A.Mauresmo *Mrs.J.Henin-Hardenne*
*1894 Mrs.G.W.Hillyard *Miss E.L.Austin*	1924 Miss K.McKane *Miss H.N.Wills*	1956 Miss S.J.Fry *Miss A.Buxton*	1982 Miss M.Navratilova *Mrs.J.M.Lloyd*	2007 Miss V.E.S.Williams *Miss M.S.Bartoli*
*1895 Miss C.R.Cooper *Miss H.Jackson*	1925 Miss S.R.F.Lenglen *Miss J.C.Fry*	*1957 Miss A.Gibson *Miss D.R.Hard*	1983 Miss M.Navratilova *Miss A.Jaeger*	2008 Miss V.E.S.Williams *Miss S.J.Williams*
1896 Miss C.R.Cooper *Mrs.W.H.Pickering*	1926 Mrs.L.A.Godfree *Miss E.M.de Alvarez*	1958 Miss A.Gibson *Miss F.A.M.Mortimer*	1984 Miss M.Navratilova *Mrs.J.M.Lloyd*	2009 Miss S.J.Williams *Miss V.E.S.Williams*
1897 Mrs.G.W.Hillyard *Miss C.R.Cooper*	1927 Miss H.Wills *Miss E.M.de Alvarez*	*1959 Miss M.E.A.Bueno *Miss D.R.Hard*	1985 Miss M.Navratilova *Mrs.J.M.Lloyd*	2010 Miss S.J.Williams *Miss V.Zvonareva*
*1898 Miss C.R.Cooper *Miss M.L.Martin*	1928 Miss H.N.Wills *Miss E.M.de Alvarez*	1960 Miss M.E.A.Bueno *Miss S.Reynolds*	1986 Miss M.Navratilova *Miss H.Mandlikova*	2011 Miss P.Kvitova *Miss M.Sharapova*
1899 Mrs.G.W.Hillyard *Miss C.R.Cooper*	1929 Miss H.N.Wills *Miss H.H.Jacobs*	*1961 Miss F.A.M.Mortimer *Miss C.C.Truman*	1987 Miss M.Navratilova *Miss S.M.Graf*	2012 Miss S.J.Williams *Miss A.R.Radwanska*
1900 Mrs.G.W.Hillyard *Miss C.R.Cooper*	1930 Mrs.F.S.Moody *Miss E.M.Ryan*	1962 Mrs.J.R.Susman *Mrs.C.Sukova*	1988 Miss S.M.Graf *Miss M.Navratilova*	2013 Miss M.S.Bartoli *Miss S.Lisicki*
1901 Mrs.A.Sterry *Mrs.G.W.Hillyard*	*1931 Miss C.Aussem *Miss H.Krahwinkel*	*1963 Miss M.Smith *Miss B.J.Moffitt*	1989 Miss S.M.Graf *Miss M.Navratilova*	2014 Miss P.Kvitova *Miss E.C.M.Bouchard*
1902 Miss M.E.Robb *Mrs.A.Sterry*	*1932 Mrs.F.S.Moody *Miss H.H.Jacobs*	1964 Miss M.E.A.Bueno *Miss M.Smith*	1990 Miss M.Navratilova *Miss Z.L.Garrison*	2015 Miss S.J.Williams *Miss G.Muguruza*
*1903 Miss D.K.Douglass *Miss E.W.Thomson*	1933 Mrs.F.S.Moody *Miss D.E.Round*	1965 Miss M.Smith *Miss M.E.A.Bueno*	1991 Miss S.M.Graf *Miss G.B.Sabatini*	2016 Miss S.J.Williams *Miss A.Kerber*
1904 Miss D.K.Douglass *Mrs.A.Sterry*	*1934 Miss D.E.Round *Miss H.H.Jacobs*	1966 Mrs.L.W.King *Miss M.E.A.Bueno*	1992 Miss S.M.Graf *Miss M.Seles*	2017 Miss G.Muguruza *Miss V.E.S.Williams*
1905 Miss M.G.Sutton *Miss D.K.Douglass*	1935 Mrs.F.S.Moody *Miss H.H.Jacobs*	1967 Mrs.L.W.King *Mrs.P.F.Jones*	1993 Miss S.M.Graf *Miss J.Novotna*	2018 Miss A.Kerber *Mrs.S.J.Williams*
1906 Miss D.K.Douglass *Miss M.G.Sutton*	*1936 Miss H.H.Jacobs *Miss S.Sperling*	1968 Mrs.L.W.King *Miss J.A.M.Tegart*	1994 Miss I.C.Martinez *Miss M.Navratilova*	2019 Miss S.Halep *Mrs.S.J.Williams*
1907 Miss M.G.Sutton *Mrs.R.L.Chambers*	1937 Mrs.D.E.Round *Miss J.Jedrzejowska*	1969 Mrs.P.F.Jones *Mrs.L.W.King*	1995 Miss S.M.Graf *Miss A.I.M.Sanchez Vicario*	
*1908 Mrs.A.Sterry *Miss A.M.Morton*	*1938 Mrs.F.S.Moody *Miss H.H.Jacobs*	*1970 Mrs.B.M.Court *Mrs.L.W.King*	1996 Miss S.M.Graf *Miss A.I.M.Sanchez Vicario*	
*1909 Miss P.D.H.Boothby *Miss A.M.Morton*	*1939 Miss A.Marble *Miss K.E.Stammers*	1971 Miss E.F.Goolagong *Mrs.B.M.Court*		

MAIDEN NAMES OF LADIES' CHAMPIONS (In the tables the following have been recorded in both married and single identities)

Mrs. R. Cawley .... Miss E. F. Goolagong	Mrs. G. W. Hillyard .... Miss B. Bingley	Mrs. G. E. Reid .... Miss K. Melville	
Mrs. R. L. Chambers .... Miss D. K. Douglass	Mrs. P. F. Jones .... Miss A. S. Haydon	Mrs. P. D. Smylie .... Miss E. M. Sayers	
Mrs. B. M. Court .... Miss M. Smith	Mrs. L. W. King .... Miss B. J. Moffitt	Mrs. S. Sperling .... Fräulein H. Krahwinkel	
Mrs. B. C. Covell .... Miss P. L. Howkins	Mrs. M. R. King .... Miss P. E. Mudford	Mrs. A. Sterry .... Miss C.R. Cooper	
Mrs. D. E. Dalton .... Miss J. A. M. Tegart	Mrs. D. R. Larcombe .... Miss E. W. Thomson	Mrs. J. R. Susman .... Miss K. Hantze	
Mrs. W. du Pont .... Miss M.E. Osborne	Mrs. J. M. Lloyd .... Miss C. M. Evert		
Mrs. L. A. Godfree .... Miss K. McKane	Mrs. F. S. Moody .... Miss H.N. Wills		
Mrs. R.L. Cawley .... Miss H. F. Gourlay	Mrs. O.V. Morozova .... Miss O.V. Morozova		
Mrs. J. Henin-Hardenne .... Miss J. Henin	Mrs. L. E. G. Price .... Miss S. Reynolds		

GENTLEMEN'S DOUBLES CHAMPIONS & RUNNERS-UP

1879	L.R.Erskine and H.F.Lawford *F.Durant and G.E.Tabor*		
1880	W.C.Renshaw and J.E.Renshaw *O.E.Woodhouse and C.J.Cole*		
1881	W.C.Renshaw and J.E.Renshaw *W.J.Down and H.Vaughan*		
1882	J.T.Hartley and R.T.Richardson *J.G.Horn and C.B.Russell*		
1883	C.W.Grinstead and C.E.Welldon *C.B.Russell and R.T.Milford*		
1884	W.C.Renshaw and J.E.Renshaw *E.W.Lewis and E.L.Williams*		
1885	W.C.Renshaw and J.E.Renshaw *C.E.Farrer and A.J.Stanley*		
1886	W.C.Renshaw and J.E.Renshaw *C.E.Farrer and A.J.Stanley*		
1887	P.B.Lyon and H.W.W.Wilberforce *J.H.Crispe and E.Barratt-Smith*		
1888	W.C.Renshaw and J.E.Renshaw *P B.Lyon and H.W.W.Wilberforce*		
1889	W.C.Renshaw and J.E.Renshaw *E.W.Lewis and G.W.Hillyard*		
1890	J.Pim and F.O.Stoker *E.W.Lewis and G.W.Hillyard*		
1891	W.Baddeley and H.Baddeley *J.Pim and F.O.Stoker*		
1892	H.S.Barlow and E.W.Lewis *W.Baddeley and H.Baddeley*		
1893	J.Pim and F.O.Stoker *E.W.Lewis and H.S.Barlow*		
1894	W.Baddeley and H.Baddeley *H.S.Barlow and C.H.Martin*		
1895	W.Baddeley and H.Baddeley *E.W.Lewis and W.V.Eaves*		
1896	W.Baddeley and H.Baddeley *R.F.Doherty and H.A.Nisbet*		
1897	R.F.Doherty and H.L.Doherty *W.Baddeley and H.Baddeley*		
1898	R.F.Doherty and H.L.Doherty *H.A.Nisbet and C.Hobart*		
1899	R.F.Doherty and H.L.Doherty *H.A.Nisbet and C.Hobart*		
1900	R.F.Doherty and H.L.Doherty *H.R.Barrett and H.A.Nisbet*		
1901	R.F.Doherty and H.L.Doherty *D.Davis and H.Ward*		
1902	S.H.Smith and F.L.Riseley *R.F.Doherty and H.L.Doherty*		
1903	R.F.Doherty and H.L.Doherty *S.H.Smith and F.L.Riseley*		
1904	R.F.Doherty and H.L.Doherty *S.H.Smith and F.L.Riseley*		
1905	R.F.Doherty and H.L.Doherty *S.H.Smith and F.L.Riseley*		
1906	S.H.Smith and F.L.Riseley *R.F.Doherty and H.L.Doherty*		
1907	N.E.Brookes and A.F.Wilding *B.C.Wright and K.Behr*		
1908	A.F.Wilding and M.J.G.Ritchie *A.W.Gore and H.R.Barrett*		
1909	A.W.Gore and H.R.Barrett *S.N.Doust and H.A.Parker*		
1910	A.F.Wilding and M.J.G.Ritchie *A.W.Gore and H.R.Barrett*		
1911	M.O.M.Decugis and A.H.Gobert *M.J.G.Ritchie and A.F.Wilding*		
1912	H.R.Barrett and C.P.Dixon *M.O.Decugis and A.H.Gobert*		
1913	H.R.Barrett and C.P.Dixon *F.W.Rahe and H.Kleinschroth*		
1914	N.E.Brookes and A.F.Wilding *H.R.Barrett and C.P.Dixon*		
1919	R.V.Thomas and P.O.Wood *R.Lycett and R.W.Heath*		
1920	R.N.Williams and C.S.Garland *A.R.F.Kingscote and J.C.Parke*		
1921	R.Lycett and M.Woosnam *F.G.Lowe and A.H.Lowe*		
1922	R.Lycett and J.O.Anderson *G.L.Patterson and P.O.Wood*		
1923	R.Lycett and L.A.Godfree *Count M.de Gomar and E.Flaquer*		
1924	F.T.Hunter and V.Richards *R.N.Williams and W.M.Washburn*		
1925	J.R.Borotra and R.Lacoste *J.F.Hennessey and R.J.Casey*		
1926	H.J.Cochet and J.Brugnon *V.Richards and H.O.Kinsey*		
1927	F.T.Hunter and W.T.Tilden *J.Brugnon and H.J.Cochet*		
1928	H.J.Cochet and J.Brugnon *G.L.Patterson and J.B.Hawkes*		
1929	W.L.Allison and J.W.Van Ryn *J.C.Gregory and I.G.Collins*		
1930	W.L.Allison and J.W.Van Ryn *J.T.G.H.Doeg and G.M.Lott*		
1931	G.M Lott and J.W.Van Ryn *H.J.Cochet and J.Brugnon*		
1932	J.R.Borotra and J.Brugnon *G.P.Hughes and F.J.Perry*		
1933	J.R.Borotra and J.Brugnon *R.Nunoi and J.Satoh*		
1934	G.M.Lott and L.R.Stoefen *J.R.Borotra and J.Brugnon*		
1935	J.H.Crawford and A.K.Quist *W.L.Allison and J.W.Van Ryn*		
1936	G.P.Hughes and C.R.D.Tuckey *C.E.Hare and F.H.D.Wilde*		
1937	J.D.Budge and G.C.Mako *G.P.Hughes and C.R.D.Tuckey*		
1938	J.D.Budge and G.C.Mako *H.E.O.Henkel and G.von Metaxa*		
1939	R.L.Riggs and E.T.Cooke *C.E.Hare and F.H.D.Wilde*		
1946	T.P.Brown and J.A.Kramer *G.E.Brown and D.R.Pails*		
1947	R.Falkenburg and J.A.Kramer *A.J.Mottram and O.W.T.Sidwell*		
1948	J.E.Bromwich and F.A.Sedgman *T.P.Brown and G.P.Mulloy*		
1949	R.A.Gonzales and F.A.Parker *G.P.Mulloy and F.R.Schroeder*		
1950	J.E.Bromwich and A.K.Quist *G.E.Brown and O.W.T.Sidwell*		
1951	K.B.McGregor and F.A.Sedgman *J.Drobny and E.W.Sturgess*		
1952	K.B.McGregor and F.A.Sedgman *E.V.Seixas and E.W.Sturgess*		
1953	L.A.Hoad and K.R.Rosewall *R.N.Hartwig and M.G.Rose*		
1954	R.N.Hartwig and M.G.Rose *E.V.Seixas and M.A.Trabert*		
1955	R.N.Hartwig and L.A.Hoad *N.A.Fraser and K.R.Rosewall*		
1956	L.A.Hoad and K.R.Rosewall *N.Pietrangeli and O.Sirola*		
1957	G.P.Mulloy and J.E.Patty *N.A.Fraser and L.A.Hoad*		
1958	S.V.Davidson and U.C.J.Schmidt *A.J.Cooper and N.A.Fraser*		
1959	R.S.Emerson and N.A.Fraser *R.G.Laver and R.Mark*		
1960	R.H.Osuna and R.D.Ralston *M.G.Davies and R.K.Wilson*		
1961	R.S.Emerson and N.A.Fraser *R.A.J.Hewitt and F.S.Stolle*		
1962	R.A.J.Hewitt and F.S.Stolle *B.Jovanovic and N.Pilic*		
1963	R.H.Osuna and A.Palafox *J.C.Barclay and P.Darmon*		
1964	R.A.J.Hewitt and F.S.Stolle *R.S.Emerson and K.N.Fletcher*		
1965	J.D.Newcombe and A.D.Roche *K.N.Fletcher and R.A.J.Hewitt*		
1966	K.N.Fletcher and J.D.Newcombe *W.W.Bowrey and O.K.Davidson*		
1967	R.A.J.Hewitt and F.D.McMillan *R.S.Emerson and K.N.Fletcher*		
1968	J.D.Newcombe and A.D.Roche *K.R.Rosewall and F.S.Stolle*		
1969	J.D.Newcombe and A.D.Roche *T.S.Okker and M.C.Reissen*		
1970	J.D.Newcombe and A.D.Roche *K.R.Rosewall and F.S.Stolle*		
1971	R.S.Emerson and R.G.Laver *A.R.Ashe and R.D.Ralston*		
1972	R.A.J.Hewitt and F.D.McMillan *S.R.Smith and E.J.van Dillen*		
1973	J.S.Connors and I.Nastase *J.R.Cooper and N.A.Fraser*		
1974	J.D.Newcombe and A.D.Roche *R.C.Lutz and S.R.Smith*		
1975	V.K.Gerulaitis and A.Mayer *C.Dowdeswell and A.J.Stone*		
1976	B.E.Gottfried and R.C.Ramirez *R.L.Case and G.Masters*		
1977	R.L.Case and G.Masters *J.G.Alexander and P.C.Dent*		
1978	R.A.J.Hewitt and F.D.McMillan *P.B.Fleming and J.P.McEnroe*		
1979	P.B.Fleming and J.P.McEnroe *B.E.Gottfried and R.C.Ramirez*		
1980	P.McNamara and P.F.McNamee *R.C.Lutz and S.R.Smith*		
1981	P.B.Fleming and J.P.McEnroe *R.C.Lutz and S.R.Smith*		
1982	P.McNamara and P.F.McNamee *P.B.Fleming and J.P.McEnroe*		
1983	P.B.Fleming and J.P.McEnroe *T.E.Gullikson and T.R.Gullikson*		
1984	P.B.Fleming and J.P.McEnroe *P.Cash and P.McNamee*		
1985	H.P.Guenthardt and B.Taroczy *P.H.Cash and J.B.Fitzgerald*		
1986	T.K.Nystrom and M.A.O.Wilander *G.W.Donnelly and P.B.Fleming*		
1987	K.E.Flach and R.A.Seguso *S.Casal and E.Sanchez*		
1988	K.E.Flach and R.A.Seguso *J.B.Fitzgerald and A.P.Jarryd*		
1989	J.B.Fitzgerald and A.P.Jarryd *R.D.Leach and J.R.Pugh*		
1990	R.D.Leach and J.R.Pugh *P.Aldrich and D.T.Visser*		
1991	J.B.Fitzgerald and A.P.Jarryd *J.A.Frana and L.Lavalle*		
1992	J.P.McEnroe and M.D.Stich *J.F.Grabb and R.A.Reneberg*		
1993	T.A.Woodbridge and M.R.Woodforde *G.D.Connell and P.J.Galbraith*		
1994	T.A.Woodbridge and M.R.Woodforde *G.D.Connell and P.J.Galbraith*		
1995	T.A.Woodbridge and M.R.Woodforde *R.D.Leach and S.D.Melville*		
1996	T.A.Woodbridge and M.R.Woodforde *B.H.Black and G.D.Connell*		
1997	T.A.Woodbridge and M.R.Woodforde *J.F.Eltingh and P.V.N.Haarhuis*		
1998	J.F.Eltingh and P.V.N.Haarhuis *T.A.Woodbridge and M.R.Woodforde*		
1999	M.S.Bhupathi and L.A.Paes *P.V.N.Haarhuis and J.E.Palmer*		
2000	T.A.Woodbridge and M.R.Woodforde *P.V.N.Haarhuis and S.F.Stolle*		
2001	D.J.Johnson and J.E.Palmer *J.Novak and D.Rikl*		
2002	J.L.Bjorkman and T.A. Woodbridge *M.S.Knowles and D.M.Nestor*		
2003	J.L.Bjorkman and T.A. Woodbridge *M.S.Bhupathi and M.N.Mirnyi*		
2004	J.L.Bjorkman and T.A. Woodbridge *J.Knowle and N.Zimonjic*		
2005	S.W.I.Huss and W.A.Moodie *R.C.Bryan and M.C.Bryan*		
2006	R.C.Bryan and M.C.Bryan *F.V.Santoro and N.Zimonjic*		
2007	A.Clement and M.Llodra *R.C.Bryan and M.C.Bryan*		
2008	D.M.Nestor and N.Zimonjic *J.L.Bjorkman and K.R.Ullyett*		
2009	D.M.Nestor and N.Zimonjic *R.C.Bryan and M.C.Bryan*		
2010	J.Melzer and P.Petzschner *R.S.Lindstedt and H.V.Tecau*		
2011	R.C.Bryan and M.C.Bryan *R.S.Lindstedt and H.V.Tecau*		
2012	J.F.Marray and F.L.Nielsen *R.S.Lindstedt and H.V.Tecau*		
2013	R.C.Bryan and M.C.Bryan *I.Dodig and M.P.D.Melo*		
2014	V.Pospisil and J.E.Sock *R.C.Bryan and M.C.Bryan*		
2015	J.J.Rojer and H.Tecau *J.R.Murray and J.Peers*		
2016	P-H.Herbert and N.P.A.Mahut *J.Benneteau and E.Roger- Vasselin*		
2017	L.Kubot and M.P.D.Melo *O.Marach and M.Pavic*		
2018	M.C.Bryan and J.Sock *R.Klaasen and M.Venus*		
2019	J.S.Cabal and R.F.Farah *N.P.A.Mahut and E.Roger- Vasselin*		

LADIES' DOUBLES CHAMPIONS & RUNNERS-UP

1913 Mrs.R.J.McNair and Miss P.D.H.Boothby
Mrs.A.Sterry and Mrs.R.L.Chambers

1914 Miss E.M.Ryan and Miss A.M.Morton
Mrs.D.T.R.Larcombe and Mrs.F.J.Hannam

1919 Miss S.R.F.Lenglen and Miss E.M.Ryan
Mrs.R.L.Chambers and Mrs.D.T.R.Larcombe

1920 Miss S.R.F.Lenglen and Miss E.M.Ryan
Mrs.R.L.Chambers and Mrs.D.T.R.Larcombe

1921 Miss S.R.F.Lenglen and Miss E.M.Ryan
Mrs.A.E.Beamish and Mrs.G.E.Peacock

1922 Miss S.R.F.Lenglen and Miss E.M.Ryan
Mrs.A.D.Stocks and Miss K.McKane

1923 Miss S.R.F.Lenglen and Miss E.M.Ryan
Miss J.W.Austin and Miss E.L.Colyer

1924 Mrs.G.Wightman and Miss H.Wills
Mrs.B.C.Covell and Miss K.McKane

1925 Miss S.Lenglen and Miss E.Ryan
Mrs.A.V.Bridge and Mrs.C.G.McIlquham

1926 Miss E.M.Ryan and Miss M.K.Browne
Mrs.L.A.Godfree and Miss E.L.Colyer

1927 Miss H.N.Wills and Miss E.M.Ryan
Miss E.L.Heine and Mrs.G.E.Peacock

1928 Mrs.M.R.Watson and Miss M.A.Saunders
Miss E.H.Harvey and Miss E.Bennett

1929 Mrs.M.R.Watson and Mrs.L.R.C.Michell
Mrs.B.C.Covell and Mrs.W.P.Barron

1930 Mrs.F.S.Moody and Miss E.M.Ryan
Miss E.A.Cross and Miss S.H.Palfrey

1931 Mrs.D.C.Shepherd-Barron and Miss P.E.Mudford
Miss D.E.Metaxa and Miss J.Sigart

1932 Miss D.E.Metaxa and Miss J.Sigart
Miss E.M.Ryan and Miss H.H.Jacobs

1933 Mrs.R.Mathieu and Miss E.M.Ryan
Miss W.A.James and Miss A.M.Yorke

1934 Mrs.R.Mathieu and Miss E.M.Ryan
Mrs.D.B.Andrus and Mrs.C.F.Henrotin

1935 Miss W.A.James and Miss K.E.Stammers
Mrs.R.Mathieu and Mrs.S.Sperling

1936 Miss W.A.James and Miss K.E.Stammers
Mrs.M.Fabyan and Miss H.H.Jacobs

1937 Mrs.R.Mathieu and Miss A.M.Yorke
Mrs.M.R.King and Mrs.J.B.Pittman

1938 Mrs.M.Fabyan and Miss A.Marble
Mrs.R.Mathieu and Miss A.M.Yorke

1939 Mrs.M.Fabyan and Miss A.Marble
Miss H.H.Jacobs and Miss A.M.Yorke

1946 Miss A.L.Brough and Miss M.E.Osborne
Miss P.M.Betz and Miss D.J.Hart

1947 Miss D.J.Hart and Mrs.R.B.Todd
Miss A.L.Brough and Miss M.E.Osborne

1948 Miss A.L.Brough and Mrs.W.du Pont
Miss D.J.Hart and Mrs.R.B.Todd

1949 Miss A.L.Brough and Mrs.W.du Pont
Miss G.Moran and Mrs.R.B.Todd

1950 Miss A.L.Brough and Mrs.W.du Pont
Miss S.J.Fry and Miss D.J.Hart

1951 Miss S.J.Fry and Miss D.J.Hart
Miss A.L.Brough and Mrs.W.du Pont

1952 Miss S.J.Fry and Miss D.J.Hart
Miss A.L.Brough and Miss M.C.Connolly

1953 Miss S.J.Fry and Miss D.J.Hart
Miss M.C.Connolly and Miss J.A.Sampson

1954 Miss A.L.Brough and Mrs.W.du Pont
Miss S.J.Fry and Miss D.J.Hart

1955 Miss F.A.Mortimer and Miss J.A.Shilcock
Miss S.J.Bloomer and Miss P.E.Ward

1956 Miss A.Buxton and Miss A.Gibson
Miss E.F.Muller and Miss D.G.Seeney

1957 Miss A.Gibson and Miss D.R.Hard
Mrs.K.Hawton and Mrs.M.N.Long

1958 Miss M.E.A.Bueno and Miss A.Gibson
Mrs.W.du Pont and Miss M.Varner

1959 Miss J.M.Arth and Miss D.R.Hard
Mrs.J.G.Fleitz and Miss C.C.Truman

1960 Miss M.E.A.Bueno and Miss D.R.Hard
Miss S.Reynolds and Miss R.Schuurman

1961 Miss K.J.Hantze and Miss B.J.Moffitt
Miss J.P.Lehane and Miss M.Smith

1962 Miss B.J.Moffitt and Mrs.J.R.Susman
Mrs.L.E.G.Price and Miss R.Schuurman

1963 Miss M.E.A.Bueno and Miss D.R.Hard
Miss R.A.Ebbern and Miss M.Smith

1964 Miss M.Smith and Miss L.R.Turner
Miss B.J.Moffitt and Mrs.J.R.Susman

1965 Miss M.E.A.Bueno and Miss B.J.Moffitt
Miss F.G.Durr and Miss J.P.Lieffrig

1966 Miss M.E.A.Bueno and Miss N.A.Richey
Miss M.Smith and Miss J.A.M.Tegart

1967 Miss R.Casals and Mrs.L.W.King
Miss M.E.A.Bueno and Miss N.A.Richey

1968 Miss R.Casals and Mrs.L.W.King
Miss F.G.Durr and Mrs.P.F.Jones

1969 Mrs.B.M.Court and Miss J.A.M.Tegart
Miss P.S.A.Hogan and Miss M.Michel

1970 Miss R.Casals and Mrs.L.W.King
Miss F.G.Durr and Miss S.V.Wade

1971 Miss R.Casals and Mrs.L.W.King
Mrs.B.M.Court and Miss E.F.Goolagong

1972 Mrs.L.W.King and Miss B.F.Stove
Mrs.D.E.Dalton and Miss F.G.Durr

1973 Miss R.Casals and Mrs.L.W.King
Miss F.G.Durr and Miss B.F.Stove

1974 Miss E.F.Goolagong and Miss M.Michel
Miss H.F.Gourlay and Miss K.M.Krantzcke

1975 Miss A.K.Kiyomura and Miss K.Sawamatsu
Miss F.G.Durr and Miss B.F.Stove

1976 Miss C.M.Evert and Miss M.Navratilova
Mrs.L.W.King and Miss B.F.Stove

1977 Mrs.R.L.Cawley and Miss J.C.Russell
Miss M.Navratilova and Miss B.F.Stove

1978 Mrs.G.E.Reid and Miss W.M.Turnbull
Miss M.Jausovec and Miss V.Ruzici

1979 Mrs.L.W.King and Miss M.Navratilova
Miss B.F.Stove and Miss W.M.Turnbull

1980 Miss K.Jordan and Miss A.E.Smith
Miss R.Casals and Miss W.M.Turnbull

1981 Miss M.Navratilova and Miss P.H.Shriver
Miss K.Jordan and Miss A.E.Smith

1982 Miss M.Navratilova and Miss P.H.Shriver
Miss K.Jordan and Miss A.E.Smith

1983 Miss M.Navratilova and Miss P.H.Shriver
Miss R.Casals and Miss W.M.Turnbull

1984 Miss M.Navratilova and Miss P.H.Shriver
Miss K.Jordan and Miss A.E.Smith

1985 Miss K.Jordan and Mrs.P.D.Smylie
Miss M.Navratilova and Miss P.H.Shriver

1986 Miss M.Navratilova and Miss P.H.Shriver
Miss H.Mandlikova and Miss W.M.Turnbull

1987 Miss C.G.Kohde-Kilsch and Miss H.Sukova
Miss H.E.Nagelsen and Mrs.P.D.Smylie

1988 Miss S.M.Graf and Miss G.B.Sabatini
Miss L.I.Savchenko and Miss N.M.Zvereva

1989 Miss J.Novotna and Miss H.Sukova
Miss L.I.Savchenko and Miss N.M.Zvereva

1990 Miss J.Novotna and Miss H.Sukova
Miss K.Jordan and Mrs.P.D.Smylie

1991 Miss L.I.Savchenko and Miss N.M.Zvereva
Miss B.C.Fernandez and Miss J.Novotna

1992 Miss B.C.Fernandez and Miss N.M.Zvereva
Miss J.Novotna and Mrs.A.Neiland

1993 Miss B.C.Fernandez and Miss N.M.Zvereva
Mrs.A.Neiland and Miss J.Novotna

1994 Miss B.C.Fernandez and Miss N.M.Zvereva
Miss J.Novotna and Miss A.I.M.Sanchez Vicario

1995 Miss J.Novotna and Miss A.I.M.Sanchez Vicario
Miss B.C.Fernandez and Miss N.M.Zvereva

1996 Miss M.Hingis and Miss H.Sukova
Miss M.J.McGrath and Mrs.A.Neiland

1997 Miss B.C.Fernandez and Miss N.M.Zvereva
Miss N.J.Arendt and Miss M.M.Bollegraf

1998 Miss M.Hingis and Miss J.Novotna
Miss L.A.Davenport and Miss N.M.Zvereva

1999 Miss L.A.Davenport and Miss C.M.Morariu
Miss M.de Swardt and Miss E.Tatarkova

2000 Miss S.J.Williams and Miss V.E.S.Williams
Mrs.A.Decugis and Miss A.Sugiyama

2001 Miss L.M.Raymond and Miss R.P.Stubbs
Miss K.Clijsters and Miss A.Sugiyama

2002 Miss S.J.Williams and Miss V.E.S.Williams
Miss V.Ruano Pascual and Miss P.L.Suarez

2003 Miss K.Clijsters and Miss A.Sugiyama
Miss V.Ruano Pascual and Miss P.L.Suarez

2004 Miss C.C.Black and Miss R.P.Stubbs
Mrs.A.Huber and Miss A.Sugiyama

2005 Miss C.C.Black and Mrs.L.Huber
Miss S.Kuznetsova and Miss A.Muresmo

2006 Miss Z.Yan and Miss J.Zheng
Miss V.Ruano Pascual and Miss P.L.Suarez

2007 Miss C.C.Black and Mrs.L.Huber
Miss K.Srebotnik and Miss A.Sugiyama

2008 Miss S.J.Williams and Miss V.E.S.Williams
Miss L.M.Raymond and Miss S.J.Stosur

2009 Miss S.J.Williams and Miss V.E.S.Williams
Miss S.J.Stosur and Miss R.P.Stubbs

2010 Miss V.King and Miss Y.V.Shvedova
Miss E.S.Vesnina and Miss V.Zvonareva

2011 Mrs.K.Peschke and Miss K.Srebotnik
Miss S.Lisicki and Miss S.J.Stosur

2012 Miss S.J.Williams and Miss V.E.S.Williams
Miss A.Hlavackova and Miss L.Hradecka

2013 Miss S-W.Hsieh and Miss S.Peng
Miss A.Barty and Miss C.Dellacqua

2014 Miss S.Errani and Miss R.Vinci
Miss T.Babos and Miss K.Mladenovic

2015 Miss M.Hingis and Miss S.Mirza
Miss E.Makarova and Mrs E.S.Vesnina

2016 Miss S.J.Williams and Miss V.E.S.Williams
Miss T.Babos and Miss Y.Shvedova

2017 Miss E.Makarova and Mrs.E.S.Vesnina
Miss H-C.Chan and Miss M.Niculescu

2018 Miss B.Krejcikova and Miss K.Siniakova
Miss N.Melichar and Mrs.K.Peschke

2019 Miss S-W.Hsieh and Miss B.Strycova
Miss G.Dabrowski and Miss Y.Xu

MIXED DOUBLES CHAMPIONS & RUNNERS-UP

1913 H.Crisp and Mrs.C.O.Tuckey
J.C.Parke and Mrs.D.T.R.Larcombe

1914 J.C.Parke and Mrs.D.T.R.Larcombe
A.F.Wilding and Miss M.Broquedis

1919 R.Lycett and Miss E.M.Ryan
A.D.Prebble and Mrs.R.L.Chambers

1920 G.L.Patterson and Miss S.R.F.Lenglen
R.Lycett and Miss E.M.Ryan

1921 R.Lycett and Miss E.M.Ryan
M.Woosnam and Miss P.L.Howkins

1922 P.O.Wood and Miss S.R.F.Lenglen
R.Lycett and Miss E.M.Ryan

1923 R.Lycett and Miss E.M.Ryan
L.S.Deane and Mrs.W.P.Barron

1924 J.B.Gilbert and Miss K.McKane
L.A.Godfree and Mrs.W.P.Barron

1925 J.Borotra and Miss S.R.F.Lenglen
U.L.de Morpurgo and Miss E.M.Ryan

1926 L.A.Godfree and Mrs.L.A.Godfree
H.O.Kinsey and Miss M.K.Browne

1927 F.T.Hunter and Miss E.M.Ryan
L.A.Godfree and Mrs.L.A.Godfree

1928 P.D.B.Spence and Miss E.M.Ryan
J.H.Crawford and Miss D.J.Akhurst

1929 F.T.Hunter and Miss H.N.Wills
I.G.Collins and Miss J.C.Fry

1930 J.H.Crawford and Miss E.M.Ryan
D.D.Prenn and Miss H.Krahwinkel

1931 G.M.Lott and Mrs.L.A.Harper
I.G.Collins and Miss J.C.Ridley

1932 E.G.Maier and Miss E.M.Ryan
H.C.Hopman and Miss J.Sigart

1933 G.von Cramm and Miss H.Krahwinkel
N.G.Farquharson and Miss G.M.Heeley

1934 R.Miki and Miss D.E.Round
H.W.Austin and Mrs.W.P.Barron

1935 F.J.Perry and Miss D.E.Round
H.C.Hopman and Mrs.H.C.Hopman

1936 F.J.Perry and Miss D.E.Round
J.D.Budge and Mrs.M.Fabyan

1937 J.D.Budge and Miss A.Marble
Y.F.M.Petra and Mrs.R.Mathieu

1938 J.D.Budge and Miss A.Marble
H.E.O.Henkel and Mrs.M.Fabyan

1939 R.L.Riggs and Miss A.Marble
F.H.D.Wilde and Miss N.B.Brown

1946 T.P.Brown and Miss A.L.Brough
G.E.Brown and Miss D.M.Bundy

1947 J.E.Bromwich and Miss A.L.Brough
C.F.Long and Mrs.G.F.Bolton

1948 J.E.Bromwich and Miss A.L.Brough
F.A.Sedgman and Miss D.J.Hart

1949 E.W.Sturgess and Mrs.R.A.Summers
J.E.Bromwich and Miss A.L.Brough

1950 E.W.Sturgess and Miss A.L.Brough
G.E.Brown and Mrs.R.B.Todd

1951 F.A.Sedgman and Miss D.J.Hart
M.G.Rose and Mrs.G.F.Bolton

1952 F.A.Sedgman and Miss D.J.Hart
E.J.Morea and Mrs.M.N.Long

1953 E.V.Seixas and Miss D.J.Hart
E.J.Morea and Miss S.J.Fry

1954 E.V.Seixas and Miss D.J.Hart
K.R.Rosewall and Mrs.W.du Pont

1955 E.V.Seixas and Miss D.J.Hart
E.J.Morea and Miss A.L.Brough

1956 E.V.Seixas and Miss S.J.Fry
G.P.Mulloy and Miss A.Gibson

1957 M.G.Rose and Miss D.R.Hard
N.A.Fraser and Miss A.Gibson

1958 R.N.Howe and Miss L.Coghlan
K.Nielsen and Miss A.Gibson

1959 R.G.Laver and Miss D.R.Hard
N.A.Fraser and Miss M.E.A.Bueno

1960 R.G.Laver and Miss D.R.Hard
R.N.Howe and Miss M.E.A.Bueno

1961 F.S.Stolle and Miss L.R.Turner
R.N.Howe and Miss E.Buding

1962 N.A.Fraser and Mrs.W.du Pont
R.D.Ralston and Miss A.S.Haydon

1963 K.N.Fletcher and Miss M.Smith
R.A.J.Hewitt and Miss D.R.Hard

1964 F.S.Stolle and Miss L.R.Turner
K.N.Fletcher and Miss M.Smith

1965 K.N.Fletcher and Miss M.Smith
A.D.Roche and Miss J.A.M.Tegart

1966 K.N.Fletcher and Miss M.Smith
R.D.Ralston and Mrs.L.W.King

1967 O.K.Davidson and Mrs.L.W.King
K.N.Fletcher and Miss M.E.A.Bueno

1968 K.N.Fletcher and Mrs.B.M.Court
A.Metreveli and Miss O.V.Morozova

1969 F.S.Stolle and Mrs.P.F.Jones
A.D.Roche and Miss J.A.M.Tegart

1970 I.Nastase and Miss R.Casals
A.Metreveli and Miss O.V.Morozova

1971 O.K.Davidson and Mrs.L.W.King
M.C.Riessen and Mrs.B.M.Court

1972 I.Nastase and Miss R.Casals
K.G.Warwick and Miss E.F.Goolagong

1973 O.K.Davidson and Mrs.L.W.King
R.C.Ramirez and Miss J.S.Newberry

1974 O.K.Davidson and Mrs.L.W.King
M.J.Farrell and Miss L.J.Charles

1975 M.C.Riessen and Mrs.B.M.Court
A.J.Stone and Miss B.F.Stove

1976 A.D.Roche and Miss F.G.Durr
R.L.Stockton and Miss R.Casals

1977 R.A.J.Hewitt and Miss G.R.Stevens
F.D.McMillan and Miss B.F.Stove

1978 F.D.McMillan and Miss B.F.Stove
R.O.Ruffels and Mrs.L.W.King

1979 R.A.J.Hewitt and Miss G.R.Stevens
F.D.McMillan and Miss B.F.Stove

1980 J.R.Austin and Miss T.A.Austin
M.R.Edmondson and Miss D.L.Fromholtz

1981 F.D.McMillan and Miss B.F.Stove
J.R.Austin and Miss T.A.Austin

1982 K.M.Curren and Miss A.E.Smith
J.M.Lloyd and Miss W.M.Turnbull

1983 J.M.Lloyd and Miss W.M.Turnbull
S.B.Denton and Mrs.L.W.King

1984 J.M.Lloyd and Miss W.M.Turnbull
S.B.Denton and Miss K.Jordan

1985 P.F.McNamee and Miss M.Navratilova
J.B.Fitzgerald and Mrs.P.D.Smylie

1986 K.E.Flach and Miss K.Jordan
H.P.Guenthardt and Miss M.Navratilova

1987 M.J.Bates and Miss J.M.Durie
D.A.Cahill and Miss N.A-L.Provis

1988 S.E.Stewart and Miss Z.L.Garrison
K.L.Jones and Mrs.S.W.Magers

1989 J.R.Pugh and Miss J.Novotna
M.Kratzmann and Miss J.M.Byrne

1990 R.D.Leach and Miss Z.L.Garrison
J.B.Fitzgerald and Mrs.P.D.Smylie

1991 J.B.Fitzgerald and Mrs.P.D.Smylie
J.R.Pugh and Miss N.M.Zvereva

1992 C.Suk and Mrs.A.Neiland
J.F.Eltingh and Miss M.J.M.M.Oremans

1993 M.R.Woodforde and Miss M.Navratilova
T.J.C.M.Nijssen and Miss M.M.Bollegraf

1994 T.A.Woodbridge and Miss H.Sukova
T.J.Middleton and Miss L.M.McNeil

1995 J.A.Stark and Miss M.Navratilova
C.Suk and Miss B.C.Fernandez

1996 C.Suk and Miss H.Sukova
M.R.Woodforde and Mrs.A.Neiland

1997 C.Suk and Miss H.Sukova
A.Olhovskiy and Mrs.A.Neiland

1998 M.N.Mirnyi and Miss S.J.Williams
M.S.Bhupathi and Miss M.Lucic

1999 L.A.Paes and Miss L.M.Raymond
J.L.Bjorkman and Miss A.S.Kournikova

2000 D.J.Johnson and Miss K.Y.Po
L.G.Hewitt and Miss K.Clijsters

2001 L.Friedl and Miss D.Hantuchova
M.C.Bryan and Mrs.L.Huber

2002 M.S.Bhupathi and Miss E.A.Likhovtseva
K.R.Ullyett and Miss D.Hantuchova

2003 L.A.Paes and Miss M.Navratilova
A.Ram and Miss A.Rodionova

2004 W.Black and Miss C.C.Black
T.A.Woodbridge and Miss A.H.Molik

2005 M.S.Bhupathi and Miss M.C.Pierce
P.Hanley and Miss T.Perebiynis

2006 A.Ram and Miss V.Zvonareva
R.C.Bryan and Miss V.E.S.Williams

2007 J.R.Murray and Miss J.Jankovic
J.L.Bjorkman and Miss A.H.Molik

2008 R.C.Bryan and Miss S.J.Stosur
M.C.Bryan and Miss K.Srebotnik

2009 M.S.Knowles and Miss A-L.Groenefeld
L.A.Paes and Miss C.C.Black

2010 L.A.Paes and Miss C.C.Black
W.A.Moodie and Miss L.M.Raymond

2011 J.Melzer and Miss I.Benesova
M.S.Bhupathi and Miss E.S.Vesnina

2012 M.Bryan and Miss L.M.Raymond
L.A.Paes and Miss E.S.Vesnina

2013 D.M.Nestor and Miss K.Mladenovic
B.Soares and Miss L.M.Raymond

2014 N.Zimonjic and Miss S.J.Stosur
M.N.Mirnyi and Miss H-C.Chan

2015 L.A.Paes and Miss M.Hingis
A.Peya and Miss T.Babos

2016 H.Kontinen and Miss H.M.Watson
R.F.Farah and Miss A-L.Groenefeld

2017 J.R.Murray and Miss M.Hingis
H.Kontinen and Miss H.M.Watson

2018 A.Peya and Miss N.Melichar
J.R.Murray and Miss V.A.Azarenka

2019 I.Dodig and Miss L.Chan
R.S.Lindstedt and Miss J.Ostapenko

GENTLEMEN'S WHEELCHAIR SINGLES CHAMPIONS & RUNNERS-UP

2016 G.Reid
S.Olsson

2017 S.Olsson
G.Fernandez

2018 S.Olsson
G.Fernandez

2019 G.Fernandez
S.Kunieda

GENTLEMEN'S WHEELCHAIR DOUBLES CHAMPIONS & RUNNERS-UP

2006 S.Saida and S.Kunieda
M.Jeremiasz and J.Mistry

2007 R.Ammerlaan and R.Vink
S.Kunieda and S.Saida

2008 R.Ammerlaan and R.Vink
S.Houdet and N.Peifer

2009 S.Houdet and M.Jeremiasz
R.Ammerlaan and S.Kunieda

2010 R.Ammerlaan and S.Olsson
S.Houdet and S.Kunieda

2011 M.Scheffers and R.Vink
S.Houdet and M.Jeremiasz

2012 T.Egberink and M.Jeremiasz
R.Ammerlaan and R.Vink

2013 S.Houdet and S.Kunieda
F.Cattaneo and R.Vink

2014 S.Houdet and S.Kunieda
M.Scheffers and R.Vink

2015 G.Fernandez and N.Peifer
M.Jeremiasz and G.Reid

2016 A.T.Hewett and G.Reid
S.Houdet and N.Peifer

2017 A.T.Hewett and G.Reid
S.Houdet and N.Peifer

2018 A.T.Hewett and G.Reid
J.Gerard and S.Olsson

2019 J.Gerard and S.Olsson
A.T.Hewett and G.Reid

LADIES' WHEELCHAIR SINGLES CHAMPIONS & RUNNERS-UP

2016 Miss J.Griffioen
Miss A.van Koot

2017 Miss D.de Groot
Miss S.Ellerbrock

2018 Miss D.de Groot
Miss A.van Koot

2019 Miss A.van Koot
Miss D.de Groot

LADIES' WHEELCHAIR DOUBLES CHAMPIONS & RUNNERS-UP

2009 Miss K.Homan and Miss E.M.Vergeer
Miss D.Di Toro and Miss L.Shuker

2010 Miss E.M.Vergeer and Miss S.Walraven
Miss D.Di Toro and Miss L.Shuker

2011 Miss E.M.Vergeer and Miss S.Walraven
Miss J.Griffioen and Miss A.van Koot

2012 Miss J.Griffioen and Miss A.van Koot
Miss L.Shuker and Miss J.J.Whiley

2013 Miss J.Griffioen and Miss A.van Koot
Miss Y.Kamiji and Miss J.J.Whiley

2014 Miss Y.Kamiji and Miss J.J.Whiley
Miss J.Griffioen and Miss A.van Koot

2015 Miss Y.Kamiji and Miss J.J.Whiley
Miss J.Griffioen and Miss A.van Koot

2016 Miss Y.Kamiji and Miss J.J.Whiley
Miss J.Griffioen and Miss A.van Koot

2017 Miss Y.Kamiji and Miss J.J.Whiley
Miss M.Buis and Miss D.de Groot

2018 Miss D.de Groot and Miss Y.Kamiji
Miss S.Ellerbrock and Miss L.Shuker

2019 Miss A.van Koot and Miss D.de Groot
Miss M.Buis and Miss G.Capocci

QUAD WHEELCHAIR SINGLES CHAMPIONS & RUNNERS-UP

2019 D.Alcott
A.Lapthorne

QUAD WHEELCHAIR DOUBLES CHAMPIONS & RUNNERS-UP

2019 D.Alcott and A.Lapthorne
K.Sugeno and D.Wagner

BOYS' SINGLES CHAMPIONS & RUNNERS-UP

1947 K.Nielsen *S.V.Davidson*	1966 V.Korotkov *B.E.Fairlie*	1985 L.Lavalle *E.Velez*	2004 G.Monfils *M.Kasiri*

1947 K.Nielsen
S.V.Davidson
1948 S.O.Stockenberg
D.Vad
1949 S.O.Stockenberg
J.A.T.Horn
1950 J.A.T.Horn
K.Mobarek
1951 J.Kupferburger
K.Mobarek
1952 R.K.Wilson
T.T.Fancutt
1953 W.A.Knight
R.Krishnan
1954 R.Krishnan
A.J.Cooper
1955 M.P.Hann
J.E.Lundquist
1956 R.E.Holmberg
R.G.Laver
1957 J.I.Tattersall
I.Ribeiro
1958 E.H.Buchholz
P.J.Lall
1959 T.Lejus
R.W.Barnes
1960 A.R.Mandelstam
J.Mukerjea
1961 C.E.Graebner
E.Blanke
1962 S.J.Matthews
A.Metreveli
1963 N.Kalogeropoulos
I.El Shafei
1964 I.El Shafei
V.Korotkov
1965 V.Korotkov
G.Goven

1966 V.Korotkov
B.E.Fairlie
1967 M.Orantes
M.S.Estep
1968 J.G.Alexander
J.Thamin
1969 B.M.Bertram
J.G.Alexander
1970 B.M.Bertram
F.Gebert
1971 R.I.Kreiss
S.A.Warboys
1972 B.R.Borg
C.J.Mottram
1973 W.W.Martin
C.S.Dowdeswell
1974 W.W.Martin
Ash Amritraj
1975 C.J.Lewis
R.Ycaza
1976 H.P.Guenthardt
P.Elter
1977 V.A.W.Winitsky
T.E.Teltscher
1978 I.Lendl
J.Turpin
1979 R.Krishnan
D.Siegler
1980 T.Tulasne
H.D.Beutel
1981 M.W.Anger
P.H.Cash
1982 P.H.Cash
H.Sundstrom
1983 S.B.Edberg
J.Frawley
1984 M.Kratzmann
S.Kruger

1985 L.Lavalle
E.Velez
1986 E.Velez
J.Sanchez
1987 D.Nargiso
J.R.Stoltenberg
1988 N.Pereira
G.Raoux
1989 L.J.N.Kulti
T.A.Woodbridge
1990 L.A.Paes
M.Ondruska
1991 K.J.T.Enquist
M.Joyce
1992 D.Skoch
B.Dunn
1993 R.Sabau
J.Szymanski
1994 S.M.Humphries
M.A.Philippoussis
1995 O.Mutis
N.Kiefer
1996 V.Voltchkov
I.Ljubicic
1997 W.Whitehouse
D.Elsner
1998 R.Federer
I.Labadze
1999 J.Melzer
K.Pless
2000 N.P.A.Mahut
M.Ancic
2001 R.Valent
G.Muller
2002 T.C.Reid
L.Quahab
2003 F.Mergea
C.Guccione

2004 G.Monfils
M.Kasiri
2005 J.Chardy
R.Haase
2006 T.De Bakker
M.Gawron
2007 D.Young
V.Ignatic
2008 G.Dimitrov
H.Kontinen
2009 A.Kuznetsov
J.Cox
2010 M.Fucsovics
B.Mitchell
2011 L.Saville
L.Broady
2012 F.Peliwo
L.Saville
2013 G.Quinzi
H.Chung
2014 N.Rubin
S.Kozlov
2015 R.Opelka
M.Ymer
2016 D.Shapovalov
A.de Minaur
2017 A.Davidovich Fokina
A.Geller
2018 C.H.Tseng
J.Draper
2019 S.Mochizuki
C.Gimeno Valero

BOYS' DOUBLES CHAMPIONS & RUNNERS-UP

1982 P.H.Cash and J.Frawley
R.D.Leach and J.J.Ross
1983 M.Kratzmann and S.Youl
M.Nastase and O.Rahnasto
1984 R.Brown and R.V.Weiss
M.Kratzmann and J.Svensson
1985 A.Moreno and J.Yzaga
P.Korda and C.Suk
1986 T.Carbonell and P.Korda
S.Barr and H.Karrasch
1987 J.Stoltenberg and T.A.Woodbridge
D.Nargiso and E.Rossi
1988 J.R.Stoltenberg and T.A.Woodbridge
D.Rikl and T.Zdrazila
1989 J.E.Palmer and J.A.Stark
J-L.De Jager and W.R.Ferreira
1990 S.Lareau and S.Leblanc
C.Marsh and M.Ondruska
1991 K.Alami and G.Rusedski
J-L.De Jager and A.Medvedev
1992 S.Baldas and S.Draper
M.S.Bhupathi and N.Kirtane
1993 S.Downs and J.Greenhalgh
N.Godwin and G.Williams
1994 B.Ellwood and M.Philippoussis
V.Platenik and R.Schlachter

1995 J.Lee and J.M.Trotman
A.Hernandez and M.Puerta
1996 D.Bracciali and J.Robichaud
D.Roberts and W.Whitehouse
1997 L.Horna and N.Massu
J.Van de Westhuizen and W.Whitehouse
1998 R.Federer and O.L.P.Rochus
M.Llodra and A.Ram
1999 G.Coria and D.P.Nalbandian
T.Enev and J.Nieminem
2000 D.Coene and K.Vliegen
A.Banks and B.Riby
2001 F.Dancevic and G.Lapentti
B.Echagaray and S.Gonzales
2002 F.Mergea and H.V.Tecau
B.Baker and B.Ram
2003 F.Mergea and H.V.Tecau
A.Feeney and C.Guccione
2004 B.Evans and S.Oudsema
R.Haase and V.Troicki
2005 J.Levine and M.Shabaz
S.Groth and A.Kennaugh
2006 K.Damico and N.Schnugg
M.Klizan and A.Martin
2007 D.Lopez and M.Trevisan
R.Jebavy and M.Klizan

2008 C-P.Hsieh and T-H.Yang
M.Reid and B.Tomic
2009 P-H.Herbert and K.Krawietz
J.Obry and A.Puget
2010 L.Broady and T.Farquharson
L.Burton and G.Morgan
2011 G.Morgan and M.Pavic
O.Golding and J.Vesely
2012 A.Harris and N.Kyrgios
M.Donati and P.Licciardi
2013 T.Kokkinakis and N.Kyrgios
E.Couacaud and S.Napolitano
2014 O.Luz and M.Zormann
S.Kozlov and A.Rublev
2015 N.H.Ly and S.Nagal
R.Opelka and A.Santillan
2016 K.Raisma and S.Tsitsipas
F.Auger-Aliassime and D.Shapovalov
2017 A.Geller and Y.H.Hsu
J.Rodionov and M.Vrbensky
2018 Y.Erel and O.Virtanen
N.Mejia and O.Styler
2019 J.Forejtek and J.Lehecka
L.Draxl and G.Nanda

GIRLS' SINGLES CHAMPIONS & RUNNERS-UP

1947 Miss G.Domken *Miss B.Wallen*	1965 Miss O.V.Morozova *Miss R.Giscarfe*	1983 Miss P.Paradis *Miss P.Hy*	2000 Miss M.E.Salerni *Miss T.Perebiynis*	2017 Miss C.Liu *Miss A.Li*
1948 Miss O.Miskova *Miss V.Rigollet*	1966 Miss B.Lindstrom *Miss J.A.Congdon*	1984 Miss A.N.Croft *Miss E.Reinach*	2001 Miss A.Widjaja *Miss D.Safina*	2018 Miss I.Swiatek *Miss L.Kung*
1949 Miss C.Mercelis *Miss J.S.V.Partridge*	1967 Miss J.H.Salome *Miss E.M.Strandberg*	1985 Miss A.Holikova *Miss J.M.Byrne*	2002 Miss V.Douchevina *Miss M.Sharapova*	2019 Miss D.Snigur *Miss A.Noel*
1950 Miss L.Cornell *Miss A.Winter*	1968 Miss K.S.Pigeon *Miss L.E.Hunt*	1986 Miss N.M.Zvereva *Miss L.Meskhi*	2003 Miss K.Flipkens *Miss A.Tchakvetadze*	
1951 Miss L.Cornell *Miss S.Lazzarino*	1969 Miss K.Sawamatsu *Miss B.I.Kirk*	1987 Miss N.M.Zvereva *Miss J.Halard*	2004 Miss K.Bondarenko *Miss A.Ivanovic*	
1952 Miss F.J.I.ten Bosch *Miss R.Davar*	1970 Miss S.A.Walsh *Miss M.V.Kroshina*	1988 Miss B.A.M.Schultz *Miss E.Derly*	2005 Miss A.R.Radwanska *Miss T.Paszek*	
1953 Miss D.Kilian *Miss V.A.Pitt*	1971 Miss M.V.Kroshina *Miss S.H.Minford*	1989 Miss A.Strnadova *Miss M.J.McGrath*	2006 Miss C.Wozniacki *Miss M.Rybarikova*	
1954 Miss V.A.Pitt *Miss C.Monnot*	1972 Miss I.S.Kloss *Miss G.L.Coles*	1990 Miss A.Strnadova *Miss K.Sharpe*	2007 Miss U.Radwanska *Miss M.Brengle*	
1955 Miss S.M.Armstrong *Miss B.de Chambure*	1973 Miss A.K.Kiyomura *Miss M.Navratilova*	1991 Miss B.Rittner *Miss E.Makarova*	2008 Miss L.M.D.Robson *Miss N.Lertcheewakarn*	
1956 Miss A.S.Haydon *Miss I.Buding*	1974 Miss M.Jausovec *Miss M.Simionescu*	1992 Miss C.R.Rubin *Miss L.Courtois*	2009 Miss N.Lertcheewakarn *Miss K.Mladenovic*	
1957 Miss M.G.Arnold *Miss E.Reyes*	1975 Miss N.Y.Chmyreva *Miss R.Marsikova*	1993 Miss N.Feber *Miss R.Grande*	2010 Miss K.Pliskova *Miss S.Ishizu*	
1958 Miss S.M.Moore *Miss A.Dmitrieva*	1976 Miss N.Y.Chmyreva *Miss M.Kruger*	1994 Miss M.Hingis *Miss M-R.Jeon*	2011 Miss A.Barty *Miss I.Khromacheva*	
1959 Miss J.Cross *Miss D.Schuster*	1977 Miss L.Antonoplis *Miss M.Louie*	1995 Miss A.Olsza *Miss T.Tanasugarn*	2012 Miss E.Bouchard *Miss E.Svitolina*	
1960 Miss K.J.Hantze *Miss L.M.Hutchings*	1978 Miss T.A.Austin *Miss H.Mandlikova*	1996 Miss A.Mauresmo *Miss M.L.Serna*	2013 Miss B.Bencic *Miss T.Townsend*	
1961 Miss G.Baksheeva *Miss K.D.Chabot*	1979 Miss M.L.Piatek *Miss A.A.Moulton*	1997 Miss C.C.Black *Miss A.Rippner*	2014 Miss J.Ostapenko *Miss K.Schmiedlova*	
1962 Miss G.Baksheeva *Miss E.P.Terry*	1980 Miss D.Freeman *Miss S.J.Leo*	1998 Miss K.Srebotnik *Miss K.Clijsters*	2015 Miss S.Zhuk *Miss A.Blinkova*	
1963 Miss D.M.Salfati *Miss K.Dening*	1981 Miss Z.L.Garrison *Miss R.R.Uys*	1999 Miss I.Tulyagnova *Miss L.Krasnoroutskaya*	2016 Miss A.S.Potapova *Miss D.O.Yastremska*	
1964 Miss J.M.Bartkowicz *Miss E.Subirats*	1982 Miss C.Tanvier *Miss H.Sukova*			

GIRLS' DOUBLES CHAMPIONS & RUNNERS-UP

1982 Miss E.A.Herr and Miss P.Barg *Miss B.S.Gerken and Miss G.A.Rush*	1995 Miss C.C.Black and Miss A.Olsza *Miss T.Musgrove and Miss J.Richardson*	2007 Miss A.Pavlyuchenkova and Miss U.Radwanska *Miss M.Doi and Miss K.Nara*
1983 Miss P.A.Fendick and Miss P.Hy *Miss C.Anderholm and Miss H.Olsson*	1996 Miss O.Barabanschikova and Miss A.Mauresmo *Miss L.Osterloh and Miss S.Reeves*	2008 Miss P.Hercog and Miss J.Moore *Miss I.Holland and Miss S.Peers*
1984 Miss C.Kuhlman and Miss S.C.Rehe *Miss V.Milvidskaya and Miss L.I.Savchenko*	1997 Miss C.C.Black and Miss I.Selyutina *Miss M.Matevzic and Miss K.Srebotnik*	2009 Miss N.Lertcheewakarn and Miss S.Peers *Miss K.Mladenovic and Miss S.Njiric*
1985 Miss L.Field and Miss J.G.Thompson *Miss E.Reinach and Miss J.A.Richardson*	1998 Miss E.Dyrberg and Miss J.Kostanic *Miss P.Rampre and Miss I.Tulyaganova*	2010 Miss T.Babos and Miss S.Stephens *Miss I.Khromacheva and Miss E.Svitolina*
1986 Miss M.Jaggard and Miss L.O'Neill *Miss L.Meskhi and Miss N.M.Zvereva*	1999 Miss D.Bedanova and Miss M.E.Salerni *Miss T.Perebiynis and Miss I.Tulyaganova*	2011 Miss E.Bouchard and Miss G.Min *Miss D.Schuurs and Miss H.C.Tang*
1987 Miss N.Medvedeva and Miss N.M.Zvereva *Miss I.S.Kim and Miss P.M.Moreno*	2000 Miss I.Gaspar and Miss T.Perebiynis *Miss D.Bedanova and Miss M.E.Salerni*	2012 Miss E.Bouchard and Miss T.Townsend *Miss B.Bencic and Miss A.Konjuh*
1988 Miss J.A.Faull and Miss R.McQuillan *Miss A.Dechaume and Miss E.Derly*	2001 Miss G.Dulko and Miss A.Harkleroad *Miss C.Horiatopoulos and Miss B.Mattek*	2013 Miss B.Krejcikova and Miss K.Siniakova *Miss A.Kalinina and Miss I.Shymanovich*
1989 Miss J.M.Capriati and Miss M.J.McGrath *Miss A.Strnadova and Miss E.Sviglerova*	2002 Miss E.Clijsters and Miss B.Strycova *Miss A.Baker and Miss A-L.Groenefeld*	2014 Miss T.Grende and Miss Q.Ye *Miss M.Bouzkova and Miss D.Galfi*
1990 Miss K.Habsudova and Miss A.Strnadova *Miss N.J.Pratt and Miss K.Sharpe*	2003 Miss A.Kleybanova and Miss S.Mirza *Miss K.Bohmova and Miss M.Krajicek*	2015 Miss D.Galfi and Miss F.Stollar *Miss V.Lapko and Miss T.Mihalikova*
1991 Miss C.Barclay and Miss L.Zaltz *Miss J.Limmer and Miss A.Woolcock*	2004 Miss V.A.Azarenka and Miss V.Havartsova *Miss M.Erakovic and Miss M.Niculescu*	2016 Miss U.M.Arconada and Miss C.Liu *Miss M.Bolkvadze and Miss C.McNally*
1992 Miss M.Avotins and Miss L.McShea *Miss P.Nelson and Miss J.Steven*	2005 Miss V.A.Azarenka and Miss A.Szavay *Miss M.Erakovic and Miss M.Niculescu*	2017 Miss O.Danilovic and Miss K.Juvan *Miss C.McNally and Miss W.Osuigwe*
1993 Miss L.Courtois and Miss N.Feber *Miss H.Mochizuki and Miss Y.Yoshida*	2006 Miss A.Kleybanova and Miss A.Pavlyuchenkova *Miss K.Antoniychuk and Miss A.Dulgheru*	2018 Miss X.Wang and Miss X.Wang *Miss C.McNally and Miss W.Osuigwe*
1994 Miss E.De Villiers and Miss E.E.Jelfs *Miss C.M.Morariu and Miss L.Varmuzova*		2019 Miss S.Broadus and Miss A.Forbes *Miss K.Bartone and Miss O.Selekhmeteva*